Children with Learning and Behavior Problems:

A Behavior Management Approach

WILLIAM I. GARDNER
University of Wisconsin

Allyn and Bacon, Inc., Boston

To William Clifford,
a warm and sensitive man and
to Rillah Siddie, a gracious lady who taught others
to share themselves by sharing herself.

Contents

Contents

Preface

Until recently few children with severe learning and behavior difficulties were provided community-based and public-supported educational programs during the preschool and early school years.
They either remained in the home without adequate educational
experiences or were placed in institutional living arrangements.
The child with less severe problems in learning and personal adjustment frequently was enrolled in early education programs designed for the normal child. In too many instances the child with
difficulties was soon dismissed as being too slow to learn, too disruptive, too hyperactive, insufficiently socialized, or too detached.
The adverse effects of such chronic failure experiences on the
psychological development of the child were both profound and
long lasting.

But conditions are improving and will continue to improve
in the 1970's. Early education programs for the young child with
learning and behavior difficulties are becoming more readily available. Vigorous actions by child advocacy groups have stimulated
community public and private agencies to attempt to provide more
appropriate early education experiences for all children. Through
its Education of the Handicapped Act the U.S. Office of Education
is supporting the initiation and evaluation of a number of exem-
plary community programs. Regular nursery, kindergarten, and
primary education programs are opening their classes once again
to children with a wide range of individual differences in learning
and behavior adjustment.

Most educational, psychological, and child development
specialists in these programs, however, have been trained to deal

with the normally developing and easily managed child. They are searching for new approaches and more effective techniques for use with children who present the severe difficulties of psychological development.

This book describes one such approach. It presents the basic social learning principles and related teaching and behavior management strategies needed to create an effective and pleasant learning experience for young children who have been awarded such labels as mentally retarded, emotionally disturbed, learning disabled, brain injured, and socially maladjusted. This approach to behavior development and modification will be of interest to parents and professionals alike who are involved on an individual basis with the young child with severe learning and behavior problems. Major attention is also provided the child as he functions in a group education setting. The book is comprehensive in its presentation of the basic concepts of social learning, but it is written in an introductory and non-technical manner. This language feature, along with numerous examples of applications to a wide variety of problem areas, facilitates usage of the book by those with only minimal background in the psychology of learning.

Consistent with the advocation of a structured, direct-teaching approach, the book emphasizes that young children can acquire positive emotional and attitudinal characteristics and can become spontaneous, creative, and self-directed only to the extent that they gain successful task and interpersonal experiences. A child cannot be creative without initial sound exposure to a wide range of successful experiences. A child will have little to be enthusiastic or spontaneous about if he is not provided learning experiences which insure successful skill attainment in a wide range of behavioral areas. The book provides the reader with numerous practical procedures for insuring that young children will become successful learners—and furthermore, will come to enjoy learning.

My sincere appreciation is extended to the hundreds of young children with learning and behavior difficulties with whom I have had personal experience. I am constantly amazed at the vitality of such young children even though they may be confronted with severe and chronic barriers to learning new ways of behaving. I have been reinforced literally thousands of times by the smiles of children who were learning effectively, and were beginning to enjoy it, after their environments had been individually structured to facilitate such learning. It is my hope that more people will see more smiles on the faces of more children as a result of the systematic application of the behavior management procedures described in this book.

W. I. G.

PART I

Basic Concepts of Behavior Management

CHAPTER 1

A Behavior Management View
of Children with Learning
and Behavior Problems

Early childhood is a highly critical period in the psychological development of the individual. During the early years, basic patterns of perceptual, motor, cognitive, language, emotional, and social behaviors are acquired. Unusual difficulty in development in any of these behavioral areas can have a most devastating and long-lasting effect on the subsequent development of more complex skills and on the general adaptation of the child to his social and physical environments.

Many young children do experience unusual difficulty in learning. The absence or slow development of various basic developmental skills has a progressive accumulative effect which renders learning and psychological adjustment more difficult as the child grows older. If, for example, a child does not acquire basic perceptual and motor skills due to faulty neurological, sensory, or muscular factors, or as a result of a poorly designed learning environment, he is at a distinct disadvantage; he is unable to acquire more complex skills which require the basic ones as prerequisites. Until the child develops the basic perceptual-motor skills to draw an identifiable facsimile of a circle he cannot draw a person. Until he acquires basic eye-hand coordination skills, he cannot color, cut with scissors, string beads, or complete puzzles. If a child fails to acquire basic skills for imitating the behavior of others, he will experience extreme difficulty in acquiring language. The child without speech will have difficulty interacting with others. This interpersonal difficulty impedes the development of other cognitive, social, and emotional skills as well as more complex modes of interpersonal relationships. The retardation of these skill areas in turn disrupts the entire early psychological development of the child. The older the child becomes the greater the negative effects of the learning difficulties.

A child cannot learn to be spontaneous and relaxed unless he is being successful. He cannot learn to like himself unless he can please others with his success. He cannot learn to be sensitive to others unless others have been sensitive to him. He cannot learn to make realistic choices unless behavioral alternatives are available to him. The fewer the behaviors present in a child's repertoire, the less he will be able to behave in a suitable manner in a variety of different situations. If the child is unable to cut out pictures or designs, to draw and color, to dress and feed himself, to make simple and complex visual and auditory discriminations, to play cooperatively with others, or to enjoy assisting a peer in solving a problem, the child cannot choose to engage in any of these modes of behavior. He can acquire individual freedom of choice only to the extent that he has a range of behaviors in his repertoire.

The more limited the behavioral repertoire of the child in comparison to the level of development characteristic of a peer of comparable chronological age the more likely it becomes that the child will acquire such inappropriate modes of responding as stereotyped and self-destructive behaviors, withdrawal patterns, intense anxiety reactions, disinterest, interpersonal difficulties, general avoidance behaviors, and hyperactivity. These observations emphasize the critical necessity of providing the child with successful child development experiences at an early age—and continuously throughout childhood.

THE WIDE RANGE OF INDIVIDUAL DIFFERENCES

It must be recognized that even young children with the most unusual and severe learning and behavior difficulties can and do learn. They may acquire a wide range of simple as well as complex behavior patterns. They may learn to walk, to distinguish red from green, to comply with parental requests, to speak, to dress themselves, to be excessively fearful, to be aggressive, to understand signs, to play cooperatively with others, to refuse to cooperate, and to be sensitive to others. The types of behaviors acquired and the rate and consistency of learning these behaviors, however, vary considerably among children with problems. Some children experience little difficulty in acquiring some behavior patterns—for example, gross motor skills of walking, running, jumping—but nevertheless experience considerable difficulty in learning other types of behaviors such as verbal expression skills or the fine motor skills involved in cutting and writing.

Some children acquire very complex and highly disruptive behavior problems, and as a result are difficult to manage. Others are easy to get along with. Some are quite attentive to adult concern; others are relatively detached from social interaction. These and related factors emphasize both the individuality as well as the wide range of differences among children with problems of early development.

EFFECTS OF EXCESSIVE FAILURE EXPERIENCES

Although various neurological, sensory, and other physical deficits or limitations may account for or contribute to many of the problematic behavior characteristics of children, it is ev dent that an *inappropriate learning environment* assumes a sign ficant role in others. Children with learning and behavior problems experience failure more frequently than do other children. They do not acquire various skills as rapidly nor do they rea h the levels of performance or maturity that are expected by the home and school environments. As a result the children may receive limited positive consequences from the social environment. Parents, siblings, and teachers are not likely to provide frequen and spontaneous expressions of delight, satisfaction, approval, acceptance, or affection toward the child who fails to make expected progress. Unless the learning environment is well-designed with the child's specific learning and behavior characteristics in focus, the child is most likely to receive an excessive amount of criticism, punishment, rejection, social isolation, and personal harshness. Those in the child's environment provide him with these negative experiences because of their own disappointments and frustrations over the child's learning and behavior problems. These excessive failure experiences result in extremes of emotional reactions. The child is likely to become explosive, or fearful, or excessively shy and detached. Parents and teachers frequently are powerless to deal with the multitude of problems which arise.

The child with excessive failure experiences is likely to become quite cautious about entering into relationships or activities. It is not unusual for the child, after failure or whenever he is required to do things that are unpleasant to him, to display excessive emotionality (for example, to cry easily and frequently, to be fearful, or to engage in intense emotional outbursts). Excessive patterns of withdrawal or hesitancy over becoming involved with people or activities are often present because previous involvement has resulted so frequently in failure. The child learns to avoid similar experiences.

Accomplishments which are rather simple for most children may be exceedingly difficult for other children with learning problems. It is not unusual for parents and teachers to prod the child to "try harder" both at inappropriate times and in an excessive manner. This social pressure results frequently in intensifying the child's conflicts and producing accompanying disruptive emotional reactions.

In other cases the social environment may be too protective and may expect too little from the child with obvious developmental difficulties. Excessive and unnecessary assistance may be provided as a matter of course, with the result that the child becomes overly dependent on others for this assistance.

Finally, it is not unusual for the family and school environments to be highly inconsistent in the kinds of learning experiences provided the child. Adults will be patient and understanding on one occasion and explosive, demanding, or disinterested on another. It is not unusual for such negative behaviors to be followed by excessive expressions of attention, overconcern, and oversolicitousness. Such inconsistency is confusing to children and further intensifies their difficulties. They become even less able to cope with the requirements placed on them by the home and school environments.

Several researchers have suggested that young children with unusual or excessive learning and behavior problems acquire many inappropriate behavior patterns, or fail to acquire desirable modes of behaving, because the learning environments have not been sufficiently sensitive to the highly individual characteristics of these children. *Children do learn in these poorly structured environments, but too frequently they do not learn the behavioral characteristics which are deemed desirable.* As noted, patterns of noninvolvement, hyperactivity, emotional outburst, aggressiveness, low frustration tolerance, temper tantrums, shyness, and unpredictable reaction to social approval are more likely to develop. Children's poor self-concepts result from excessive failure experiences. The children learn to view themselves as inadequate and deficient, and others learn to view them as being unwilling and unable to accomplish anything. McClain (1969) speculates that a child's inappropriate behavior pattern ". . . reflects a failure to have learned positive social skills due to an impoverished environment as well as the inconsistent reinforcement or absence of

reinforcement of socially approved behavior. Coupled with this
. . . is the overwhelming reinforcement of negative behavior."
(p. 122)

The experiences of Hamblin and his associates (1971)
with young children with severe learning and behavior difficulties
lead to a similar impression that

> . . . learning environments can vary tremendously in value
> and in potency. Some are orthogenic, that is they help the
> child acquire pro–normal patterns; others are pathogenic,
> they cause the child to lose pro–normal patterns and they
> foster withdrawal or the development of bizarre, disruptive
> patterns. Furthermore, the various orthogenic and pathogenic
> environments apparently vary in potency. Some foster a
> higher rate of learning than others. (p. 67)

PROBLEM BEHAVIORS MAY BE AVOIDED

Behavioral characteristics of children with severe learning and
behavior difficulties will be described more fully in Chapter 2.
The following chapters also will decribe principles and procedures influencing appropriate behavior development and functioning in a manner consistent with prevention or remediation of
many of these difficulties. The *behavior management** system
presented in this book assumes the enthusiastic position that
children with problems of development not only can avoid many
unsatisfactory behavior patterns but also can acquire many contrasting desired patterns if provided appropriately designed and
stimulating learning environments. *Although there are obvious
limitations to what any child can learn,* the individualized approach of the behavior management system insures that the child's
potentials are not inadvertently overlooked by pessimistic concepts
of deficits or limitations.

The behavior management system presented throughout
this book is equally as relevant to the task of development and
improvement of any of the basic skills and behavior patterns with
which early education programs are concerned as it is to the reduction or elimination of the undesirable behavior patterns mentioned

---

* The teacher attempts to manage the learning environment provided
for the child so that he may learn and behave in an optimal manner.
The concept of *behavior management* is used in preference to similar
frequently used terms of *behavior modification* and *behavior therapy,*
as it best describes the active role which the teacher must assume to insure that the child is provided with suitable learning experiences.

above. The principles and procedures discussed will provide guidance for the teacher in developing educational programs for the following types of concerns:

How can I get a child interested in learning?

How can I keep him involved in his eye-hand coordination exercises?

How can I increase her attention to the speech sounds? She has severe articulation problems but she won't attend to me when I attempt to get her to practice the appropriate sounds.

How can I best arrange her experiences so that she will attempt to copy letters and numbers?

How can I teach him to recognize simple words?

How can I arrange the teaching environment so that he won't make so many mistakes in matching colors, objects, and shapes?

How can I get her to persist at a task that is a little difficult for her?

He is so hesitant about sharing his ideas with others. How can I encourage him to do so?

TERMS AND CONCEPTS

A number of general labels have been used to refer to young children who experience significant difficulty acquiring, retaining, and effectively using those behavioral skills and patterns which are typical of children of similar chronological age. These include such terms as *handicapped, disabled, exceptional, atypical, impaired, disordered, special,* and *developmentally delayed.* Additionally, these children have been provided a wide range of more specific labels denoting diagnostic categories which represent patterns of symptomatic behavior and presumed related internal causes. Examples of these labels include *mentally retarded, emotionally disturbed, minimally brain damaged, autistic, learning disabled, language disordered,* and *perceptually impaired.* Children have been provided these specific diagnostic labels on the basis of certain of their psychological or behavioral characteristics. A child is observed to have difficulty in understanding speech or in interacting with peers. These and similar observable behavior patterns used to diagnose and classify a child typically are assumed to be the surface symptoms of some underlying internal factors which cause the difficulty—the mental retardation, the autism, the learning disability, or the emotional disturbance.

The present book will not use such terms or related diagnostic categories *except in a descriptive manner.* These labels contribute little to the task of devising those developmental education programs which will best foster the learning and performance of appropriate patterns of behavior. The label of "mentally retarded" may be used to refer to a child who learns new behaviors considerably more slowly than typical. It will not be used in this book to explain "why" the child does not learn as rapidly as most of his peers of equal chronological age. Instead, emphasis will focus both on a detailed description of the behavioral characteristics of each individual child and on the learning conditions which hold promise of contributing to a higher level of behavioral functioning of a specific child.

The terms *children with developmental difficulties* and *children with learning and behavior problems* will be used interchangeably throughout the book. These will be used as *general descriptive terms* to refer to children who present severe and unusual problems of learning and of adapting to various physical, social, and interpersonal situations. It should be recognized, however, that these labels, as well as others previously listed, have potentially negative connotations. Whenever a term or label which implies some problem or difficulty area is applied to a child, there is always a danger of assuming that all children so labeled are of a specific type or kind. The following section examines this and other dangers inherent in applying labels and emphasizes the need for a pragmatic and flexible system for describing children and their problems.

DANGERS INHERENT IN USE OF LABELS

Blame Placed on Child

An initial danger of using such labels as retarded, disturbed, deviant, dysfunctional, or disordered is that the blame for learning and adaptation difficulties may be placed upon the children so labeled. Such a practice mistakenly emphasizes that something is wrong with *the child* when he presents unusual developmental, behavioral, learning, emotional, or social adaptation problems. Some internal pathology—mental retardation, emotional disturbance, learning disability—is assumed to cause the problems. The frequent effect of such practices is to shift the focus of difficulty (and blame) *from* the educational or learning program and place the responsibility for his difficulties *on* the child. This takes place even though the most critical factors which could be used to influence behavior change frequently reside in the child's environment and not within the child's diagnosed pathology or deviation.

9

Overlooked Uniqueness

One of the most frequent consequences of labeling a child as having some internal pathology is that specific and unique individual characteristics are overlooked. The individuality of the child is ignored on too many occasions in an attempt to find the "real" internal cause of his problems. This is done by providing him with labels denoting circumscribed deviations such as "poor ego development," "phobia," "pent-up hostility," "hyperactivity," "disrupting," "habit disorder," or, as noted, by assigning him to special diagnostic categories such as "emotionally handicapped," "immature," "learning disabled," "brain damaged," or "mentally handicapped." All children so labeled are assumed to have the same characteristics and often are provided the same type of learning program.

False assumptions and overgeneralizations frequently result from the practice of placing children in diagnostic categories. For example, it is not unusual for parents and teachers to assume that the child cannot learn because he is retarded or brain damaged. "Oh, he's mentally retarded. Now I understand why he can't learn." "John has been diagnosed as having minimal brain dysfunction. You'll just have to work around his hyperactivity, distractibility, short attention span, and low frustration tolerance." "Sue is emotionally disturbed. She's unable to recognize words because of her emotional block." Such reasoning uses the behavioral difficulties that characterize a child to explain why he has such difficulties. This approach emphasizes the child's presumed deficits and results in a rather pessimistic view of the child's potentialities.

The label or diagnosis of mental retardation, to continue the previous example:

—does not explain why a child does not learn.
—does not indicate the specifics of what the child can indeed learn.
—does not indicate what specific behaviors a child does exhibit.
—does not identify the conditions under which optimal learning will occur for that particular child.

As a result of these limitations and dangers, the behavior management approach views mental retardation as a descriptive label which suggests that a child has not acquired a behavioral repertoire at the rate or level which is characteristic of children of comparable age.

In a similar vein, such diagnostic labels as emotional disturbance, learning disability, and minimal brain dysfunction do not explain why a child has difficulty in tasks requiring visual-motor skills, or in maintaining composure when confronted with frustration. Nor do these labels indicate why a child may have trouble learning to read or why he cries easily and frequently, has frequent disagreements with his peers, or is unhappy.

Generalized Patterns of Difficulty

Labels also imply that children behave in a given manner under all conditions and at all times. This simply is not true. A child labeled as hyperactive may be quite attentive and inactive, for example, while watching TV or when listening to a favorite record. A "retarded" child may be quite "normal" in some endeavors, perhaps in gross motor activities. The "shy" child may be shy only around adults, casual acquaintances, and strangers. He may be quite outgoing around some of his close friends. The "learning disabled" child may have extreme difficulty with auditory perception most of the time. Under special conditions of stimulus presentation he may have little difficulty.

In summary, diagnostic labels provide nothing more than summary or short-hand terms for problematic behavior patterns of children. Although there may be some common characteristics among children so designated, the *differences far outnumber* the similarities. Grouping children under such umbrella terms on the basis of a few behavioral similarities creates the danger that the similarities will be overemphasized and the individual differences will be minimized or ignored. Since a group of children may all be designated as emotionally disturbed, for example, it is easy to imply that there are some educational strategies that should be used with all such children. It may be assumed further that these strategies differ in kind or degree from those educational strategies used with children provided other diagnostic labels such as mentally retarded or learning disabled. *There is no evidence that either of these assumptions is true.*

A BEHAVIOR MANAGEMENT FOCUS

The behavior management position represented in this book is contrary to these internal pathology assumptions and related practices. As the following chapters will reveal, the child with developmental difficulties can best learn in an environment that is organized around his specific and unique characteristics. The task of devising such a program is best accomplished in the absence of any preconceptions or overgeneralizations, which frequently accompany diagnostic labeling and categorization, about what the child can or cannot do. A focus on the child's assumed internal deviations is highly inconsistent with an educational focus which asks, "I wonder how a behavior management program can be arranged for a specific child or for a group of children to facilitate optimal learning of a wide array of both specific behavioral skills and broader personality characteristics?" The behavior management approach described in this book emphasizes that the child *can indeed learn.* The activity of developing the most effective learning environment can proceed in a more sensitive and constructive manner if meaningful educational factors are considered instead of focusing on nonfunctional ones which emphasize internal deviation.

The behavior management approach recognizes that most children learn many of the early skills of language, perception, self-care, socialization, and emotional expression and control in the absence of any formally structured training program. Even though many children may not learn successfully under these unstructured conditions, it is assumed that given a more highly structured, individually designed, and systematically presented set of learning experiences these children with learning difficulties will be able to acquire many of the behaviors which otherwise would be missed. This position thus assumes that at least some of the learning deficits and behavioral difficulties in most instances may reside in the environment and not necessarily within the child.

Children are unique and must be treated individually regardless of similarities within their various patterns of difficulties. One child, regardless of the disability label awarded him, may best learn in an environment that has minimal distracting auditory stimulation. Another child may require frequent repetitions of a new behavior prior to its becoming a reliable aspect of his repertoire. Another child may be a rapid learner in some behavioral areas but a slow and inefficient learner in others. Without question there are limitations to what any child can learn. Since there are no absolute means of determining what a child can acquire prior to exposing him to well-designed learning experiences, the parent and teacher should remain open and flexible concerning the child's limitations and potentials.

Static information, diagnostic labels denoting internal psychic pathology, and all related concepts should be discarded as educationally meaningless. Only that information and those concepts which contribute to educational and behavior management endeavors should be provided consideration. The chapters to follow will provide a more detailed discussion of concepts which focus on the assets and potentialities of the child and which provide direction to procedures designed to maximize the child's behavioral development and functioning.

CHARACTERISTICS OF A BEHAVIOR MANAGEMENT APPROACH

The present section will describe the basic characteristics of a behavior management approach and will illustrate differences in concepts and practices from other viewpoints of how learning and behavior problems develop and of what can be done to deal with them.

Focus on Behavior

The major characteristic of the behavior management approach is its focus on influencing the *behavior* of the child as he interacts in a social environment. Behavior is viewed as what the child does do that can be observed by others. This behavior may be viewed by others as normal and acceptable or as deviant and unacceptable. A child is described as aggressive, for example, on the basis of various of his behaviors which parents, teacher, and others define as aggressive. An "unhappy" child is so labeled on the basis of various observable emotional, social, and interpersonal child behaviors. A child is described as inattentive in view of his response to aspects of his environment other than or in addition to those required by the teacher or parent. The manner in which he responds to other persons at other times may result in a child being called cordial, cooperative, and friendly. Another child on the basis of behaviors which are observed by others may be viewed as lonely, sad, or detached. The focus of an educational behavior management program is to influence these observable patterns of behavior.

The behavior approach finds it useful to view general and complex child behaviors as representing various repertoires or classes of behavior. The total behavior of a child may be described in terms of such classes as verbal behaviors, motor behaviors, emotional behaviors, and social behaviors. Or he may be described in terms of more circumscribed behavior patterns such as his self-concept behaviors, independence behaviors, patience behaviors, self-control behaviors, or his lack-of-confidence behaviors. In describing the child in terms of observable behavior patterns, the teacher is in an ideal position to ask such relevant questions as: How can I influence the child's self-concept behaviors, his independence behaviors, his persistence behaviors, or his self-control behaviors? She focuses on what she can observe about the child and does not become side-tracked into a theoretical analysis of presumed internal factors.

Child Can Learn

The behavior management approach assumes the enthusiastic position that children with learning and behavior problems not only can learn but also can become efficient and enthusiastic learners under appropriately structured learning conditions. The approach assumes that the child can learn many of the specific developmental skills such as dressing, grooming, talking, toileting, playing, cutting, and coloring, as well as more general and complex socially desirable behavior patterns. In dealing with more complex behaviors, the position assumes that when provided appropriate experiences over an extended period of time the child with developmental difficulties

—may learn to make deliberate decisions.
—may develop behaviors of responsibility.
—may develop basic skills of self-management.
—may learn to be sensitive to the rights and feelings of others.
—may learn to respect rules without rebelliousness.
—may learn to relate in a group in a meaningful manner.
—may acquire a range of healthy emotional reactions and may become happy, free of excessive anxiety, and affectionately attached to adults and peers.

Child-Centered Approach

The behavior management approach, as implied, is child-centered. The child with developmental difficulties is first an individual. Emphasis is placed on understanding each child by studying this child in his social environment. If the child is to become more independent and competent, his uniqueness must be respected and facilitated. Young children with learning and behavior problems vary widely in behavioral and physical characteristics. Realistic expectations concerning what a specific child may learn and the rate of his learning are possible only after thorough appraisal of each child and of his previous and present learning experiences. As no two children have exactly the same patterns of abilities and limitations, it is necessary to view each child in a highly individual manner. With many children, it will be necessary to provide various learning experiences to determine what the child can learn and to identify the best conditions under which learning will occur.

Present Environment Is Important

The present social environment and the related stimulation to which the child is exposed are assumed to be critical in influencing present behavior. This environment, and only this present environment, can be used by the teacher to influence the child's behavioral development and functioning. She can do nothing about previous learning experiences. She can do something about present ones. Teacher, peers, the physical conditions of the classroom, and family members all contribute to the present experiences of the child. Causes of behavior are viewed as those present events which are effective in influencing the occurrence or nonoccurrence of various behaviors. Significant changes in the manner in which a child behaves usually come about slowly and reflect the cumulative results of numerous learning experiences.

Although major focus is placed on environmental influence, it is recognized that some behaviors are influenced greatly by physical factors. These influences can be temporary, such as fatigue, hunger, or a brief low blood sugar level. Others are more lasting: a hormonal or enzyme deficiency, an injury, or a sensory deficit such as a visual or a hearing loss. Obviously, these and other pertinent physical factors must be considered both when designing an educational program for a child and in any attempt to account for various of his behavioral characteristics. In such cases, after appropriate medical evaluation and treatment, the learning environment can be designed in an effort to maximize its behavior development components. Medical evaluation may establish the presence of brain injury but may be unable to provide any treatment to influence the learning skills of the child. The learning environment must then focus on the behavioral characteristics of the child as they exist in the present (some of which may be a direct result of the brain injury) and be designed to make use of or to compensate for these characteristics in promoting more appropriate behavior development and functioning.

The position that behavior is frequently under the influence of events in the present environment of the child is contrary to the popular belief that learning difficulties and bothersome or problematic behavior result from some internal pathology or some single or small number of past traumatic experiences. It is true that most present behavior does represent the end result of numerous learning experiences. Some complex behavior patterns represent the cumulative effect of hundreds or even thousands of previous experiences. A child who is highly aggressive, argumentative, disruptive, or difficult to manage due to his negativism does not behave in this manner as a result of, for example, some "emotional disturbance" or of some few past experiences. Rather, it is assumed that these behavior patterns have been acquired over a lengthy period as a result of literally hundreds or even thousands of social experiences with other adults, siblings, and peers.

Likewise, a child who is attentive, highly interested, and easily stimulated to engage in new behaviors does not exhibit these characteristics because he is "normal," or "good," or "talented." These behaviors, as suggested, have evolved out of numerous previous learning experiences. A child does not behave as he does because he is naughty, mean, or emotionally disturbed. He is influenced by his present environment. This present environment indeed has acquired its influence as a result of the numerous past experiences of the child. Abnormal behavior is not symptomatic of some internal pathology. It is a symptom—that is, the result—of past inappropriate learning experiences.

But most behavior patterns *can be* changed in most instances if, and only if, the present environment changes. Psychological and environmental events, many of which may be identified and influenced by the teacher, are promoting and maintaining present behavior. As complex behavior patterns develop gradually over a series of experiences, events involved in the initial development of a behavior pattern may be quite different from those events which presently maintain it. At any time a given experience may exert only a minute influence on the strengthening or the maintenance of various complex behavior patterns. But, as noted, 100, 200, 500, or even 1000 such experiences can gradually result in an obnoxious, argumentative, aggressive child; or, more appropriate experiences may result in a cooperative, attentive, enthusiastic child.

Little if any beneficial purpose is served by efforts to identify hypothetical internal causes, or even historical causes, as nothing can be done to change them. The teacher can only deal with present events which comprise the child's present environment. Present behavior, regardless of how undesirable it may be, continues to occur in the present as it represents the best adaptation that the child can make to conditions as they exist now. This does not imply, however, that the child cannot learn more desirable means of behaving under changed environmental conditions.

A major strategy to "understanding" the occurrence of present behavior patterns is that of focusing on what the child's behavior produces in the present, on those conditions under which it occurs, and on the strength of this behavior. If a child makes a distracting clucking noise while the teacher is reading a story, for example, focus should be placed on the function or purpose for the child which this behavior serves in the present. Does it produce social attention from the teacher or from peers? Does the behavior serve to remove the child from an unpleasant classroom situation? Such consequences of behavior, as will be described later, assume central importanec in understanding many behavior patterns. A focus on the present may result in a desired modification of the child's behavior.

Seven-year-old Cal has intense temper tantrums when aggravated by his older brother. To understand how the older brother has come to influence Cal in this manner, the numerous previous experiences involving Cal and his brother must be described. However, if one wishes to develop a behavior management program to modify this behavior pattern, attention must focus on the present. What does the older brother do to Cal? What are the results of Cal's temper tantrums? These and similar concerns will result in a behavior management program to modify the behavior of both Cal and his older brother. It is not necessary to understand how a particular problem behavior developed out of past experiences in order to effectively change the behavior in the present.

It is true that with extreme developmental deviations a child may appear to be unresponsive to his present environment. The child who is described as autistic typically is quite difficult to influence. In most cases, however, a focus on the child as he responds in his present environment can result in some appropriate behavior development. The reports of Wolf *et al.* (1964), Wolf *et al.* (1967), Lovaas (1967), and Lovaas *et al.* (1967) illustrate this positivistic statement. Children with limited and highly deviant behavior patterns were provided behavior management programs which resulted in the development of a wide range of desired social behavior patterns. A brief account of some of the procedures used in work with similar children is presented in Chapter 12.

Environmental Influences Vs. Internal Causes

Some educators view a child's problem behaviors as reflecting various internal needs. This position is reflected in the following observations: "Calvin misbehaves in order to get attention. He has such a high need for affection." "The dependent child clings to mother because she needs the security of mother's presence." "The emotionally disturbed child needs to know that others like him so he must be given love, acceptance, and attention regardless of how he behaves. A structured environment which holds him responsible for his behavior would interfere with his need for attention and assurance."

The child's behavior is explained as a surface manifestation of the presumed internal-need states: the child clings to mother because he needs love. The educational focus of such an internal-need approach is directed toward influencing the internal-need states. It is assumed that these states are the real causes of the child's learning and behavior problems. Once these hypothetical need states change, so it is assumed, the child's behavior in turn will improve.

Some children are clingers. They seem constantly to be demanding the attention of adults. It is easy to assume that such behavior is a reflection of some internal-need state and to attempt to meet this need lest the child be damaged. Some children become upset when not in the presence of adults. It is easy to assume that these children have a fear of rejection and require close attention and concern.

The behavior management approach, with its major focus on what the child does in various situations, differs somewhat from the internal-cause position. It recognizes that all children are social as they live in a social world. Children influence, and are influenced by, the attention, approval, affection, praise, and acceptance of others. Individual differences obviously exist. Some children are only minimally influenced by social events while others are greatly influenced. Some children prefer to be in the presence of both children and adults; others have a decided preference for adults. But as behavioral characteristics these actions are the result of a large number of previous learning experiences; they are not viewed by the behavior management approach as resulting from some assumed internal-need condition. The child may cling to mother to attract her attention. The attention may in fact reduce uncomfortable feelings and thus increase the likelihood that the child will continue to cling to mother. However, this attention merely serves to increase the clinging behavior instead of increasing the child's independence. The child could be taught to engage in more independent behavior with a carefully designed behavior management program which would produce desired amounts of mother's attention. As a result independence behaviors would be acquired by the child. In this relationship both mother and child are satisfied.

There is considerable evidence that behavioral characteristics can be influenced in such a direct manner by rearranging the child's environment. This direct approach is preferred to the indirect one dealing with presumed internal-need states.

Principles of Social Learning

The behavior management approach to influencing the behavior of young children with developmental difficulties is based on principles of social learning and related concepts of behavior development and change. The major concept underlying the approach, that of positive reinforcement, emphasizes the positive, humanistic orientation of the approach. The major premise suggests that a child can best acquire a wide range of desired behavior patterns, including emotional and attitudinal ones, in an environment which emphasizes positive consequences of desired behavior and which keeps negative consequences at an absolute minimum.

Rules of Successful Learning

The social learning principles and related concepts provide a set of rules for structuring successful learning experiences. Some of these rules suggest that many behaviors of the child are influenced by the consequences which the behavior produces. These behaviors are referred to by learning theorists as *operant* or *instrumental* in nature. These operants refer to what the child *does* as he interacts with his social and physical environment. These are behaviors which, in a sense, operate on the environment to produce certain consequences. These behaviors also may be said to be instrumental in producing various consequences. Rules for influencing operant behavior will be presented in Chapters 4, 5, and 6.

A child's emotional behaviors are influenced by a different set of rules. These rules are derived from principles of respondent conditioning. Instead of being influenced by consequences, emotional (respondent) behaviors are influenced by preceding events. The rules involved in the learning of emotional behaviors will be presented in Chapter 7.

The goal in application of these rules of learning is to increase the child's competency level in dealing with a wide range of problem situations. "What would I like the child to do?" is emphasized instead of "I wish he would not do that." "Do not do that," becomes, "John, let's do this." If a child is encouraged to be cooperative, he is less likely to be disruptive or noncompliant. If reinforced sufficiently for attending, the child will not be wandering about the classroom during work time. If he is smiling, he cannot be whining and crying. The structure in such program experiences is reflected in the consistency which exists between various behaviors and various consequences which the behaviors produce. The child learns what to expect. Through guided ex-

19

periences he discovers the relationship between specific behaviors and particular kinds of consequences. He discovers that inappropriate behavior is not to his benefit and responds readily to the structure which guides him into discovering more adaptable means of behaving.

Abnormal Learning Experiences

The behavior management emphasis on development of appropriate behavior patterns is in contrast to many other approaches which focus on various deviations or pathologies assumed to underlie the learning and social adaptation problems of children. As suggested, the child's behavior is not viewed as abnormal, bad, mysterious, pathological, or deviant, nor as being related to a set of causes which differ from those which underlie normal behavior patterns. It is assumed that the same principles of behavior which account for the development of desired behaviors also are involved in the development of inappropriate modes of behaving. Inappropriate, unwanted, or undesirable behavior results from "abnormal" learning experiences—that is, experiences which encourage the wrong behaviors.

A given set of learning experiences may be quite successful in promoting appropriate behavior development for children who do not exhibit developmental difficulties. However, these same experiences may result in numerous problems for children who do demonstrate developmental difficulties. Many children may learn quite well in a classroom in which they are permitted to move freely from one activity to another. In contrast, children with difficulties in focusing attention may find this a disastrous classroom environment. A more highly structured situation in which redundant stimuli are reduced may result in more effective learning. This emphasizes the necessity of tailoring the early learning experiences around a child's individual characteristics.

Another example of abnormality in children with learning and behavior problems is a child who behaves in a highly aggressive and disruptive manner. No constructive purpose is served by viewing the child's aggressive behavior nor the child himself as abnormal. His behavior is merely behavior which the social environment has influenced. The environment in which the child developed the behavior pattern has provided abnormal or inappropriate experiences for that child—that is, those experiences which have resulted in the undesired aggressive behaviors. These behaviors will change as the child's social learning environment is normalized to provide systematic experiences designed to promote more desirable means of interaction. This represents another illustration that the behavior management approach does not place the blame on the child for difficulties in learning or in adjustment to the requirements of the social environment.

The child is not viewed as bad, evil, or deliberately negative. If he is "spoiled," it is only because the social environment intentionally or inadvertently has reinforced him on numerous occasions for "spoiled" behavior. No child ever intentionally decides to become retarded, obnoxious, grouchy, socially difficult, or autistic. Concepts of internal deviancy or pathology must be discarded and replaced by those which result in strategies for improving the present social learning environment.

A behavior management approach places emphasis on those events which appear to influence various behavior patterns. For example, a child may appear to enjoy provoking the parent or adult into becoming upset or angry. He may demand certain things to the point that the adult becomes irritated and screams at the child. On the surface, it may appear that the child is a "little devil" or that he is "expressing evil tendencies." The social learning principles which underlie a behavior management approach, however, would assume an entirely different position.

An attempt would be made to reconstruct the critical social learning experiences in the child's history which have strengthened the child's aggravating ways of behaving. An analysis also would be made of the present events which trigger the behavior and those reinforcing aspects which serve to insure that the behavior continues to occur. It may be hypothesized, for example, that whenever the adult becomes upset this reinforces the "spoiled" behavior in some manner. It may be that on occasion the child's demanding behavior pays off—the child gets his way. Or it may be that the adult provides various forms of social attention only after becoming upset at the child. Under these conditions the child may learn that "after I upset the teacher, she will be nice to me for a while." The child's behavior thus may be altered by a minor change in the teacher's behavior. She begins to be nice to the child following appropriate behavior and to ignore him as he misbehaves. The child now is likely to learn desired behavior which results in the positive consequence of "teacher being nice." His "spoiled" behavior will occur less frequently since it no longer serves any purpose for the child.

Natural Environment

The natural environments of home and school are assumed to be the best settings in which to deal with various problems of learning and adaptation. If the child is overly aggressive toward siblings at home, this problem behavior should be managed in the home setting. If the child has difficulty getting along with peers, this problem should be managed in the school environment in the presence of peers. Programs which remove the child from these natural environments and place him in other less natural areas for special treatment are deemed appropriate only in highly selective cases. In most instances, if appropriately structured, the natural environments contain the elements needed for appropriate behavior development and functioning. Numerous illustrations will be provided which document this position that learning and behavior problems most frequently can be dealt with in the home and school settings in which these problems occur. Further, teachers and parents can become effective in designing and implementing behavior management programs. It will be seen that frequently only minor changes in the social experiences which parents and teachers provide will lead to desirable and long-term changes in the child's way of behaving.

Emphasis on Self-Direction

The behavior management approach seeks to develop self-direction, self-control, and independence in every young child to the highest level possible. These are not skills or behavioral characteristics which develop automatically as the child grows older. These behavior patterns can, however, be facilitated by a sensitive learning environment which systematically encourages them in a step-by-step manner.

The child should be provided as much responsibility for his behavior as he is able to fulfill at any given time. With this orientation, the child whose behavior is unacceptable or aggravating is not responded to in an angry or punitive manner. The social environment may be firm and consistent in presenting behavioral expectations but as nagging is reduced to a minimum, a basis is provided for positive social interaction. Such an approach seldom uses such an expression as "Don't do that." "Stop that," is reduced and replaced by a strategy of providing direction and positive reinforcement for desired behavior. As the child is exposed to various consequences, he learns to choose those behaviors which result in consequences that are most pleasing to him, and to refrain from behavior that produces unpleasant consequences. He learns to be responsible for his own behavior.

Potentials Are Not Predetermined

The specifics of what a child can or cannot do at any given time in the future or under any given set of conditions is not decided on an *a priori* basis. Reporting that a five-year-old child is mildly re-tarded merely provides a general description of his present level of functioning in those areas sampled by the objective tests used in establishing this diagnosis. Such a description *does not* relate what the child will be able to learn in the future or the specifics of the behavior management program which will best facilitate new learning. What a child can learn can be determined only by exposing the child to a learning environment that is optimally tailored with the specific characteristics of a given child as a focus. No child, from a behavior management position, is ever deprived of an effective learning program just because he is labeled as retarded, or emotionally disturbed, or autistic; nor is he categori-cally placed in a predetermined special environment for children so labeled.

Focus on How to Influence Behavior

The behavior management approach is concerned with "how" teachers, parents, and others may influence the behavior of chil-dren and not primarily with "what" behavior patterns a child should acquire. The approach does not offer any guides or rules concerning what a child should learn. The behaviors which are deemed desirable for a child must be decided upon prior to the initiation of a learning experience. Once these behavioral objec-tives or goals have been identified, principles and practices of behavior management can then be used to design a learning program to assist the child in reaching these goals. "Should a child be polite?" "Should he remain quiet?" "Should he be happy?" "Should he dress himself without assistance?" "Should he learn to read?" "Should he learn to share possessions with others?" "Should he learn to comply without objection to adult requests?" These and thousands of similar questions must be decided upon by parents and teachers. Once the parent or teacher has decided that "politeness" is a desirable behavioral objective, the behavior management approach provides guides and proce-dures for use in an educational program designed to strengthen polite behaviors.

Some behavior goals are viewed by almost everyone as being desirable for all children. Almost everyone would agree that children should learn an adequate verbal language system, or should learn basic skills of self-care such as dressing, grooming, or feeding. But the desirability of many other behaviors is open to varying opinions. Should all children dress neatly, develop table manners, learn grammatically correct English, sit quietly while the teacher is talking, learn to share possessions? On the basis of various legal, ethical, philosophic, religious, cultural, economic, and other conceptual and emotional factors parents and teachers may respond negatively to these and similar questions. These factors form the basis for quite different behavioral goals. Again, the behavior management system is concerned primarily with *how* to influence behavior and is useful to the teacher after she has decided upon *what* behaviors should be influenced.

In future discussion the terms *desirable behavior, appropriate behavior*, and *acceptable behavior* are used to refer to those behaviors with which those who comprise the child's social environments will be pleased. *Undesirable, inappropriate*, and *unacceptable* are used to refer to the child's behaviors which will be objectionable or cause negative reactions in the child's environment. The specific behaviors viewed as desirable or as undesirable, of course, will vary across different social environments.

Educational specialists generally agree, however, that children learn better when home and school agree upon the behavior patterns which are desirable. Such an agreement produces consistency in the child's life, and reduces the difficulties confronting him. He feels more secure and competent since he can predict what is expected of him even though he moves from home setting to the school setting. Any obvious inconsistency between school and home settings can only add to the child's learning and behavior difficulties. This emphasizes the desirability of systematic communication and cooperative programs between home and school. The nature of such programs will be discussed in Chapter 13.

A PREVIEW

The following chapters will consist of a description of more specific concepts and related procedures of the behavior management approach and its applications to specific problems of learning and behavior adaptation. After a description of the more prevalent behavior characteristics of young children which interfere with effective learning and behaving, the social learning principles and related procedures of influencing behavior will be presented. These chapters will focus on the following questions:

—*How can new behaviors which the child has never engaged in be acquired?*
—*How can existing behaviors which occur too infrequently be strengthened?*
—*What can be done to insure that behaviors learned in the educational setting will also occur in other settings?*

—*What can be done to insure that behaviors acquired in the education setting will be maintained over extended periods of time?*
—*What can be done to insure that the child will behave in a discriminating fashion?*
—*How can inappropriate behaviors be reduced or eliminated?*

Behavioral evaluation procedures used in a behavior management program will precede a step-by-step examination of how to organize a specific program of behavior management. General guidelines for implementing such a program will be followed by chapters on specific applications to a range of behavioral areas.

CHAPTER 2

A Description of General
and Specific Learning
and Behavior Problems

Children with severe learning and behavior difficulties have much in common with all young children: they rarely exhibit any kinds of behaviors that are not also seen in the typical child. At the same time, the child with developmental difficulties exhibits different intensities and combinations of behavior patterns that do create problems for the child and his social environment. These are patterns of behavior which render both the teaching and learning processes more difficult undertakings. This chapter will provide brief descriptions of some of the more obvious behavioral and learning characteristics which must be recognized and dealt with by teachers and parents if successful behavior management programs are to be devised and implemented.

The patterns to be described here are not proposed as characteristic of all children with severe learning and behavior difficulties. Quite the contrary, some children show highly individual and limited problem behavior patterns. But others display many of the behavior patterns to be detailed and thus experience extensive problems in learning and in behaving.

In viewing these areas of difficulty, the teacher must avoid dismissing them as inevitable or as unalterable components of some assumed disease or pathology. "Oh, Sue cannot persist at a task or tolerate frustration because she is emotionally disturbed," or, "He can't remember because he is mentally retarded." Such explanations serve no useful purpose for the teacher or the child.

The areas of difficulty with which a child struggles should be defined precisely and dealt with in a direct manner. If a child shows limitations in curiosity behavior, persistence, and in imitation skills, the behavior management program must attempt to facilitate the development and strengthening of these characteristics. He may not be attentive; the program should be designed to teach him to be more attentive. He may be apathetic; the program should be designed to increase his involvement. He may engage in disruptive emotional behavior upon slight frustration; the program should be designed to teach him better emotional control. A moderately retarded child may become enthusiastic, attentive, curious, and imitative even though he lacked many of these behavior patterns when initially enrolled in a behavior management program. These and other problem behavior areas cannot be expected to disappear or improve in some undefined manner, but the desired behavior patterns can be fostered and strengthened when dealt with in a programmatic manner.

GENERAL AND SPECIFIC LEARNING DIFFICULTIES

Some children demonstrate very general learning difficulties. There is rather even, albeit depressed, learning and performance across all developmental areas. A child may show relatively equal retardation in the development of language skills, self-help skills, socialization skills, perceptual skills, problem-solving skills, and of skills of emotional expression and control. Other children develop normally in some areas but exhibit specific and severe difficulties in others. It is also true that children may present various combinations of general and specific difficulties. A five-year-old mentally retarded child may be characterized in most areas by a rate of functioning which is typical of a three-year-old; however, in some areas he may be much more advanced or much more depressed. A recent experience illustrates this. A five-year-old girl with no expressive speech had been described following a detailed diagnostic study as being moderately retarded with severe expressive speech difficulties. Close observation in a series of developmental education situations revealed levels of development in many areas which were quite above that expected on the basis of her performance on various formal intelligence tests. She was well within age range in tasks which did not require use of expressive speech.
There may be very uneven behavior development even within a single behavior dimension such as perception or language. Auditory perception may be good; visual perception may

be poor. Expressive language may be poor; receptive language may be good. Speech expression may be far below gestural communication skills. The level of one skill should not be used as an index of the level of behavioral development of another skill. The child can be understood only by a careful and detailed evaluation of his functioning along numerous behavioral dimensions. This must be done by using formal and informal observational procedures. The peculiar learning histories, the neurological, physical, and sensory limitations, and the behaviors being maintained by the present environment all influence what a child may learn and demonstrate at any time.

It becomes evident that the child with developmental difficulties must be treated in a unique manner if optimal behavior development is to result. The teacher cannot depend upon the presence of many of the basic skills of attention, curiosity, persistence, interest, or discrimination. She may find with some children that these basic skills must be taught prior to being concerned with the development of other more complex skills. For example, if the teacher is interested in teaching basic dressing skills, color discrimination, or some other sensory-motor skills, she must first insure that the child has sufficient attention skills, persistence, frustration tolerance, and imitation skills. If these more basic skills are minimal, the teaching experience will be a frustrating one to teacher and child alike. The initial educational program must be designed to strengthen these prerequisite skills.

ATTENTION DEFICITS, DISTRACTIBILITY AND HYPERACTIVITY

Effective learning of many skills requires that a child focus his attention on various aspects of the learning task. If he is to learn to distinguish a red color from a blue color he must focus attention on one and then on the other. He also must persist in his attention behavior and refrain from excessive attending, or otherwise responding, to other aspects of his present environment.

One of the most basic and major deficits of many children with developmental difficulties is in the area of attention behavior. Children labeled as mentally retarded, emotionally disturbed, brain damaged, and perceptually handicapped have been described as having short attention spans and as being distractible. In addition, the highly correlated behavior pattern of hyperactivity is frequently described. The child is unable to engage in many activities in a concentrated fashion. He moves from one aspect of his stimulus environment to another. His perseverance is limited.

The child has difficulty in focusing on specific events long enough for these events to acquire any consistent influence on his behavior.

In discussing these interrelated behavioral characteristics observed in many young children with learning and behavior problems, it is essential to note that they are not absolute characteristics. A child may be nonattentive and hyperactive in some situations and not in others. He may exhibit good attention and activity control for periods of days or weeks and then lose this control for some time. Additionally, as is true of all human characteristics, there is considerable variation among children with the same diagnostic label. Some children who are mentally retarded, brain injured, and perceptually handicapped may be highly distractible and hyperactive. Other children so labeled may have good skills of attention and activity control.

When a child is described as not attending, reference is made (1) to a specific type of stimulation to which the child is to respond in a discriminating fashion and (2) to the observation that he is responding to other aspects of the environment. His responses are being controlled by events other than those which the teacher presents in an effort to "get his attention."

> The teacher may suggest, "Jill, look at the picture on your table and find one like this," as she holds up a picture of a black dog. Jill looks at the picture momentarily and quickly turns to Jim who is humming softly to himself. She then turns her attention to a sudden noise in the hall. As she turns her head in the direction of the noise, she catches a glimpse of a favorite toy which she earlier had left on the floor. As she moves to retrieve the toy, the teacher redirects her attention again with the request, "Jill, sit down and look at the picture."

This example illustrates that the hyperactive and distractible child has not acquired general skills of focusing on selected aspects of a situation in which a multitude of stimuli are present. Instead, she responds to many different stimulus events, but frequently for only short periods of time. The child is described as unable to focus attention. There is strong competition among stimuli. This competition may be within a specific sense such as the visual area or between senses such as the visual and auditory areas.

It becomes essential for effective learning that a child acquire behavior skills of attending. Further, it is essential that certain aspects of the child's stimulus environment come to have greater influence over attentional responses than other aspects. For example, it is necessary that the teacher's voice and the picture which she is holding gain Jill's attention instead of other events which are irrelevant to the lesson being presented. With the distractible child, this differential control of attentional responses frequently has not been acquired. Unless the child can respond differentially to different stimuli, learning does not occur. Or if the skill is only poorly developed, highly inefficient learning results. The child attends to one event for an insufficient length of time and then moves to another event. Or he responds to events that are irrelevant to the learning task that is being presented. Program suggestions for influencing attention skills in the hyperactive child are presented in Chapter 12.

LIMITATIONS IN CURIOSITY BEHAVIOR

Observation of a typical group of preschool children reveals a considerable amount of exploratory behavior when the children are exposed to new or novel aspects of their environment. It is felt by many that a child has a natural tendency to explore his environment and in this manner to learn about it. Some psychologists suggest that children are intrinsically motivated to be creative, spontaneous, and curious. Deci (1972) commented:

> I am fascinated with a child's unflagging curiosity. He explores everything; for him objects exist to be touched, smelled, and tasted, and where possible, eaten. He learns, and learning excites and delights him. (p. 57)

Children with various learning and behavior difficulties frequently demonstrate a limited amount of curiosity behavior. Much of this limited curiosity which the children reveal as they enter a developmental education program is related to their previous learning experiences. Children learn to avoid or to withdraw from new situations as they are unable to predict what the consequences of such exploration might be. Such behavioral restrictions may have resulted from an excessive number of unpleasant experiences associated with previous exploratory or curiosity behavior. New situations produce fear or a more general state of discomfort and children come to avoid these situations.

It is also true that curiosity behavior may have been reduced as it has not been encouraged by the social environment. Parents have been afraid that the child might hurt himself or that "he will get into too many things" and thus have restricted his exploratory behavior. As he has explored he has been told, "No, don't do that. Stop that." In other instances the adults may have ignored his curiosity behavior or else have viewed it as bothersome and have intentionally shut the child out of any attention when such curiosity has occurred. In doing so, a behavior pattern of curiosity and exploration has been restricted. Program suggestions for encouraging curiosity behaviors will be presented in Chapter 11.

MOTIVATIONAL DEFICITS AND LIMITED PERSISTENCE

The young child is typically quite involved in many aspects of his environment. He responds well to teacher suggestions, enters into new situations with enthusiasm, and maintains his interest and enjoyment of many things that are present. These characteristics render early education endeavors enjoyable for parent and teacher.

But a problem for many children with developmental difficulties arises in the area of a general motivational deficit. The following descriptions illustrate this deficit: "He is not interested in many things," "He doesn't seem to be motivated to enter into relationships," "He easily gets discouraged," "Nothing seems to hold his interest for too long," "The usual things that spark enthusiasm in the young child don't motivate him." As a result the teacher must attend specifically to this problem of motivation. She must arrange the environment so that task involvement will become satisfying to the child.

Children with learning and behavior problems are not only less likely to become involved in learning tasks but also show a lack of persistence once a learning task is presented. While some children will typically persist for some time at a cutting task, a coloring activity, or putting puzzles together and will characteristically show enthusiasm and concentration, the child with learning difficulties all too frequently remains with a task or activity only for short periods. It is not unusual for the child to discard a task quickly when confronted with difficulty, to become frustrated easily, to be prone to become excessively emotional, and to lose interest. He may toss the materials aside or have a temper tantrum. He readily shifts his attention to other things in his environment.

Becoming involved and continuing involvement in given tasks have too frequently in the past resulted in failure for many children. The child has not been able to please himself or others and there have not been sufficient pleasant consequences associated with persistence in the face of difficulty. Involvement in a difficult task is a cue to the child that failure is likely. Such recognition of difficulty creates an unpleasant emotional reaction which the child terminates by leaving the task. Suggestions for encouraging greater interest in and persistence at a range of activities and relationships will be discussed in Chapters 4 and 7.

○ MEMORY DIFFICULTIES

Many children learn rapidly during the preschool years and are able to retain their new learning and expand it into more complex behavior patterns. Once a behavior has been acquired, the teacher can depend upon it being remembered.

In contrast, the child with developmental difficulties may exhibit obvious memory difficulties. He seems to know something one day but forgets it the next. "He just doesn't seem to remember what he learns. I have to go over and over it. It surely slows me down because I never know if the children will know tomorrow what they learned today." Program procedures for enhancing memory skills will be discussed in Chapters 9 and 11.

DEFICITS IN IMITATION LEARNING SKILLS

The young child acquires many of his speech, social, and other behaviors through imitation learning. He learns to imitate the behaviors of significant others since such behavior results in pleasant consequences. He mimics the sounds, the movements, the interactions of parents, teachers, and peers whom he likes. The more closely he imitates the behaviors of others, the more frequent and enthusiastic the social attention he receives from others. The behavior models which are provided thus significantly influence what he learns as well as the rate at which he acquires many skills.

Many children with developmental difficulties have poorly developed skills of imitation, a deficit which could be due to numerous factors. Early attempts at imitation by the young child may not be encouraged by his social environment. Attention skills may be poorly developed and in turn interfere with the child's perception of consistent behavior to imitate. In other cases, excessive emotional behaviors may disrupt the child's relationship with others and provide less desired behavior to imitate. As a result, the behavior of others is not attended to or modeled nearly as frequently as is typically true. The child is deprived of many of the basic skills (which are acquired by the typical child through imitation) upon which more complex skills are based. A program for influencing imitation skills is described in Chapter 11.

DIFFICULTIES IN TRANSFER OF LEARNING

Behaviors learned in one setting by most children readily generalize to another. The child learns to say certain words, engage in sensory-motor skills, or to interact in a certain manner with adults and peers. These behaviors occur not only in those situations in which they were acquired initially but also in numerous other similar situations.

Many children, however, experience unusual difficulty in generalization. The child is unable to make the transfer from one situation to another. Behavior learned in one setting appears to be highly specific and the child must be retaught the skill in new situations. This difficulty creates additional problems for the child with learning and behavior problems as excessive time is required to insure that behaviors will be acquired in numerous situations. Program suggestions for improving generalizaiton skills will be described in Chapter 5.

INCIDENTAL LEARNING DEFICITS

Most children acquire many of their behavioral patterns in the typical unstructured or unplanned experiences which represent the give and take of family life. As the child enters into more formal nursery, kindergarten, and elementary school programs, many experiences are presented in a more structured fashion. Even here, however, a great percentage of the learning that occurs is acquired incidentally to the formal teaching. This occurs as the child is able to attend to, become involved in, and find enjoyable many aspects of his environment which are in addition to those experiences which are presented in an organized and planned fashion by the teacher.

Many children with learning and behavior problems experience difficulty in incidental learning. Behavioral skills acquired incidentally by the typical child must be carefully programmed to insure that the child with developmental difficulties will acquire these skills. It is not unusual for a teacher to realize, "Why, he doesn't even know how to play," or, "I have to teach many things that most children just learn by growing up." These incidental learning deficits frequently reflect the result of other deficit behavior areas such as attentional deficits, curiosity deficits, motivation deficits, excessive fearfulness, and the like. Program suggestions for facilitating incidental learning skills will be presented in Chapter 11.

EXCESSIVE DISRUPTIVE AND/OR COMPETING AVOIDANCE BEHAVIOR

Effective learning requires skills of attention, persistence, and control of competing behaviors which could be distracting. Many children with developmental difficulties exhibit strong behavior patterns which significantly interfere with effective learning. This may include such disruptive behaviors as stereotyped movements, hyperactivity, excessive perseveration, and talking at inappropriate times. Additionally, some children have acquired strong patterns of avoidance behavior with obvious disruptive emotional components. They become upset when exposed to a learning task or when placed in a situation requiring such behaviors as attention, persistence, concentration, and effort. Program procedures for reducing these disruptive behaviors are discussed in Chapters 6, 7, and 12.

LOW FRUSTRATION TOLERANCE AND EXCESSIVE EMOTIONAL REACTIONS

As children grow through the preschool years, they are able to function appropriately under an increasing amount of frustration. There is an increase in patience as well as in the level of frustration which can be experienced without engaging in temper outbursts.

Many children with learning and behavior problems are quite prone to react in a disruptive emotional manner to numerous aspects of their environment. They are characterized by a relatively low tolerance for frustration. The presentation of a new task that requires more attention and persistence than they are accustomed to, a delay in meeting their demands, the least sign of failure or rejection, a change in the kind or amount of positive consequences from that which is expected, or a minor confrontation with adult or peer are all likely to result in excessive emotional reactions. The child has difficulty delaying gratification, waiting his turn, or accepting the fact that he cannot have everything he wishes at the moment he wants it. He may pout, scream, become angry, anxious, distractible, and hyperactive. The interruptions are frequently so intense that effective learning and social interaction are disrupted. These reactions interfere with attention to relevant aspects of a learning program, with efforts toward persistence and concentration, or with obtaining any pleasure out of completing a task. These behaviors render highly unlikely a variety of other adaptive behaviors. Program suggestions for increasing the frustration tolerance of children are discussed in Chapters 7, 11, and 12.

PATTERNS OF DEPENDENCY

One of the outstanding features of child growth is a progressive increase in independence. The child learns to do things for himself and by himself. He depends increasingly less on others for assistance and direction. In contrast, many children with developmental difficulties are quite prone to develop patterns of dependency which persist for extended periods of time. The child is unable to do much without the presence or assistance of adults. He requests an excessive amount of adult attention and support and is apt to become fearful when adults are not prodding or assisting him. The child clings to the adult and prefers to be close to the adult instead of being with other children. Suggestions for reducing dependency and rendering the child more independent are described in Chapter 12.

PATTERNS OF APATHY OR INACTIVITY

Young children typically are curious, involved, active, and persistent in their exploration and interaction with their physical and social environment. Many children with developmental difficulties, however, are characterized by a general limited responsiveness to the environment. If not directed into activities by others the child sits in inactivity. He is described as listless and apathetic.

The child may be fearful of involvement due to previous excessively painful experiences. In other instances, he may have received little attention for becoming involved in activities or may even have been reinforced for relative inactivity.

Whenever such a child becomes involved, he generally shows a limited range of emotional reactions along with a minimal intensity of emotional responsiveness. He may not resist involvement—he just waits until he is directed. Program procedures for increasing the general responsiveness of an inactive child are described in Chapters 7, 11, and 12.

SLOW RATE OF ACQUIRING NEW BEHAVIORS

Due to many of the above described behavioral characteristics of children with developmental difficulties, new behaviors frequently are acquired at a rather slow rate. The attentional deficits, the imitation deficits, the motivation deficits, the memory difficulties, the presence of strong disruptive emotional behaviors, and other similar deficits result in inefficient learning.

In addition, language and perceptual difficulties are frequent. Language difficulties of one kind or another are present in the vast majority of children with developmental difficulties. The child may be generally depressed in language skills, he may show highly specific language deficits, or he may experience difficulty in using the language skills that are in his repertoire.

Many children have difficulty in making various sensory discriminations or in translating such discriminations into effective motor behaviors. Visual, auditory, and kinesthetic difficulties occur with high frequency and interfere with learning of a wide range of behaviors. The failures associated with these difficulties in turn create disruptive emotional reactions and related motivational difficulties. The behavior management program for a child frequently must focus on many of these difficulty areas prior to or in conjunction with efforts to teach the child other social, motor, cognitive, self-help, emotional, preacademic, and academic skills.

PART II

Principles and Procedures for Producing Behavior Change

CHAPTER 3

Influencing Behavior Patterns

The home and school environments of the child contain a wide range of events which influence *how* a child will behave as well as *when and where* these behaviors are likely to occur. A brief look at a preschool classroom might reveal the following activities:

> *The teacher, Mrs. Schmidt, points to a puzzle and suggests, "Put the dog together, Phil." Susan jumps out of her chair and yells at Jim who is in the play area across the room. The teacher aide, Miss Debany, seated with three children in another section of the room, smiles at Jill and exclaims, "Oh, you can really color well." Mrs. Schmidt exclaims, "Scott, stop that and sit down!" Jill smiles at Tom when he gives her a toy.*

Within this brief time span, a number of things are occurring which illustrate the dynamic aspects of the social learning process. The environment contains many events which may assume various roles in this process.

Some of these events facilitate learning; others may actively interfere with effective learning. Some events come to influence the time and place of specific patterns of behavior. Other events serve to strengthen and to insure that specific behaviors will be maintained. Still other events serve to discourage a child from engaging in certain behavior. Some events influence unsettling emotional reactions while others serve to soothe and satisfy the child. There are certain rules which, when followed by the parent and teacher, will influence child behavior in a specific manner. The effective adult, whether parent or teacher, whether in the home or in a more formal school setting, uses these rules to insure that the child will learn those behaviors which he should acquire.

CLASSES OF ENVIRONMENTAL EVENTS

Events Influencing Emotional Behavior

Many events in the environment influence the child's *emotional* behavior. A child who behaves in a fearful manner around strangers represents an example of the influence of such events. The fear response occurs whenever strangers are present. The fearfulness developed out of the child's previous experiences and can be understood in terms of certain learning principles. The same principles accounting for the development of this fearful behavior can be used to influence more positive emotional characteristics of the child. For example, these principles can be used in structuring learning experiences to insure that a child learns to like an activity or to enjoy a person. The way in which a child learns various emotional behaviors and the manner in which certain events in the child's environment can come to influence these behaviors will be discussed in Chapter 7.

Positive Reinforcing Events

Other events in the environment influence the development of a wide range of self-help, motor, socialization, language, and similar behavior patterns. Such events influence behavior when they occur after the child does something. These consequences which follow behavior and strengthen it are called *reinforcers* or *reinforcing events*.

Behavior	*Pleasant (Reinforcing) Consequences*
Tom gives Jill the toy car.	Jill smiles at Tom.
John looks at the teacher when she calls his name.	The teacher smiles and suggests, "You may put your work up."
Sue says the word "Ball" when shown a picture of a ball.	The language therapist enthusiastically exclaims, "That's right!"
Sara puts her toys away.	Mother hugs her and exclaims, "What a big helper you are!"

The child will learn to behave in that manner which results in these reinforcing and similar pleasant consequences. Jill's smile, which followed Tom's sharing of his toy, increases the likelihood of such behavior on his part in the future. The smile may serve to reinforce or strengthen this behavior.

It is valuable to recognize that the type of reinforcing events which are most effective in promoting learning vary greatly from child to child and under certain circumstances, from one time to another for any specific child. A consequence such as adult approval or praise may be highly reinforcing to Melissa but be of little interest to her playmate, Toni. A teacher's smile at a given time in a child's development may be highly reinforcing for one child but not so for another child. Adult attention may be highly enjoyable to a child on most occasions, but at times for the same child such attention may have a neutral or even an aggravating effect.

Discriminative Events

A third class of environmental events fulfills a *discriminatory* role. These antecedent events come before behavior occurs and serve to signal the time and place at which certain behaviors are likely to result in certain consequences. The same behavior occurring at other times or in other places may not result in positive consequences and thus would be less likely to reoccur under those circumstances. The child who does behave appropriately by engaging in the desired behavior at the right time and place is said to be behaving in a discriminating manner. He learns not only how to behave, but also when or under what conditions to engage in various behaviors.

Antecedent (Cue)	*Behavior*
Jill sees the candy.	Jill reaches for the candy.
The teacher says, "Mindy, look at me."	Mindy looks at the teacher.
The teacher says, "John finish your work."	John returns to his desk and begins working.
Mother announces, "Dinner is ready."	Sue stops her coloring and runs to the table.

A teacher's request, "John, finish your work," has acquired influence over the behavior involved in work completion as this behavior pattern has been reinforced (resulted in desirable consequences) on numerous occasions in the past. Behaviors other than those involved in work completion, under these conditions, have not resulted in similar positive consequences and are less likely to interfere with work completion.

Aversive Events

Another class of events has painful or unpleasant characteristics. These events may have quite different effects on the behavior of a child depending upon whether the behavior is followed by (1) the *occurrence* of these unpleasant consequences or (2) the *removal* of these unpleasant consequences.

Punishing events. Behavior which results in the occurrence of unpleasant consequences is less likely to be repeated under similar conditions in the future. Behavior which results in the loss or reduced availability of pleasant consequences is also less likely to reoccur. The arrangement whereby such unpleasant consequences follow certain behaviors is called *punishment*.

John's behavior of pulling the toy away from Joe was followed immediately by the painful consequence of being hit in the stomach. Sue's whining behavior resulted in her loss of the privilege of watching TV. In both instances of punishment, the behavior which produced the unpleasant consequences would be less likely to reoccur under similar conditions in the future.

Negative reinforcing events. Other behaviors may be followed by the removal of unpleasant conditions which are present at the time the behavior occurs. As a result, these behaviors are more likely to reoccur under similar circumstances in the future. The procedure by which behavior is influenced through removal of unpleasant conditions is called *negative reinforcement*.

In each case below, those behaviors which terminated the unpleasant conditions were strengthened. Sara's calling her mother, Don's whining, Jill's crying, and teacher's frowning and threatening all are more likely to occur under the same or similar circumstances in the future since each removed an unpleasant condition; Cathy stopped teasing Sara, Nan gave the book to Don and left the room, Mother stayed with Jill, and Jack stopped talking.

Behavior	*Unpleasant (Punishing) Consequences*
John pulled the toy away from Joe.	Joe hit John in the stomach.
Sue began to whine when asked to get ready for bed.	Sue lost her privilege of watching the late movie on TV.
Jill moved from the table when asked by the teacher to remain seated.	The teacher aide promptly placed Jill in a chair in the corner facing the wall. She could not interact with the class for ten minutes.
Steve refused to put the toys on the shelf.	Mrs. Jones required Steve to sit at his desk during recess period.

Unpleasant Condition	*Behavior and Consequence*
Cathy is teasing Sara.	Sara calls her mother. Cathy stops teasing.
Nan attempts to take the book from Don.	Don begins to whine. Nan turns the book loose and leaves the room.
Mother announces that she is leaving Jill with a sitter.	Jill begins to sob and clings to Mother. Mother stays at home.
Jack is talking too loudly during independent work period.	Teacher frowns at Jack, shakes her finger at him and threatens to punish him. Jack stops talking.

Neutral Events

Numerous events in the life of the child may have no systematic effect on his behavior. Many of these *neutral* events can acquire, however, any of the behavior influence characteristics noted above. A neutral event may become aversive, reinforcing, may come to produce either positive or negative emotional behavior, or may serve as cues for other behaviors. The actual characteristics acquired will depend upon the manner in which these neutral events are associated with other events which presently influence behavior in a specific manner.

A teacher may request, "Sue, look at me." The child may continue playing with her toys and give no indication that the verbal request had any influence on what she was doing. In this instance, the request was a neutral stimulus event since it had no specific influence on the child's behavior.

If the teacher wishes to change the influence which the verbal request has on the child, she may follow a procedure of *behavior shaping*. This may involve the following steps: (1) the child is physically guided, or prompted, through the response pattern of looking at the teacher following the verbal cue "Sue, look," and (2) after looking at the teacher the child is provided an immediate consequence such as a pat on the back, a piece of food, or some other event which is reinforcing to the child. After a few repetitions of this sequence, the neutral event of "Sue, look at me," may come to function as a specific discriminative cue. The child learns to look up whenever teacher makes a request. This learning takes place as the behavior of looking at the teacher immediately following these specific cues results in positive consequences.

As another example, a teacher's praise initially may have little consistent reinforcing effect on Tim's behavior. However, after frequent association of teacher's praise with other events, which are in fact reinforcing to Tim (such as a pat on the back or food), the teacher's approval may become reinforcing. In this manner, a neutral event may become highly effective in strengthening and maintaining other behavior patterns of the child. The procedures of behavior shaping and the method of increasing the reinforcement qualities of neutral events will be described in more detail in later chapters.

Social Models

The social models in the child's life are another important class of events which influence the behavioral patterns of the child. He may develop desirable and undesirable behaviors alike through *imitating* the observed behavior of those around him. If the peers, siblings, or adults in the child's life are loud, anxious, short-tempered, and aggressive, the child is quite likely, through imitation, to adopt some of these behavior patterns. If the social models are relaxed and pleasant, the child is more likely to acquire these behavioral patterns. In view of the possible influence of behavioral models, adults must behave in the presence of their children as they wish the children to behave. If most effective behavior development is to occur, children must be exposed to the appropriate behaviors of other children and adults. A more detailed discussion of the principles of imitation learning is presented in Chapters 5 and 7.

Behavioral Contingencies

It is useful to think of the relationship which exists between behavior and its environmental consequences as representing a *behavioral contingency*. A statement of a behavioral contingency includes a specification of the behavior which will produce a specific consequence. The behavioral contingency may refer to relationships which involve either positive or negative consequences. The behavior management program is designed so that the teacher may control many of these behavioral contingencies. She may arrange for positive consequences to follow desired behavior or she may decide to remove positive consequences following inappropriate behavior. She may arrange for aversive events to follow or be presented contingent upon inappropriate responses or she may arrange for the removal of aversive consequences following desired behavior. To the extent that she has control over present contingencies or can influence future contingencies, the teacher will be able to influence the development and reliable occurrence of desired behaviors.

LEARNING UNDESIRABLE BEHAVIORS

It should be emphasized prior to further discussion of the principles and procedures of influencing behavior that a child may learn to misbehave just as he may learn desired behavior patterns. He may *learn* inappropriate behavior patterns even though parents and teacher are not attempting intentionally to teach such behaviors. As suggested earlier, it is perhaps true that children with learning and behavior problems are more prone than other children to develop inappropriate behavior patterns. This is a result of their physical, neurological, or sensory difficulties and related learning deficits and experiences resulting from these problems. The manner in which the parent or teacher handles problem behaviors as they occur initially will greatly influence which of these behavior patterns will become stronger and thus more frequent and which will occur only infrequently or disappear.

A hyperactive behavior pattern, for example, may be intensified or decreased, depending upon the consequences which such behavior produces from the child's environment. This was illustrated by Allen and her colleagues (1967) in their work with a 4½ year-old boy who displayed a tendency to move constantly from one play activity to another while attending a preschool program. After obtaining a measure of the frequency of moving from one activity to another under typical classroom conditions, the teacher began to provide social attention only after the boy had remained with a single play activity for one minute. Social attention from the teacher was maintained until the boy moved into a different play activity. Under these new conditions the child showed a significant increase in his attending behavior, with much less movement from one activity to another. Reintroducing the typical classroom conditions of providing social attention most frequently when the boy was moving from one activity to another resulted in a return to the initial hyperactivity level. After this, the teacher attended to him only after one minute, and later only after two minutes, of sticking to a single play-activity. The child's hyperactivity was again reduced significantly under these new conditions of social attention.

In another illustration, a physically-disabled child may learn to whine and fuss until mother dresses him or he may learn to dress himself without a fuss. The particular behavior will depend upon the specific consequences which the contrasting behavior patterns produce. A child may learn to sit at his desk and engage in an assigned perceptual-motor task, just as he may learn to be noisy and out of his seat during this work time. In an effort to get a highly active boy to settle down, a teacher may hold him in her lap as she encourages him to complete a visual-motor task. She may be increasing the likelihood of hyperactive noisy behavior by the close personal attention which such behavior produced. The same learning principles are involved in the development of these and similar undesired behavior patterns as are involved in the development of appropriate ways of behaving. In view of this, there is no question that the home and school environments, in spite of intentions and plans to the contrary on the part of parents and teachers, do inadvertently strengthen many of the problematic behaviors which characterize many young children. It is not unusual for parents and teachers to attend to a child when he is misbehaving but to ignore him as long as he is behaving satisfactorily. In this manner misbehavior may be strengthened.

When a child is sitting, attending, working, cooperating, or playing, he is provided praise, approval, or other forms of social attention too infrequently. In contrast, the child who is disruptive, refuses to cooperate, is overly aggressive toward others, does not attend, or is hyperactive is likely to receive an abundance of immediate attention following these behaviors. This attention, even when in a scolding, threatening, or reprimanding manner, may well serve to strengthen the very behavior which such consequences are intended to control or eliminate.

Madsen and his colleagues (1968) provide evidence that the more frequently teachers asked young children to sit down after getting out of their seats at inappropriate times, the more frequently the children stood up. The social attention provided by the teacher, even though intended as a mild reprimand, increased rather than decreased the undesired behavior.

A child who refuses to cooperate is not infrequently the center of attention from teacher and peers alike. Those children who do participate cooperatively in class routine are likely to be ignored by that teacher who is not cognizant of the effects which her behavior will have on those children's behavior. In this social setting, inappropriate behavior, rather than appropriate behavior, may become a more likely occurrence as it produces more intense, immediate, and prolonged social attention. It is not being suggested that a child plans to or even that he intentionally misbehaves in order to provoke the teacher; on the contrary, children most frequently are totally unaware of the factors which influence the occurrence of their behavior. Nevertheless, behaviors which result in social consequences are more likely to reoccur than those which produce no consequences.

> A child learns inappropri-
> ate behavior patterns in the
> same manner that he learns
> appropriate ways of behav-
> ing.

INCONSISTENCY CREATES PROBLEMS

Inconsistency by parents and teachers in requiring certain behaviors from the child creates conditions for development of inappropriate ways of behaving. A child may learn to voice excessive and unwarranted objection to teacher and parental requests by the inconsistent manner in which the objections are handled by these adults. A teacher who fluctuates between following through at times on what she requires the child to do and in giving in to the child's objection (e.g., stalling, negativistic comments, whining, crying) at other times is merely teaching the child to object inappropriately to those teacher requests which he does not like. These experiences teach the child to become uncooperative, to whine, or to engage in temper tantrums or attention-getting behavior. These inappropriate behavior patterns occasionally pay off; they remove the unpleasant requests made by the teacher. The child learns not to pay too much attention to what adults say or else he learns that responsibilities or agreements do not have to be honored. Rules and limits are not taken seriously since they apply only part of the time—and then only inconsistently.

Children with learning and behavior problems should be provided with well-delineated restrictions and freedoms. A child who knows what to expect—what various behaviors will result in what specific consequences—is a child who will be free to use his resources for positive learning experiences. He will not spend excessive time "objecting," "testing the limits," or attempting to find out if mother or teacher is really serious this time when she makes a request.

It is probably true that a child who does experience learning and behavior difficulties requires, even more than the non-handicapped child, a consistent and supportive learning environment if he is to avoid learning an excessive number of undesirable behavior patterns. In view of this situation, both parent and teacher should be highly selective in the behavioral expectations which are set for each child at any given time. They should have a sound basis for their expectations of each child so that there is reasonable assurance that the child can engage in the behaviors expected under the specific conditions provided. With this assurance the adults will be justified in their expectations on most occasions and will provide the child with a consistent, predictable, and successful learning experience. After favorable experiences in a structured and consistent environment, the child will become assured that requests will not be made that will be impossible or too difficult for him to fulfill. The child will become a more cooperative, self-assured, and successful learner.

CLASSES OF PROBLEMATIC BEHAVIOR

The major goals of an early education experience are (1) to influence the development and consistent occurrence of an increasingly complex set of new behavior patterns and (2) to eliminate or reduce in strength behavioral reactions which create problems for the child and others in this social environment. A child is viewed as having problems whenever he does not learn or behave as he is expected to by the home or school environments. If the child does not behave as expected, teachers, parents, and others comprising the child's social environment will react in a manner which reflects their disappointment or concern. These expectations by parents and teachers may be based on a variety of chronological, mental, physical, legal, ethical, or other considerations. A four-year-old child is expected to do certain things in relation to specific situations. He is expected to feed himself, to dress with minimal assistance, to play with other children, to have language skills permitting verbal interaction. A child with a mental age of three is expected to be able to discriminate a doll from a ball upon verbal request and to color a picture with reasonable accuracy.

Behavioral Deficits

Regardless of the basis for these deficits, parents and teachers do expect a child to behave in a specified manner both in structured learning or performance situations and in unstructured settings. The child is given a spoon and encouraged to feed himself. He does not do so. Another child is given a box of blocks of various shapes and colors and asked to sort the red circles and blue squares in a separate pile. He fails to complete this task even though he does seem to distinguish red from blue. A third child does not pay attention to the teacher during language class. He wanders around the room instead. Josh sits and stares in a blank fashion at a cartoon movie while his peers respond with laughter and animated pleasure. All of these children exhibit *behavioral deficits* when viewed from the point of view of what the social environment expects or wishes the child to be able to do. Each child in these examples does not behave in the manner expected of him by the situation. A discrepancy exists between what the child does and what the situation requires. He either lacks the necessary skills, or, if they are present, the skills occur in an inconsistent and unacceptable manner.

Basis for Behavioral Deficits

Depending on the behavior deficits which he presents, a child may be described as exhibiting a general learning deficit, perceptual-motor deficits, language deficits, deficits in self-care behaviors, or a combination of these and other problems. Within any of these behavior areas, the deficits may represent one or a combination of the following:

1. *The desired behavior may be completely absent.* The child may never have engaged in the behavior. The child may never have been able to distinguish a red ball from a blue ball or to write his name. He may be unable to engage in certain behaviors at a given time because he never has had an opportunity to learn the desired behaviors. He may not be able to dress himself because mother has always done it for him. He may be unable to engage in simple perceptual-motor tasks or in social interaction as a result of high-rate stereotyped behavior such as body rocking. He may be unable to use scissors, to distinguish red from green, or to speak in complete sentences because he has never been exposed to an environment which provided for the development of these behaviors.

In other instances the learning experiences which were provided may have been inadequate to teach that child the behavior patterns which were desired but absent. Mother may have attempted to teach the child to distinguish red from blue or to see the difference between a circle and a square, but failed to accomplish her goal as a result of the way in which she presented the task. The educational goal in these instances where the desired behavior is absent is to provide a more satisfactory teaching program to insure the development of the absent behavior.

2. *The desired behavior may be in the child's repertoire but may not occur on a consistent basis.* The child may be able to engage in the behavior but does not. He has done so on some occasions in the past. The child may not want to dress himself or be interested in playing with other children even though he has dressed himself previously and has played with other children on past occasions. The goal is to increase the consistency of the behavior by associating its occurrence with reinforcing consequences.

3. *The desired behavior occurs but only under restricted conditions.* The child will talk when mother is present but will not talk to anyone else when mother is absent. The child can read simple stories, but will not do so when other children are present. The goal in such instances is to insure that the behavior will also occur in a number of other appropriate conditions.

4. *The desired behavior may be in the child's repertoire but occurs only under conditions of frequent reinforcement.* Under less favorable conditions the behavior becomes erratic or does not occur at all. Hal will complete his table work when the teacher sits next to him and praises him frequently. He seldom completes a task when the teacher is not present. The goal is to insure that the behavior will be maintained under conditions of less frequent reinforcement.

It is true that behavioral deficits may reflect neurological or other physical conditions which restrict or greatly impede the learning or performance of the desired behavior. Care must be exercised in assuming, however, that behavioral deficits are in fact totally a result of physical limitations. The child with obvious neurological, sensory, or physical impairment may well be able to acquire new behavior patterns and to engage in them under normal conditions if provided carefully designed learning experiences. The goals of an early education program for children with deficit behavior patterns are obviously (1) to provide appropriate learning experiences which will result in the child's acquisition of desired behavior patterns which he presently does not have, and (2) to insure that these are maintained and do occur with consistency under appropriate conditions. A number of principles and related procedures to accomplish these goals are presented in the chapters to follow.

Excessive Behavior Patterns

Other behavior patterns create problems due to their *excessive* nature. Children who are demanding, who cry too easily or too frequently, who talk too much or are too loud, who are too fearful, or who are too aggressive toward their peers demonstrate excessive behavior patterns. In other instances behavior is excessive if it occurs in too many inappropriate situations. The child shows poor discrimination. Such excessive behavior patterns may not only disrupt other children and adults but also may interfere with the child's ability to learn new behaviors or to engage in other more appropriate behaviors. As an example: a child who is disruptive during music period may well have appropriate skills of attending; during Sesame Street, he may attend for long periods of time. The teacher knows from this observation that he can sit still and participate in group activities under certain conditions. But under the conditions of the music period, the disruptive behavior is stronger than the desired behavior of attending.

At the same time, such excessive behavior patterns frequently interfere with the development of more appropriate ones. During the time the child is talking loudly he cannot be listening to what the teacher is saying and thus misses his language lesson. He cannot learn the new concepts which the teacher is presenting.

It may well be that a child "knows better" than to engage in excessive behavior patterns. The child may be able to verbalize what he should do in a situation, and even be successful in engaging in such behaviors on occasion. But on other occasions inappropriate behavior occurs. The child displaying such inconsistent behavior patterns should not be viewed as naughty or intentionally disruptive. His behavior is the result of social-learning experiences and is acquired in the same manner that more appropriate behavior is acquired. The disruptive behavior pattern at times is under stronger environmental influence than is the appropriate behavior. This may reflect a difference in the previous reinforcement experiences under varying combinations of cues which become associated with the contrasting behavior patterns.

In viewing the excessive behavior patterns of young children, it also is important to recognize that most behavior is not excessive in any absolute sense. Although some behaviors are excessive regardless of where or when they occur, many behaviors may be excessive if they occur in one setting, while not being inappropriate for other situations. Additionally, some excessively occurring behavior may be quite adaptive and even characteristic of many children, but for a given child it becomes inappropriate due to its extreme rate of occurrence. Asking for teacher assistance may be encouraged for all children in a class when unusual difficulty is encountered, but seeking teacher assistance may be viewed as maladaptive when a child engages this tactic on numerous occasions throughout the school day.

It may be true that specific behavior becomes excessive

because a child has numerous behavior deficits in relation to the requirements of specific situations. The child may not have the required behavior in his repertoire; therefore, he engages excessively in what he can do. A child may engage in temper tantrum behavior because he does not have the skills demanded in a situation. Similarly, he may withdraw into stereotyped hand waving, become aggressive, begin to cry, or become hyperactive because the competing appropriate behaviors are not in his repertoire.

Some excessive behavior patterns may occur in a wide range of situations. "He always talks too loudly." "He is too aggressive in all his peer interactions." Other excessive patterns may be specific to situations or to types of situations. "He only becomes hyperactive and distractible when required to interact verbally with adults. At other times he is calm and is able to stick to his work."

Excessively occurring behaviors frequently are puzzling to the teacher due to the apparent self-defeating character of such behaviors. It is difficult to understand what is accomplished. In some instances excessive behavior patterns appear to persist in the absence of any discernible positive consequences. These patterns become even more puzzling when they persist in the face of obvious punishment. "I reprimand him every time it occurs, but it doesn't seem to do any good. He still persists in taking things away from his peers," or "I can't understand why he continues to refuse to cooperate with his peers. They reject him and won't play with him for a while." There is a tendency for many teachers to view such behaviors as resulting from some internal psychic pathology or as reflecting some "deep-down disturbance."

Again, it may be that the child simply has no suitable alternative behaviors available. While the reinforcing consequences associated with the excessive behavior may be minimal, these consequences are sufficient to maintain the excessive behavior patterns simply because the child has no alternative behaviors available for producing more desirable consequences. He must repeat perseveringly the behaviors that are available even though these do not produce the desired positive consequences.

In summary, the "inappropriateness" or the "excessiveness" of a behavior is not an inherent or all-or-none characteristic of the child's behavior. Each gains meaning only in relation to the requirements or expectations of specific situations.

The goals of an educational program designed to deal with excessive behavior patterns are:

1. Teaching the child new discriminations so that behaviors will occur under appropriate conditions and only under appropriate conditions.
2. Reducing the frequency or intensity of excessive behaviors to a level that is acceptable by teaching the child a range of ap-

propriate behaviors which can be used as alternatives to the excessively occurring behaviors.
3. Eliminating selective behaviors so that these will seldom or never reoccur.

Usefulness of Deficit-Excessive Classification

It is useful to view problem behavior areas as representative of either deficit or excessive patterns because various rules of learning and related behavior management strategies are available for dealing with each class of problematic behaviors. The general procedures used with deficit-behavior patterns are concerned with developing, strengthening, maintaining, and generalizing behavior patterns. If the problem area is one of excessive behavior, procedures relating to means of decreasing, restricting, or eliminating the behavior become pertinent. Most learning and behavior problems of children present both excessive and deficit components. A child may be unable (behavior deficit) to complete a visual-motor

Table 3.1 Problem Behaviors and Management Procedures

TYPES OF PROBLEMS	BEHAVIOR MANAGEMENT PROCEDURES	CHAPTER
Deficit Behavior		
Behavior is absent	Teaching new behaviors by shaping and chaining	5
Behavior is inconsistent	Strengthening existing behaviors through frequent reinforcement	4
Behavior is too restricted	Enhancing generalization by expanding stimulus control	5
Behavior is not maintained	Insuring maintenance through reinforcement schedules	5
Emotional behavior is absent or weak	Strengthening behavior through emotional conditioning	7
Excessive Behavior		
Behavior is too generalized	Teaching discriminations by differential reinforcement	5
Behavior is excessive	Reducing strength of behavior by extinction, punishment, or by teaching competing behaviors	6
Emotional behavior is too generalized or intense	Restricting or eliminating emotional behavior through extinction or counter conditioning	7

task.   At the same time he may display rather hyperactive and distractible (excessive) behaviors as the teacher is prompting the child to complete the task.   The educational goals in these instances are to teach successful task completion and reduce or eliminate the distractible and hyperactive behaviors.

Table 3.1 summarizes the types of deficit and excessive behavior patterns presented by young children and the related behavior management procedures for use with each.   The chapters in which further primary discussion is provided for each problem area are listed.   A separate listing is included for emotional difficulties since the rules which relate to the acquisition, persistence, and elimination of such behaviors are different from those involved in nonemotional behaviors.

CHAPTER 4

Concepts of
Positive Reinforcement

Behaviors which are followed by positive consequences will become stronger and will be more likely to reoccur in similar situations in the future than will other behaviors which have not resulted in positive consequences. This procedure which follows desired behavior with positive consequences in order to strengthen the behavior is called *positive reinforcement*. As noted previously, those consequences which do strengthen behavior are called *positive reinforcing events or positive reinforcers*. The child will learn those behaviors which will produce or enhance the availability and continuation of these events. If a child, for example, likes the company of other children, he will learn those ways of behaving which place him in the presence of his playmates and which serve to prolong this association with them. He seeks to approach and to experience over and over again the positive reinforcing events.

These reinforcing consequences of behavior may represent events which naturally result from some behaviors. A child runs into the warm summer rain and splashes in the water which results in a natural consequence of getting wet. Assuming that he finds the rain pleasurable, his behavior of running into the rain will be strengthened. The relationship between the behavior and the consequence is a natural one.

In other instances, the consequences which follow certain behaviors are not as inevitable or natural. A child may greet an adult with a smile and a "hello." The adult may smile in return and reply, "Hi! What a pretty dress you have on!" In such an experience, the child's preceding behavior is likely to be strengthened. Or, the adult may ignore the child or may actually frown at the child and reply, "Get lost! Can't you see I'm busy?" Under these conditions, the preceding child behavior may be less likely to reoccur in the future.

Finally, consequences of behavior may be presented in a systematic manner as part of a planned behavior management program. The program may be designed to provide social attention whenever a child makes an attempt to imitate a word or to provide access to a favorite toy when the child completes a specified task. In any of these events, whether natural, whether unsystematic and unpredictable, or whether planned as one component of a behavior management program, behaviors which are followed by positive consequences are more likely to be repeated under similar conditions in the future.

A child will show interest in or be motivated to become involved in various activities to the extent that these or similar situations have resulted previously in positive consequences. As will be described in a later section, a child may even be likely to engage in behaviors which he has observed in others which have resulted in positive consequences.

This procedure of influencing the strength of behavior by following it with positive events is simple, but most effective. If the parent or teacher wishes to strengthen some behavior such as attending to verbal requests, recognizing the difference between a red ball and a blue ball, sharing toys with others, or complying with requests, she must arrange for some desirable consequences to follow the desired behavior. Once it occurs, if desired behavior is not followed by favorable consequences, it is less likely to reappear.

Behavior followed by reinforcing events is likely to reoccur.

The procedure of following behavior with a reinforcing event has application both to the goals (1) of teaching a new behavior which the child presently does not have, and (2) of increasing the strength of existing behaviors. The desired behavior may be present but may not occur with sufficient consistency. The goal may be to increase the accuracy or speed of specific behaviors, for example:

> *John points to his mouth, eyes, ears, and hair sometimes when asked to do so but at other times he does not get these cor-*

rect. Jerome will look at me when I call his name on occasion but at other times he doesn't seem to realize that I am speaking to him. Susan can print the letters from A to G but misses most of them on other occasions. Susan is able to copy the geometric forms but is quite slow in doing so.

These are examples of emerging behaviors which are in the child's repertoire but which are of insufficient strength to occur in the desired manner. These existing behaviors will begin to occur more appropriately, that is, will become stronger, as they result more frequently in reinforcing consequences. The teacher should provide events which are reinforcing to John, Jerome, and Susan whenever the desired behavior occurs. As will be discussed later, the type of events which would result in strengthening behavior may well differ for each child. Praise or other forms of social approval may be most effective with John and Susan but not with Jerome. Following Jerome's desired behavior by permitting him to play with a flashlight or listen to music may be more reinforcing to him.

Allen (1972) described a behavior management program for a four-year-old girl who had a low rate of verbal output. The child had an adequately developed verbal repertoire; she just did not use this behavior to any extent, although she did talk more freely to adults than to peers. The child had many nonverbal responses which she used to communicate with others. The teachers began to provide social reinforcement for any of her verbal behavior and to ignore her when she attempted her nonverbal request. Verbal interaction with adults quickly increased in frequency. Following this support the child was reinforced selectively for verbal interaction with peers. In this manner, low-rate verbal behavior increased to the level which was comparable to that of her peer group.

NEW BEHAVIOR IS ACQUIRED SLOWLY

In most instances new behavior, appropriate and inappropriate, is acquired slowly. A child does not learn overnight to attend to and comply with adult requests or to recognize and label colors and forms any more than he suddenly learns to be too demanding or to fight with his peers. These behavior patterns evolve slowly over numerous learning experiences in which these behaviors or their approximations have resulted in reinforcement. The social environment (for example, parent, teacher) may be quite unaware of the variety of events which are reinforcing to a child. Under these conditions, the adults may be surprised and puzzled to discover that certain undesirable behavior patterns have become rather persistent.

In the early stages of learning a new behavior, the desired behavior may occur only infrequently, and even then in an inconsistent manner. Frequent and consistent reinforcement of the new behavior may be necessary for it to become a reliable part of the child's repertoire. This emphasizes the need for a well-designed behavior management program which provides for consistent reinforcement of new behaviors over an extended period of time. Although learning will take place under less desirable conditions, the learning will be slower, inconsistent, and a more arduous task for the child.

BEHAVIOR REINFORCED DIRECTLY

It is important for effective and efficient learning that the reinforcing events be provided in direct relationship to the desired behavior. Just being nice or kind or affectionate is not enough. It is not sufficient, for example, merely to provide the child with reinforcing events such as acceptance, approval, or praise in a manner unrelated to the desired behavior if the goal is that of strengthening some specific behavior. This was illustrated by an experience with a five-year-old girl who engaged in a number of disturbing social behaviors while attending a preschool program. She was described as balky, verbally insulting, occasionally foul-mouthed, and prone to tell disjointed stories about violent accidents (Hart, Reynolds, Baer, Brawley, and Harris, 1968). Although she frequently approached other children, these contacts tended to be brief. She engaged in cooperative interaction with her peers less than 5 percent of the time available in the preschool session, even though she was in close physical proximity to children about 50 percent of the time. During the initial observation period, the teachers were noted to spend slightly in excess of 20 percent of the school day interacting with the girl.

As an initial approach to increasing the amount of time spent in cooperative play with peers, the teachers increased their time spent with the child to 80 percent of each session. During this time the teachers talked to her, attended to her activities, gave her materials and toys, and generally "made a fuss over her." The increased social attention did not follow any particular kind of behavior but rather was presented randomly. Other children were attracted to the teacher's activities and thus increased the amount of time spent in proximity to the girl. The rate of cooperative play between the girl and her peers, nonetheless, remained unchanged.

The teachers then switched to socially reinforcing the child only for approximations to cooperative interactions with the other children.   Cooperative-play behavior increased within twelve days from the original 5 percent to 40 percent of the time available in each session.   This experience demonstrated that approval, praise, and other forms of social attention became most influential in increasing cooperative peer interaction when these reinforcing events were provided in a systematic manner following the occurrence of the behaviors which the teachers wished to strengthen.   It supports the statement of Bettelheim (1950) that "Love is not enough."   Even love, when provided too freely, regardless of the child's behavior, can interfere with normal development.

It is not being suggested that children should be given social attention in its numerous forms of praise, approval, affection, and the like only whenever the parent and teacher are attempting to influence some specific behavior pattern.   Social and emotional interactions should be natural and spontaneous whenever possible.   Obviously children need to experience and will benefit from the affectionate behavior of significant adults and peers.   It is desirable to indicate to a child on numerous occasions and in multiple ways that he is good, that he is liked, that he is worthwhile, that others can enjoy him and can demonstrate their interest by emotional expressions of affection, love, enthusiasm, and concern.   The child with learning and behavior problems needs the adults in his life to express to him, independently of any specific task completion or goal attainment, such feelings as "I love you," "Say, I really like you," "You are my favorite person," "I'm glad you are my friend."   But the adult must recognize that to the extent such personal attention is reinforcing to the child, behavior which immediately precedes this reinforcement will be influenced.

If the affection or other forms of attention are provided most frequently as the child is engaging in various "dependency behavior," for example, such behaviors will be strengthened.   As will be discussed in more detail in Chapter 12, it is easy for adults to show sympathy and concern to the child who is experiencing difficulty in completing various activities.   If the adult shows too much empathy and offers too much assistance whenever the child experiences difficulty, the child may be taught to depend on the adult to do things for him whenever he is faced with a difficult task.   In this manner excessive dependency behavior can be developed.

A recent experience with a young "emotionally disturbed" boy provides further illustration of the undesirable consequences of offering too much reinforcing attention to a child at the wrong time. This boy was attending a specialized day school program for children with excessive behavior management problems. He had considerable difficulty remaining at any activity for more than a few seconds at a time. The teacher of the group of six boys felt that all "emotionally disturbed" children need considerable affection and genuine concern from adults. In observing Jim in this class, it was noted that whenever he got out of his chair during periods in which he was instructed to complete various tasks at his desk the teacher would move closer to him. She would provide him with some soothing comment and gently move him back to his desk. It was apparent that such social interaction was quite reinforcing to him.

During a ten-day observation period, Jim was out of his seat most of the time receiving "warm concern" from the teacher. "He's emotionally disturbed. He needs to know that I care for him and that I will not reject him even if he is unable to control his impulses." Under these conditions the teacher was providing the boy no opportunity to learn to control his impulses. In fact, she was facilitating inadvertently the very behaviors that interfered with his development of any self-control. The teacher, after suspecting the futility of her approach to Jim, agreed to provide just as much attention in the form of acceptance and concern as ever, but mostly after appropriate compliance with her requests. Within a few days Jim was spending an increasing amount of time at his desk engaging in the preacademic tasks provided him. The teacher was now able to express her acceptance in a realistic manner following desired behavior. Jim also was able to develop some competency behavior which was a source of pride to him.

> **Reinforcing events will influence those behaviors with which they are most directly and consistently associated.**

REINFORCING EVENTS EXERT AN IMMEDIATE AND AUTOMATIC EFFECT

Jim's experience illustrates another important learning concept. It is not necessary for the child to understand or even be aware of the positive effects of consequences for them to influence the strength of associated behaviors. Jim did not "know" that his behavior of getting out of his seat was becoming stronger and more likely to reoccur because such behavior resulted in teacher attention. The strengthening effect of these consequences was *automatic*.

It is just as true that teachers and parents can be influenced automatically by consequences which follow various of their behaviors, and without being aware of the influence. Children and adults learn many unplanned behaviors, both appropriate and inappropriate, as a result of this automatic effect on behavior of various consequences. This observation emphasizes the need for designing and implementing a structured learning environment for the young child with learning and behavior difficulties and for consistently analyzing the effects which various consequences do in fact have on specific behavior patterns of children.

This automatic effect of reinforcing events emphasizes the applicability of the rule of positive reinforcement to the young, the severely retarded, and the nonverbal child as well as to the child who has language and related intellectual skills. It is not necessary that the child "know" that certain of his behaviors result in various positive consequences. The child with severe developmental difficulties may be taught to attend to verbal requests, to dress himself, to feed himself, to take care of his toilet needs, and to make basic discriminations if these behaviors are followed consistently with reinforcing events.

BEHAVIORS THAT ARE INFLUENCED BY REINFORCEMENT

Any behavior or combination of behaviors in which the child may engage as he interacts with his physical and social environments may be influenced by positive reinforcement. The behaviors which may be strengthened range from simple behaviors such as looking up when requested to do so, feeding oneself without spilling, drinking out of a cup, and distinguishing a large circle from a large square to more complex patterns such as recognizing and using letters of the alphabet, cooperative play, persistence in a difficult task, and reading stories to a group of peers. It is also true that a child's emotional behavior is influenced by positive reinforcement. The rules involved in influencing emotional behavior will be described in Chapter 7.

The following listing illustrates the types of behaviors of

young children with learning and behavior problems which have been influenced successfully by behavior management programs using positive reinforcement. Some of these programs will be described in various sections of the book.

—Teaching a nonambulatory five-year-old physically handicapped retarded child to walk with the aid of crutches (Horner, 1971).
—Teaching printing and writing skills to young children (Hopkins *et al.*, 1971; Salzberg *et al.*, 1971).
—Toilet training of four-year-old severely retarded children (Mahoney *et al.*, 1971).
—Teaching young severely retarded children to follow instructions (Whitman *et al.*, 1971).
—Increasing use of descriptive adjectives in spontaneous speech in culturally deprived children (Hart and Risley, 1968).
—Increasing social interaction of shy children (Ward and Baker, 1968).
—Decreasing resistive behavior of culturally deprived children (Wasik *et al.*, 1969).
—Reducing stereotyped autistic behavior in an autistic boy (Wolf *et al.*, 1964).
—Decrease in classroom disruptive behaviors (Bushell *et al.*, 1968).
—Decrease in crying episodes (Hart *et al.*, 1964).
—Increase in peer interaction and decrease of hyperactivity (Allen *et al.*, 1967).
—Increasing cooperative play (Hart *et al.*, 1968).
—Teaching autistic children to function as a group in a kindergarten class (Martin *et al.*, 1968).
—Improvement in motor skills (Johnston *et al.*, 1966).
—Increase in attending behavior in the classroom (Packard, 1970).
—Increasing study behavior in a school setting (Bushell *et al.*, 1968).
—Modification of extreme social withdrawal (Ross *et al.*, 1971).
—Improving verbal skills in a disadvantaged child (Reynolds and Risley, 1968).
—Improvement in excessively dependent behavior (Wahler *et al.*, 1965).
—Improved bowel control in a five-year-old child (Barrett, 1969).
—Design of a total classroom environment for young handicapped children (Bijou, 1972).
—Improvement in classroom behavior of young retarded children (Birnbrauer *et al.*, 1965).
—Modification of multiple problem behaviors in home and school settings (Patterson and Brodsky, 1966).
—Decrease in hyperactivity in a classroom situation (Patterson *et al.*, 1965).
—Elimination of obscene conduct in a classroom situation (Sulzbacher and Houser, 1968).

—Remediation of language and related academic skills in young children with learning disabilities (Hamblin *et al.*, 1971).

REINFORCING EVENTS

As teachers can influence the strength of behaviors by insuring that they are followed by reinforcing consequences, it is essential that the teacher be aware of those events which do have reinforcing consequences for specific children. The teacher must be prepared to use those consequences *which are in fact reinforcing to a specific child* for the behavior pattern being influenced. A wide range of tangible, social, activity, and token reinforcers is available for use. The school environment is rich with potential reinforcers—play materials, snack time, games, activities, peers, and special events. In many instances in teaching young children with learning and behavior difficulties, the teacher will find it necessary to create new reinforcing events which she may use with individual children. The major problem facing the teacher thus is not one of finding reinforcing events in the school environment; these are plentiful. Rather, the major task is to successfully integrate these reinforcing events into an effective learning experience for each child.

The teacher cannot rely on any highly effective common reinforcing event for use with all children. Young children may respond well to one type of consequence at one time and poorly to it at another. Thus the teacher should have available a wide range of events which can be arranged as consequences of desired behavior. If some events are not effective with a given child at a given time, or if an event loses its effectiveness, others must be available for immediate use.

Children are more likely to learn in an environment which provides a wide range of reinforcing events. Behavior patterns of enthusiasm, cooperativeness, and persistence appear to be engendered in an environment which provides the novelty of a variety of effective reinforcers. Reinforcing events, it should be remembered, are those events which are proven to influence the behavior of a specific child. It may seem reasonable to the teacher that events such as approval or extra play time would be highly reinforcing to a child, but experience in using these reinforcers with that child may demonstrate that they have little effect on his behavior. In view of this possibility, the teacher should never assume that any event is reinforcing to a child until she uses it and evaluates its effectiveness.

> **Reinforcers are those events which do in fact strengthen and maintain a child's behavior.**

And, a related rule,

> **Events which are reinforcing to one child may not be reinforcing to another.**

TYPES OF REINFORCING EVENTS

Primary Reinforcers

Some events which may be used to strengthen and maintain behavior are naturally rewarding to a child and are called *primary reinforcers*. These serve as reinforcers as a result of a basic relationship with certain physiological characteristics of the child. Food and liquid items such as candy, cookies, cereal, bread, soda pop, and milk may have primary reinforcing properties without the influence of prior learning. These and other primary types of events such as physical stimulation are quite valuable in influencing the behavior development of the younger child and of the child with the more severe learning and behavior problems.

As examples of the use of primary reinforcers, Wolf, Risley and Mees (1964) and Risley and Wolf (1967) used a variety of food items as reinforcers in a behavior management program designed to strengthen a variety of speech and social behaviors in a young child described as autistic. These teachers identified food items for which the child showed a particular preference and presented these in small bites following desired behaviors. Ideally, food items used should be those which the child cannot play with, and which the child can eat rapidly. Ice cream and sherbet are ideal food reinforcers for many young children.

Secondary Reinforcers

Other events may have little or no reinforcing effect when initially presented to a child; for example, a smile, approval, acceptance, a gold star, money, educational toys, music, the opportunity to engage in various play activities. These events may become effective reinforcers if they are associated frequently with consequences which are reinforcing to the child. A smile or praise may become reinforcing if paired frequently with the presentation, consumption, or manipulation of such tangible events as food, drink, toys, or play activity which already are reinforcing to a child. These *secondary, learned,* or *acquired reinforcers* assume a most important role in teaching and maintaining new behavior patterns as they are readily available and can be provided immediately and frequently without undue difficulty.

In developing the reinforcing characteristics of a neutral event, the teacher should:

1. Identify events which are reinforcing for the child, as examples, food, an activity, a toy.
2. When these items are presented to the child, an event which is neutral in terms of its reinforcing effects (for example, "very good") is presented simultaneously. As the child is provided a reinforcing event (a toy for example) after a desired behavior, the teacher smiles and says "very good."
3. After a number of such associations, the smile and "very good" will acquire reinforcing characteristics and then can be used independently of the toy as a reinforcer to strengthen behaviors. The critical factor in this procedure is the close and frequent association of the neutral and the reinforcing events.

> **Neutral events may become reinforcing events if paired frequently with events which are reinforcing.**

Typically, as a child becomes older, an increasing number of events become reinforcing. This development depends upon the specific experiences of each child. A child with limited experiences associating reinforcing events with neutral ones will acquire fewer secondary reinforcers. Learning new behaviors thus will be a more difficult undertaking as fewer reinforcing events will be available to strengthen new behaviors. As a result, the learning difficulties of the child will become intensified.

It should be recognized that such events as completing a task, being successful, or even that of reaching a previously set behavior goal may become reinforcing events. In fact, a child can gain increasing independence and self-responsibility only as events which are natural to various behaviors become secondary reinforcers. Task involvement, task completion, creating an art form, or any other type of accomplishment can become a reinforcing event (satisfying or pleasurable to a child) only after being associated on numerous occasions with other reinforcing consequences which have followed these activities. However, achievement and accomplishment such as dressing without assistance, or completing a project, involvement in various motor and social activities or relationships hold only minimal if any reinforcement value for many children with developmental difficulties due to their learning problems and associated excessive failure experiences.

With such children, the teacher must begin with those events that are reinforcing to each child and use them to insure that the child will be successful. As these events are paired over and over again with various aspects of task involvement and completion, with social interaction, or with any other types of behavior patterns, these activities will become reinforcing and therefore self-maintaining independent of the previous reinforcing consequences.

In summary, the teacher of children with learning difficulties must pay careful attention to the process by which neutral or even unpleasant events and activities can become reinforcing. Activities and accomplishments which appear to be intrinsically motivating or reinforcing to many children cannot be depended upon for influencing the behavior of the child with learning problems. The reinforcing characeristics of these events must be developed through careful arrangement of the learning environment. The goals of an early education program thus involve not only the strengthening of new behavior patterns but also insurance that a range of naturally available events such as involvement in activities, accomplishments, and social interaction become highly reinforcing.

Social Reinforcers

An extremely important class of secondary reinforcers is social in nature, and includes such events as smiling, providing approval, acceptance, affection, attention, praise, recognition, calling a child by his name, asking a child to participate in an activity, talking to a child, being in close physical proximity to a child, looking at a child, and more subtle forms of attention such as winking, tone of voice, and gestures. Specific behavioral examples would include comments such as "Good work," "I like that," "Great thinking," "Nice going," "Thank you," "Well done," and "Great."

Teachers will find it best to be most expressive in providing various forms of social reinforcement to some children and much more subdued and subtle with others. Some children (notably the excessively shy and inhibited child) will benefit from a healthy display of pleasure and enthusiasm following appropriate behavior. Some children "can't believe" that they could please others due to their history of failure or limited success. Thus it is valuable to display enthusiasm following success to enhance the child's positive feelings and thoughts about himself. Other children become agitated easily. Too much enthusiastic display will elicit overactivity and subsequent distracting emotional and motor behaviors. These children require a calm and reassuring mode of social attention.

A study by Harris, Johnston, Kelley and Wolf (1964) illustrates the effectiveness of social reinforcement in influencing desired behavior and in decreasing the strength of a bothersome behavior pattern in a young child. A program was designed to deal with a high rate of crawling observed in a three-year-old child attending a preschool program. Observations over a number of daily morning sessions revealed a crawling rate which exceeded 80 percent. The teachers viewed this behavior as a form of regression which followed the birth of a second child in the family.

It was observed that the teachers provided the child with considerable attention, especially when she crawled. The teachers agreed, as one aspect of a behavior management program, to ignore her crawling behavior and instead to provide her with continuous attention whenever she was upright. A normal pattern of standing, walking, and running was obtained within a week after initiation of this procedure of providing social attention. Following a return to a procedure of providing teacher attention only after crawling occurred, within two days the child regained her original 80 percent crawling rate. Reinstatement of providing attention for walking, standing, and running resulted in a normal pattern being reestablished within four days. This approach then became the social reinforcement procedure followed which in turn resulted in the continuation of normal mobility behavior.

The type of social attention which is most reinforcing will vary from child to child. Some children are highly influenced by any form of attention. It is not unusual to find that types of social attention used by adults as threat or punishment may in fact be positively reinforcing. The secondary reinforcing aspects of the attention provided in these instances add more strength to the preceding child behavior than is subtracted by the unpleasant aspects of the punishment. Thus it must be recognized that repri-

mands, ridicule, criticism, and other forms of social attention used
by the teacher in an effort to reduce behavior may in fact serve to
strengthen the very behavior which the teacher is attempting to
eliminate. In view of this possibility, the teacher must distinguish
between her own intentions in using various forms of social responsiveness and the actual effect these consequences do have on
the child's behavior.

> **Social attention may
> strengthen inappropriate as
> well as appropriate be-
> haviors.**

Attention from adults in its many varieties is potentially a
very powerful reinforcer for young children. There are few events
in the child's life that can rival the constant availability of such
social events. In fact some children become so highly dependent
upon adult attention that they isolate themselves from their peers.
Allen and her colleagues (1964) describe an interesting example
of this danger and demonstrate skillful use of adult attention in
facilitating increased peer interaction. Ann, a four-year-old girl
attending a preschool program, was described as isolating herself
from her peers and engaging in many attempts to gain and prolong
the attention of the teacher and other adults in the preschool
environment. Frequently she would play alone, engaging in various make-believe activities. Mild tic-like behaviors were present.
She was described as often speaking in breathy tones at levels so
low that it was difficult to understand what she said. She com-
plained at length about minute or invisible bumps and abrasions.

As most of the adult attention was provided Ann for
behaviors that were incompatible with play behavior with peers, a
plan was initiated to give her adult attention as she approached or
played with another child. At the initiation of this plan, Ann
spent about 10 percent of her time interacting with children and
40 percent with adults. After some three weeks during which the
teachers reinforced her socially for peer interaction, Ann was
spending some 55 to 60 percent of her time with children and
considerably less time interacting with the adults. During this
time her speech rose in tempo, pitch and volume. Complaints
about abrasions and bumps disappeared entirely. She appeared to
enjoy her increased peer interaction.

Even though it is true that many children are highly influenced by adult attention, it remains essential that teachers and

parents identify and utilize those events which influence a specific child's behavior. Young children with developmental difficulties may require frequent tangible and activity reinforcers combined skillfully with adult attention for optimal behavior development. Some children may even find adult attention to be unpleasant. Such attention may disrupt or even suppress rather than reinforce preceding behavior. Levin and Simmons (1962), in their work with boys described as emotionally disturbed, unusually hyperactive, and aggressive, provide support for this possibility. Providing indiscriminate social attention in these instances may actually disrupt rather than facilitate the way the child learns or behaves.

The younger and more severely involved child generally will require more immediate and tangible reinforcing events for effective learning than will be required by the older and more successful child. The teacher who attempts to use social reinforcement exclusively or even as her major strategy for promoting and strengthening behavior patterns of young children with learning and behavior problems will be relatively ineffective. Social reinforcement in all its many variations should be used frequently, but only if it produces more effective results than other events. As noted earlier, if social consequences are not effective reinforcers, such events should be paired frequently with other events which are reinforcing. In this manner, social attention in its many forms may become reinforcing.

> **Attention from adults may become a highly effective reinforcing event if associated with other reinforcing events.**

Social reinforcement of young children by an emotionally expressive teacher may well have a most positive effect on the entire class. A recent observation of a class of seven four- to five-year-old mildly retarded and behavior problem children attending a day school provides illustration of this. The teacher had given each child seated around a table a matching task involving geometric forms. The children were experiencing a little difficulty getting started. They were talking to each other and engaging in other disruptive behavior which interfered with the visual attending and concentration needed for successful task completion. The teacher, noting that Bill did complete his task successfully, ignored the disruptive behavior of other members of the class. She immediately moved close to Bill, patted him on the arm, as she exclaimed in a warm, expressive manner, "Bill, look at what you did. I'm so proud of you. You really got to work and finished yours." "Now do another one for me," as she placed a more difficult task on the desk for him. Other children, observing this display, immediately went to work. The teacher was quite attentive to each child's effort or task completion and just as quickly and affectionately provided approval and praise. For 15 minutes the children worked attentively and enjoyably, bursting into a smile upon task completion and looking at the teacher for the forthcoming praise.

Social reinforcement in the form of praise, approval, and positive statements may have an effect on the child's development beyond that of strengthening the specific associated behaviors. Such social events also provide the child with models of verbal statements which he may apply to himself. He may begin to label himself as "I can do," "That's great," "Good job," "I am smart," following activity involvement or completion. These positive self-referents can become quite valuable to the child in his approach to an activity and in his involvement.

Peers as Reinforcers

A child may serve as a source of reinforcement for the behavior of other children. Inappropriate as well as appropriate behavior patterns can be strengthened and maintained by the peer attention which follows such behaviors. The child who is not socially reinforcing to his peers most likely will be avoided by them. Additionally, the child who does not find other children to be socially reinforcing will isolate himself from others.

The teacher may find it necessary to develop or enhance the social-reinforcement value of a child by having him provide other children with reinforcing events which they enjoy. In this manner the child will become more reinforcing and his peers will respond more positively to him. Wiesen and Watson (1967), in an attempt to increase the cooperative social interaction between an isolated six-year-old severely retarded boy and his six peers, had his peers reinforce the boy with M&M's whenever he engaged in cooperative social behavior. The interaction between the boy and his peers increased considerably. Kirby and Toler (1970) reinforced an isolated boy for passing out reinforcers to his peers. Social interaction increased considerably; apparently, the child had become an effective social reinforcer through being associated with providing other reinforcers.

Activity Reinforcers

The opportunity to engage in various activities or the possibility of gaining access to certain events or stimulus environments can also become quite reinforcing. Behaviors may be strengthened which are followed by such activities as listening to music, looking at books, watching TV, playing games, being first in line, being a member of a group or club, being read to, running errands, resting, talking, reading, playing ten minutes longer.

This can be translated into a rule of behavior:

> *Activities which the child enjoys (behaviors which would have high preference in those situations in which the child could choose his activities) may be used to reinforce other behaviors in which the child does not choose to engage.*

This general principle has been described by Premack (1959) and has sufficient experimental and clinical support to recommend its use. Homme and his associates (1963), in observing children in a preschool program, noted that the most preferred activities included running around the class room, screaming, pushing chairs across the floor, and playing with jigsaw puzzles. Among the least likely behaviors were those of complying with the teacher's request to "sit down" or to attend to the teacher's instruction. The teacher then arranged for the children to engage in their high preference behaviors of running and screaming following small amounts of the teacher-requested behaviors of sitting and attending. After some experience with this procedure of low preference behavior leading to high preference behavior, the children quickly acquired a range of appropriate behaviors.

Every child has some activities he prefers which could be used to reinforce other activities which he does not prefer. "As soon as we clean up our mess, we shall listen to your favorite record," represents an application of this rule for children who have a high preference for music and a low preference for cleaning up. If a child enjoys finger painting, but is slow and uninvolved in other perceptual-motor tasks, permit him to finger paint for a longer period than usual after he finishes the perceptual-motor activities. If this were done consistently, the perceptual-motor activities should increase in strength.

The teacher can best make use of this rule of influencing behavior by developing a list of activities which each child prefers. Include in this list the class activities which are enjoyable to each child. Such a list may include items like play period, recess period, nap time, lunch period, talking loudly, clowning, running around, playing with toy dump truck, listening to specific records, coloring, and painting. With the list she will be in a position to

71

precede these high preference activities with any activities which are of low strength which need to be reinforced.

Addison and Homme (1966) describe an interesting procedure—a reinforcement event menu—displaying a variety of high-preference activities which would be available to children following desired behaviors. The reinforcement menu consists of stick figures engaged in various activities such as playing with dolls, coloring, playing with water, painting, or climbing a rope. The activities displayed would be drawn from observation of the child or group of children for which the menu is devised. After an assignment is completed, the child would be permitted to select one of the activities and engage in it for a designated period of time.

Daley (1969) used the reinforcing event menu with a group of mentally retarded children. Observation of the class produced 22 items which represented high preference behaviors of various members of the group. These included such activities as talking, coloring, drawing, listening to a record, dancing, walking, drawing on the chalk board, working with jigsaw puzzles, singing, moving chairs, and looking out the window. Each activity was depicted in color and enclosed in a single book with one activity per page. The children were shown the pictures and informed that when their work was finished they could select the activity of their choice. Significant improvement in low-preference behaviors was noted.

In using a reinforcement menu, it is desirable to change the activities routinely to avoid a child's possible disinterest. Also, it would be helpful to include a special event on occasion to enhance the reinforcement value of the procedure. These may include such activities as playing "dress-up," viewing cartoons, having a party, and blowing noisy horns. These events may be placed in the menu on an irregular basis so as to increase their surprise value. The teacher may also find that the effectiveness of the menu may be enhanced by colored Polaroid pictures of the children engaging in various activities which would be available to them. This procedure would increase the meaningfulness of the menu to the younger and the more severely handicapped child.

A low-preference activity will be strengthened if followed frequently by a high-preference activity.

Token Reinforcers

An additional class of secondary reinforcing events which may be used by teacher and parent to strengthen and maintain behavior patterns consists of *token reinforcers*. These are objects that have no particular initial value of their own: grades, marks, stamps, tokens, certificates, diplomas, money, and chips. In one way or another these items represent other reinforcing events which the child will experience at a later time. A token, for example, may be exchanged for other objects or activities; good grades may produce reinforcing events like praise from parents or an increase in allowance. These token events serve to bridge the time delay between the behavior to be strengthened and the later presentation of other reinforcing events. For many children with learning and behavior problems, the more tangible and physically durable these events are which bridge the gap between behavior and the subsequent final reinforcing event the more effective these token events become in strengthening and maintaining behavior.

These token events become reinforcing through previous association with the reinforcing events for which they can be exchanged. Such tokens would soon lose any reinforcing functions, however, if they no longer resulted in or could be exchanged for objects or privileges or no longer provided social reinforcement such as praise or other forms of attention from others.

In some instances it may not be feasible to provide social and certain types of tangible reinforcing consequences following behavior. Frequent social reinforcement may disturb the child or her peers. With some children social reinforcement may be ineffective in influencing desired classroom behaviors. Birnbrauer and Lawler (1964) report the development of numerous appropriate social and study behaviors in a highly disruptive, severely retarded boy. These newly acquired behaviors were soon lost when only social approval was provided. For children who require tangible reinforcers for effective learning, it may not be possible to provide these supports immediately following the desired behavior. In such cases it may be helpful to make use of a token reinforcement system. The child would be provided a small token or a check on a grid card which may be taped to his desk. The tangible token will serve to bridge the time gap between behavior and the later availability of some back-up reinforcer. These tokens would be exchanged at a later time for the tangible or activity reinforcers.

Such a token reinforcement system is relatively simple to administer. The tokens or marks are easily handled by the child and are a reminder of the reinforcer to be provided later. Behavior can be reinforced as it occurs. Tokens frequently can be provided without disrupting the task behavior. Birnbrauer and Lawler (1964) provided each child with an apron with front pockets into which the teacher could drop the token as it was provided the child. The child could easily keep his tokens without dropping them and without other children taking them. Twardosz and Sajwaj (1972) used X-marks which the teacher placed on a card which young children with learning and behavior problems wore around their necks. Other teachers have provided children with small plastic cups for each child in which they place a token as the child earns it. Heitzman (1970) used red transparent bingo markers in working with primary level children in reading and arithmetic instruction. These were deposited in individual baby-food jar banks and exchanged at a later time for a variety of reinforcers. A grid card taped in front of each child as he sits at the work table has been used successfully. The teacher marks the child's card following occurrence of the desired behavior. Other possible tokens suggested by Becker, Engelmann, and Thomas (1971) include tickets, punches on a card, a counter with a light flash or buzzer, numbers of a page, marks on the blackboard, gold stars, marbles in a jar, and marks on a ladder with 50 steps on it. These and similar experiences support the usefulness and the feasibility of using a token system of reinforcement with young children. The actual token procedure selected should be easily handled and should cause a minimum of interference with what the child is doing when the token is provided.

The tangible nature of the token is quite valuable to many children. Social praise or approval is too momentary. Once presented, there is nothing tangible to represent the approval. The concept of pleasant consequences at the end of the period or the day is too abstract to influence the child. The token, in contrast, does assist the child in making the connection between appropriate behavior at one moment and the resulting pleasant consequences at a later time.

When introducing the use of tokens, it is useful with the younger and more severely disabled child to provide tangible reinforcers such as food or trinkets initially following desired behavior. The token is next introduced as a substitute for the tangible reinforcer. The child exchanges the tokens immediately for the reinforcer. Gradually, the time is extended between the presentation of the token and the exchange for the back-up consequences. Baker, Stanish, and Fraser (1972) successfully used a token system with a group of four- to seven-year-old moderately retarded children attending a preschool program. The children were provided tokens contingent upon appropriate behavior. The procedure of establishing and maintaining the reinforcing value of the token was as follows:

As soon as the child was given a token, another member of the program staff exchanged it for a candy or other "goody." This pattern was maintained for the first day of token introduction. On the following day the children were required to hold the token momentarily before the exchange for primary reward took place. On each successive day the length of time the child was required to hold the token before exchanging it was increased until at the end of five days the children were retaining the token for 10 minutes before "cashing in." At this point small cloth pockets were tied around each child's waist and the children were instructed to save their tokens in these pockets. Over the following 5 days the delays between receiving tokens and their exchange was increased until all of the children were able to save their poker chips until the end of the morning when they would exchange them for toys, candy, and other "goodies" at a "store." The "store" consisted of a large wooden chest in which a variety of primary rewards were kept and attractively displayed during the exchange period. (pp. 17-18)

Birnbrauer and Lawler (1964) used tokens in classes for children described as severely retarded. Initially the classroom teacher used a candy reinforcer for a variety of desirable social and study behaviors. These tokens were presented as a child exhibited approximations of desired behavior. Each presentation was accompanied by social approval. Within a short period of time, the children were occasionally given a poker chip following correct behavior. After the child had saved two or three chips, he exchanged these on a one-to-one basis for candy. Gradually the teacher gave more and more tokens and less and less candy reinforcers until the child earned only tokens. These could be exchanged at the end of a class period for a variety of tangible objects such as trinkets, balloons, candy, and other edibles. During the transition phase from candy to tokens, some children received tokens and others received candy. It is interesting to note that children who had learned the value of tokens were not upset that other children were receiving immediate candy reinforcers. Children were encouraged to save the tokens for longer periods of time prior to exchange. It was not long before some children were able to work throughout the school day prior to exchange. Some were able to save from one day to the next.

After a few months experience with the token system, the teachers reported that most of the children ". . . hung up their coats upon entering the classroom, took their seats quietly, and waited for their assignments with only an occasional reminder." (p. 277)

The experiences of Bushell and his associates (1968) provide an additional illustration of the effective use of tokens with young children.   These children, ranging in age from three to six, attended a three-hour daily preschool program.   Following the first 75 minutes of classroom work, a special event (such as a short movie, trip to a nearby park, an art project, a story, and gym class) was made available to the children.   After this, additional pre-school activity was followed by a 30-minute snack period.   The special event and snack periods were available only to those children who had earned tokens during the preceding classroom activity periods.

The tokens, colored plastic washers about 1.5 inches in diameter, were provided by the teacher to children as they were engaging in appropriate classroom behavior.   The teachers moved about the classroom and gave the tokens whenever they observed children attending to instructions, working independently or in cooperation with others, remaining with and attending to assigned tasks, and reciting after completion of assignments.

Children who had earned a sufficient number of tokens were permitted to exchange them for participation in the special event and for snack items (ice cream, cookies, milk, lemonade). Children who had an insufficient number did not participate in these special events.   The teachers reported a 20 to 25 percent increase in appropriate study behavior following use of the token reinforcement procedure.   They conclude:

> A token system has much to recommend it from a practical standpoint, for there are many school activities (recess, early dismissal, extra-curricular events) which might be employed to develop and maintain higher levels of study behavior. Further, the classroom teacher responsible for the behavior of many students can manage a token system, but faces some difficulty in relying solely on verbal praise and attention as reinforcers.   (p. 61)

The following procedure has been found helpful in enhancing the effective use of a token system with young children.   An individual reinforcement menu, composed of colored Polaroid pictures of each child engaging in various reinforcing activities such as eating candy, drinking soda, listening to music, playing, painting, and playing "dress-up," is developed.   In addition, a group menu is prepared which depicts special, surprise, and unusual events.   At the beginning of the school day, each child selects from his individual book the activity which he wishes to earn. The picture is removed from the menu and mounted on a token card.   A number of blank squares are drawn at the bottom of the card and represent the number of tokens which must be earned prior to reception of the selected reinforcer.   This token card is placed on the child's table and as he engages in various appropriate behaviors the teacher places her initials in one of the squares. The card may follow the child from activity to activity. The child may exchange the card for the activity immediately upon filling all the squares or at specific times designated by the teacher. The number of squares required for each item may be the same for each class member or may vary from child to child. On occasion each child is permitted to select from the special group menu. The use of a special menu adds interest and enthusiasm to the token system.

> Tokens which represent other reinforcers may be used to strengthen behavior.

The use of a token-reinforcement system potentially has a number of positive effects on the total classroom program. Teachers are likely to become more aware of individual behavior. They focus on the repertoires of individual children and identify those components which need specific reinforcement. Individualized instruction is a natural result. If tasks presented to a child are too difficult, he receives too few tokens or perhaps none at all. If the tasks are too easy, the child will receive too many tokens. The teacher is able to make the necessary instructional adjustments.

The use of a token procedure also emphasizes the relationship between behavior and consequences. This is extremely helpful to many children with severe learning and behavior difficulties since they are relatively insensitive to behavior-reinforcement relationships. Exposure to a token-reinforcement program which pairs appropriate behavior with tangible positive consequences provides the child with experiences which contribute to the development of self-responsibility. The child is provided tangible evidence that certain behaviors provide positive consequences. He learns to select those behaviors which result in the positive events and to avoid those which do not contribute to the achievement of those consequences.

Self-Reinforcement

A child may learn to reinforce some of his own behaviors by "patting himself on the back" while engaging in or immediately upon completion of these behaviors. In fact, such self-management is the ultimate goal of a child development program. He can learn to say to himself, "That's good work," "I'm smart," "I deserve to be proud," "Good job," "I'm proud of myself" after certain of his behaviors. To facilitate the development of such self-reinforcement behaviors, the teacher should encourage the child to compliment himself after appropriate behavior. If such verbal statements are associated on numerous occasions with reinforcing events presented by others, these self-delivered compliments will become reinforcing. The child becomes more independent of external reinforcers and is able to maintain present behaviors and to acquire new behaviors on his own.

Reinforcer Sampling and Exposure

There are numerous events available to the child in the school environment which could serve potentially as reinforcers but which the child has seldom if ever experienced. The child may appear to be disinterested in many aspects of his environment which are reinforcing to many children. The reinforcing qualities of these events may be enhanced by insuring that the child observes others enjoying these events. Additionally, the child could be more actively exposed to these events and encouraged to sample or participate in them. For example, a child with limited experience with finger painting may not prefer to engage in this activity. After observing others having fun using the paints and being reinforced by praise for initial exploration, the child may come to enjoy the activity. Finger painting, in turn, may then be used as a reinforcing event to strengthen other behaviors which the teacher wishes to encourage.

Summary

In deciding upon the types of reinforcing events to use with a child, it should be recognized that the goal is to render the child as independent as possible of frequent tangible events in as many behavioral areas as possible. The goal is to shift from the use of arbitrary reinforcing events such as trinkets, toys, or tokens to the use of those social and other events which are natural to the child's environments. This would include the development of self-reinforcement skills and of rendering many behaviors intrinsically reinforcing—task completion, task involvement, achievement, creative activities, pleasing others, interacting with others. These activities gradually acquire reinforcing characteristics as they are associated frequently with other reinforcing events.

At the same time, it must be recognized that consequences which do in fact strengthen and possibly maintain behavior for any given child must be used. The teacher may find with some children that effective learning will occur only under conditions of frequent presentation of tangible events which the child can eat or manipulate. Children with many previous failures will benefit from the use of tangible reinforcers by the teacher. These events serve to remind him that he has accomplished something and that he can be successful. In such cases, the teacher should be prepared to use these reinforcers. In these instances, social attention in the form of praise and smiles along with other neutral events should be associated on every occasion with the tangible consequences. The range of reinforcing events should be increased as quickly as possible. As this is accomplished, the behavior management program will become more effective.

Finally, the teacher may find that the child who responds well to social and self-reinforcement on most occasions may require more tangible consequences when confronted with unusually difficult behavior requirements.

> **Those events which are positively reinforcing to a child must be used if learning is to occur.**

To make best use of this rule, many teachers have found it valuable to develop a list of reinforcing events for each child in her class. The list would include primary, social, and activity reinforcers as illustrated in Table 4.1. The items included in the list were gathered by observing the child, discussions with parents, and by asking the child to identify preferred items and activities. The teacher will evaluate her listing routinely and make additions and deletions as events change in effectiveness.

The following additional items are representative of those suggested by various educators as possible reinforcers for use by teachers of children with developmental difficulties.* These include *consumable* items which the child may eat or drink; *durable* items such as toys, trinkets, or hobby items which may be kept by the child or which may be used by the child for a specific period of time; *activities* such as watching TV, listening to music, and *social*

---

* Reference should be made to the following sources for more comprehensive listings: Becker, Engelmann, and Thomas (1971); Bijou and Sturges (1959); Clarizio (1971); Rosenberg (1971); Spradlin and Girardeau (1966); and Sulzer and Mayer (1972).

Table 4.1: Primary, Social, and Activity Reinforcing Events.

TYPE OF REINFORCER	NAME OF CHILDREN			
	JACK	JILL	EUDORA	KITTY
Primary	Choc. milk Pepsi cola Choc. candy Potato chips	Peanuts Hard candy Gum Cherry pop	Cookies Variety of candy Choc. milk Coca Cola	Potato chips Lollipops Soda pop
Social	Praise for being correct Recognition in group Affection	Being included in group Being the leader General attention from teacher	Physical proximity Smiles and other forms of approval Being singled out in front of group	Quiet praise Soft physical contact Praise for success
Activity	Listening to music Free play Finger paints Animal puzzles	Puppet play Coloring Cutting Playing with teacher	Puzzles Brush painting Doll play Group games	Solitary doll play Finger painting Music Swings and slides

events. The specific reinforcing events used by any teacher at any time obviously will be chosen to coincide with the individual preferences of the children in her class. The items used may include such events as:

Listening to music
Use of tape recorder
Using the telephone
Use of jump boards
Use of rail beams
Use of twist board
Throwing bean bags and ball

Passing out cookies at snack time
Painting
Using makeup kit
Using Play–Dough
Drawing with magic markers
Using earphones

Extra play period
Being first in line
A class party
Helping teacher
Food items such as candy, grapes, peanuts, corn chips, raisins, cheese sticks, and cookies
Playing toy piano
Use of a rocking chair
Manipulative games and toys such as Lego toys, Tinker toys, Erector sets, building blocks
Puzzles
Playing with typewriter
Using puppets
Finger painting
Multicolor and multiform plastic and metal trinkets
Using teacher as playmate
Talking to a classmate
Selecting the records to play
Looking out the window
Singing
Sitting next to teacher

Blowing up a balloon
Stringing beads
Watching filmstrip
Blowing bubbles
Playing in water or sand
Blowing a whistle or using other noisemakers
Watching short film
Shooting a cap pistol
Using flashlight in a darkened room
Recording voice on tape recorder
Smile, nod, gentle pat on shoulder, wink, throwing child a kiss, and a variety of comments of praise, approval, acceptance, and recognition such as "good," "fine," "great," "right," "nice," "OK," "perfect," "wonderful."
Being first at show-and-tell
Feeding a pet
Playing dress-up
Listening to a story
Showing pictures to class

WHEN SHOULD REINFORCEMENT BE PROVIDED?

In the early stages of teaching a new behavior pattern, the child will learn most effectively if reinforcing consequences are presented *immediately* following either the desired behavior or some acceptable approximations of this behavior. When the child who is without speech attempts to use sound in a meaningful manner, reinforcement must be provided at that moment. If a shy, isolated child approaches another child in an apparent attempt at social interaction, the teacher should reinforce that behavior when it occurs. This rule of immediate reinforcement following the desired behavior is especially important in teaching the young child with learning and behavior problems. Events such as being correct, completing a task, or being promised a later reinforcement cannot be depended upon to strengthen behavior as may be the case for some older children. If it is not possible to provide the reinforcer immediately, the behavior that is being reinforced should be described to the child as the consequences are provided. "You remembered to put your toys away like a big boy. I am proud of you."

> **A child will learn new be-
> haviors best if he is pro-
> vided immediate reinforce-
> ment.**

The consistent implementation of this rule presents some obvious practical problems. In working with groups of children, obviously it is not possible to reinforce immediately each and every behavior which the teacher is attempting to influence. The teacher may plan to use the activity of listening to records as a reinforcing event for the children in her class for completing individually designed table work. As some children will complete their work sooner than others, there will be a delay between task completion and the availability of the reinforcing activity. The teacher may use one or both of the following procedures to bridge the time delay between behavior and reinforcement. She may indicate as each child finishes, "Oh, I see you are finished. You may go to the music corner in just a minute or two." Or she may use a token reinforcement procedure which could consist of a small key representing a key to the music room or even a small black cardboard disk which could represent a record which each child could use later to exchange for a record which he or she will play. These tangible objects could possibly even serve as secondary reinforcers for the behavior of sitting quietly while the other children were finishing their table assignments.

HOW FREQUENTLY SHOULD THE CHILD BE REINFORCED?

In addition to the requirement of immediate reinforcement, most rapid learning will occur initially if the desired behavior is reinforced *on every occasion*. In the initial stages of teaching a child a new behavior, the teacher must be prepared to reinforce the behavior immediately each time it (or an acceptable approximation) occurs. Fulfilling these two requirements is essential for the child with extreme learning difficulties. As such children typically acquire new behaviors at a slow rate, success can best be achieved by a consistent use of these two procedures.

> A child will learn new be-
> haviors most rapidly if
> these are reinforced every
> time they occur.

It is true that children do learn many behavior patterns even though reinforcement is delayed or is presented in a haphazard manner. However, such learning will be inefficient and will require considerably more time than would be necessary under more appropriate learning conditions. The child with developmental difficulties can ill-afford an inefficient learning environment.

The relationship between the time of a behavioral consequence and the effects which the consequence exerts on behavior provide an explanation for the development of behavior patterns which are frequently puzzling to teachers and parents. "He gets into his sister's toys even though he knows he will be punished when I get home from the office," or "He insists on looking at pictures during naptime even though he loses part of his play period later in the day." In these instances it appears that the immediate consequences of playing with sister's toys or of looking at the pictures are quite reinforcing and serve to maintain such behaviors. As the negative consequences are quite delayed, it can be assumed that they are too far removed in time to offset the reinforcement effects of the behaviors which the adult views as puzzling. In some instances, the delayed punishment may be quite severe relative to the apparent value of the positive reinforcer. The critical factor is the time interval between behavior and consequence. Behavior which produces an immediate consequence will be more influenced by that consequence than by a delayed consequence. The immediacy factor, especially with young children who receive infrequent and inconsistent positive consequences, may become a more critical variable than the magnitude of consequence, especially if delay is long.

EFFECTIVENESS OF REINFORCING EVENTS

The reinforcing influence which any event has on a child's behavior at any specific time is related to a number of factors. As suggested earlier, the time and frequency relationships between behavior and a consequence are of importance. The more immediate and frequent the reinforcing event, the more likely the preceding behavior will be influenced. Other factors include:

1. *Kind of reinforcer.* Events which are reinforcing to one child may not be reinforcing to another. The implication of this is simple: the same events cannot be provided every child if maximum program effects are to be realized. These reinforcing events must be individualized. The range of events which is reinforcing for some children is quite varied and for others quite limited.

New events may become reinforcing to a child as he gains familiarity with them. Various toys, novel foods, new activities, and other events may be of minimal reinforcement value initially as the child has had only limited exposure to them. The value of these novelties may be enhanced, as described earlier, by exposing the children to them and insuring that they sample or otherwise experience the new events. It would be best to introduce them at times when the child is enjoying something familiar to him. In a popular sense, such exposure creates a "need" for the event. After pleasant association, the event becomes reinforcing in its own right and thus can be depended upon to reinforce behavior which produces it.

2. *Amount and relative value of a reinforcer.* Generally, the greater the amount of the reinforcing events provided after any specific behavior, the greater the effect it has on contributing to the strength of the behavior. Providing 30 minutes of free time following task completion should be more reinforcing than providing only five minutes. Praise, while representing a single kind of event, may be more influential if provided by a highly admired teacher than if provided by a stranger. This type of factor is represented in a frequently observed example. A group of children may learn progressively in one classroom taught by a warm, expressive, and empathetic teacher who praises frequently. In another classroom in which praise is also provided, the children are noted to make much less and systematic progress in acquiring new behavioral skills. The same kind of social events provided at relatively comparable frequency but by different persons may influence children differently.

The amount of reinforcement required to maintain behavior after it becomes a stable part of the child's repertoire frequently may be reduced below that level needed during the initial teaching of the behavior. Also the child will learn to engage in longer and longer behavior patterns for the same reinforcing events. Initially the child may be reinforced with a specific event such as a token at the completion of a specified behavior. He is given a token when he correctly places the final piece of the puzzle. Next, he may be required to place two pieces, then three, then four, and eventually may be required to finish two complete puzzles prior to being reinforced with the token.

Hamblin and his associates (1971) described this procedure of requiring an increasingly large amount of behavior prior to reinforcement in teaching verbal expression skills to an extremely inhibited child in a primary classroom. The teacher initially provided candy (M&M's) if the boy would correctly label the colors of each. After a few experiences, the same method was used to reinforce prompt naming of familiar objects which the teacher presented to the child. The teacher next required the boy to tell a story about a picture which she provided. Initially he would talk for only 15 to 30 seconds; after two weeks he was able to continue telling a story for up to six minutes. The same reinforcing event was now maintaining behavior that was over twelve times that which initially occurred.

3. *Variation in reinforcer effects.* The reinforcing effect of some events may diminish or disappear following frequent use. Praise may be effective the first few times it is provided in the morning, but may gradually diminish with additional use during the day. Playtime and other activities and events may be highly reinforcing if used sparingly but lose their effectiveness if used too often. For many reinforcers, the state of *deprivation* or *satiation* thus will influence the reinforcer effectiveness of numerous events. If a child has not experienced specific reinforcing events for a period of time, these events will become more valuable to the child. Food, social interaction, and the opportunity to play with a highly valued toy represent examples. At the same time, following periods of play, social interaction, watching TV, or listening to music the child may become satiated with the result that these activities may lose temporarily some of their reinforcing value. The teacher must be sensitive to satiation effects and change to alternate reinforcing events when these are noted.

> **Events which are reinforcing to a child at one time may not be reinforcing at another.**

and

> **A reinforcing event may become ineffective if used too frequently.**

For those reinforcers which do show a satiation effect, it may be possible to reestablish the reinforcing qualities by depriving the child of the event for a period of time. If playtime, looking at a particular book, using a specific box of building blocks, praise, or other forms of social attention show satiation effects, the teacher should withdraw these reinforcers for a period of time. In this manner, these events may be used again with increased effectiveness for limited periods of time.

> **The value of a reinforcing event can be increased by depriving the child of that event.**

and a related rule

> **The value of a reinforcing event can be increased by reducing the availability of other more preferred events.**

Token reinforcers are less likely to be influenced by satiation effects as a result of the generalized nature of the token. This is especially true in those instances in which the tokens can be exchanged for a wide variety of other reinforcing events. This feature recommends the use of tokens when tangible events are required to produce best learning.

4. *Type of responses.* A specific reinforcer will be generally more effective in strengthening simple responses than in influencing more complex behavior patterns. The kind and amount of a reinforcing event must be appropriate to the difficulty level of a behavior pattern for optimal learning to occur. There must be a reasonable match between the degree of difficulty of a given task and the type and amount of the contingent consequences. Social

approval, for example, may be a valuable event for use in strengthening an attending response but be of insufficient value for use in strengthening more complex behavior such as completion of a series of puzzles. Again, the simple and complex nature of a behavioral requirement will vary greatly from child to child, and even for any given child, from time to time. A behavior pattern such as sitting for ten minutes and coloring and cutting may be quite simple for one child to learn and will require only brief and infrequent social praise to maintain it. For another child the same behavior pattern may be most difficult and may require much more frequent reinforcers as well as events of a different kind and amount.

As implied earlier, high-value reinforcers may be needed in the early stages of teaching a child a new behavior pattern. However, as this behavior is developed, it may result in other sources of reinforcement that maintain the behavior. As this occurs, the teacher-provided reinforcing events can be removed. A child may learn new ways of playing and sharing possessions with other children under a behavior management program in which both tangible and social reinforcement are provided by the teacher. As the child develops these behavior patterns, the consequences provided by the other children may become quite sufficient in maintaining these newly acquired social interaction skills. The tangible and teacher social reinforcement can be phased out.

> **The kind and amount of reinforcing consequences should be matched to the difficulty level of the desired behavior.**

HOW SHOULD REINFORCING EVENTS BE PROVIDED?

The teacher should be careful about the manner in which the learning environment is arranged in making use of the rules of positive reinforcement. Consequences should not be provided in an authoritarian or arbitrary manner. Such an approach would suggest to the child: "If you do what I ask, I shall give you something." In this type of arrangement, the child is taught to exchange his behavior for a reward: "Pick up your toys and I shall give you some candy!" This type of arrangement or bribery usually comes after the child has refused to pick up the toys. This arrangement is highly undesirable and represents an obvious poor use of the rules of reinforcement. It teaches the child to barter with those who control the reinforcers. The reinforcers represent something given arbitrarily by an authority agent.

Using reinforcing events in a bribing fashion can result in some highly bothersome behavior patterns. Such misuse of positive reinforcement can teach a child that he can "get his way" if he engages in certain inappropriate behaviors. He may learn: "in order to get teacher or parent to give me what I want, I must begin to misbehave." The adult will then respond, "If you stop that noise and play quietly until the visitors leave, I will give you a treat." In this manner a chain of events is strengthened: *The child finds the adult in a vulnerable situation.*————▶*He begins to misbehave.*————▶*The adult bribes him to stop his misbehavior with a promise of a reward for good behavior. The child engages in appropriate behavior.*————▶*The reward is given.* The final reinforcer strengthens the entire chain of events.

> **Reinforcement is not bribery.**

Such misuse of reinforcement produces what has been labeled the "spoiled" or "self-centered" child. The child has learned that "regardless of what I do, I will get reinforced. If I do not get my way, all I have to do is to become demanding and disruptive and the social environment will provide what I want." The child has been taught that regardless of his behavior, appropriate or inappropriate, desired consequences will be forthcoming.

> **The misuse of reinforcement can result in a problem child.**

A more appropriate arrangement between behavior and consequences would be one in which the consequences are provided in as logical and natural a manner as possible. An arrangement which suggests "After we finish cleaning, we shall listen to our favorite music," or one in which a social consequence is naturally and spontaneously provided, teaches the child that certain of his behaviors produce desirable consequences. The child's reply of "Thank you" after the teacher helps the child with his coat results in a warm smile from the teacher. Both the teacher and the child are reinforced in this interchange. The teacher does not present the smile in an arbitrary or authoritarian manner nor does she give it to the child. The smile represents a natural social consequence of a social behavior. The more natural and socially relevant the manner in which reinforcing consequences occur, the more such consequences will contribute to positive behavior development. Under these socially relevant conditions the child is not "forced," "pressured," "prodded," or "bribed" into desired behaviors. The child's experiences suggest to him those behaviors which result in consequences which are of value to him. He learns to choose these behaviors and to refrain from others which result in unpleasant consequences.

> **The appropriate use of reinforcement results in a successful child.**

USE OF REINFORCEMENT PROCEDURES IN GROUPS

A natural concern expressed by teachers inexperienced in the use of positive reinforcement procedures in the classroom is "Will the children who are not being reinforced become upset?" Also, "Is it possible to use reinforcement procedures such as tokens with all children in the class? I don't see how I would ever have time for such activities." The obvious reply to these concerns is that every child in the classroom should be provided positive reinforcement frequently and consistently. The type of reinforcing events and the time and frequency of providing them will obviously differ from child-to-child and from class-to-class. Some children will require frequent social reinforcement; others will require much less attention. Some will require frequent tangible reinforcers; others may learn and perform satisfactorily with only infrequent tangible consequences. Some children with severe problem behaviors may require close reinforcement attention; other children may function more independently of teacher-provided reinforcement. A token system of reinforcement may be used with all children for some activities but not for others. In a successful program described earlier, Bushell and associates (1968) used tokens with all members of a preschool class. The tokens were awarded each child contingent upon his own appropriate behavior.

On some occasions the reinforcing events may be placed on a group contingency basis. In this type of arrangement, the class as a whole will be reinforced on the basis of some designated behaviors expected of all members of the class. Any deviation from these expected behaviors by any member of the class will result in possible loss of reinforcement by the entire class. Packard (1970) used this group contingency procedure in a program designed to increase the classroom attention of an entire class of children in a preschool setting. The teacher defined the types of attending behaviors (position of body and eyes, no inappropriate noise, following instructions) which she desired during a preacademic language class. A red light connected to a timer, was turned on by the teacher when any class members were not attending. The light was turned off when all class members were engaged in appropriate attending behavior. At the end of the class period, the entire class was provided access to a play activity (recess, gym, or a group game in the room) if attending behavior had been present for a designated percentage of the class period. If this criterion had not been met, the reinforcing activity was not provided. If this criterion had been exceeded by a certain percentage, the class was provided a bonus of additional time for play activity. The amount of time spent in attentive behavior under this group reinforcement procedure was gradually increased until a high level of attending behavior became evident.

Packard (1970) emphasized the possible effect of peer influence in a group contingency program. He wrote that

> . . . a program of reinforcing attention would be proportionately enhanced by making peer approval or disapproval contingent on a student's attention to task . . . Subjective observation and other anecdotal evidence . . . indicated considerable peer interaction of this type. Though such pressure never reached the "back–alley trouncing" stage, there were frequent instances, both during and after classes, of students not hesitating to remind or even scold a classmate for "keeping the light on," and to congratulate an improved student. (p. 26)

In another variation of the group contingency procedure, Patterson (1965) arranged a classroom program for a hyperactive boy so that the boy could earn candy and pennies for the entire class for each ten seconds he remained at his desk and worked at a task. The peers assisted the boy by not attending to him when he was working. The peers also provided considerable social praise between classes and encouraged him to continue in his appropriate attending behavior.

Ward and Baker (1968), in response to another concern which teachers have over the use of reinforcement procedures in the classroom, evaluated the effects on other class members when teachers provided selective social reinforcement to individual children who presented specific patterns of problem behaviors. Children who either presented a high frequency of disruptive classroom behaviors or who were withdrawn and nonattentive were provided frequent social attention for appropriate classroom behavior. Other class members were responded to as they had been prior to the initiation of the specific behavior management programs for these problem children. The children who received the selective social attention for appropriate behaviors showed a significant decrease in undesired behaviors. Ward and Baker concluded:

> No support was found for the argument that behavior of other pupils in a class deteriorates when the teacher's attention is somehow diverted from them in treating behavior problem children. Although teachers did slightly decrease the amount of attention given to control children, there was no significant increase in the control children's deviant behavior. (p. 327)

In summary, behavior management programs using positive reinforcement procedures may be designed for the entire class or for individual members of the class. Optimal flexibility must be maintained to insure that individual differences among children will be attended to. If the teacher is hesitant about using behavior management procedures, she should begin on a small scale. Perhaps one child should be selected initially. After some successful experience, the teacher may gradually add other children to whom she provides positive reinforcement in a specific response-contingent manner.

Reinforcement procedures can be used effectively with groups of children.

REINFORCEMENT CHARACTERISTICS OF CHILDREN WITH PROBLEMS

In evaluating the responsiveness to reinforcing events of young children with severe learning and behavior difficulties, various characteristics distinguish them from other children who progress normally in development. These include:

1. As a result of excessive failure experiences, there are likely to be fewer effective secondary reinforcing events available for use by the teacher. Those events that have become secondary reinforcers frequently are relatively weak. It will be necessary for the teacher to initiate an active program developing new secondary reinforcers and increasing the strength of existing ones.

2. The child is likely to require more immediate and frequent reinforcement for effective learning and for consistent use of behaviors which are in his repertoire. He is less able to delay gratification. Events which are in his present environment are more influential than future promised events. The teacher must have available a range of tangible and other immediately available events. She must also initiate an active program of teaching delay of reinforcement. The use of tokens and a program for reinforcing longer periods of appropriate behavior without tangible reinforcers will be helpful.

3. Social attention in its various forms is less likely to be as effective in influencing behavior as are more concrete tangible events. Reynolds and Risley (1968) and Bereiter and Engelmann (1966) all suggest that material reinforcers are disproportionately strong and that social reinforcement (attention, praise, approval) from adults is a weak reinforcer among preschool children who live in culturally-deprived homes. Adults appear to be important chiefly as dispensers of material reinforcers. Quay and his associates (1966), Patterson (1971), and Wahler (1972) suggests that children with negativistic and aggressive behavior patterns find social reinforcement from adults to be relatively ineffectual in influencing modification of their problem behavior areas. Frequent tangible reinforcers provided for appropriate behaviors and paired consistently with social attention will result in best learning. The consistent pairing of tangible and social events will result in an increase in the value of social events as positive reinforcers.

Shy and isolated children will require strong tangible reinforcers for the development of social interaction skills. These children frequently have a deficit repertoire of social skills and also may find social attention uncomfortable to them.

4. In some instances, children may be quite responsive to social reinforcement, but only when provided by highly specific

individuals (usually the mother or father). These "selective responders" are likely to demonstrate anxiety or related negative emotional reactions when not in the presence of the socially reinforcing person (Patterson and Brodsky, 1966). Social attention, praise, or approval when provided by persons other than the mother or father will have little reinforcing effect. This type of characteristic frequently is observed in children who exhibit phobic behavior associated with separation anxiety.

5. The child will have had less successful exposure to a wide range of activities which for most children hold exciting reinforcement value. His experiences have been more restrictive and more negative. He is less likely to become curious or enthusiastic over novel events as newness in his previous experiences has too frequently resulted in unpleasant consequences. Procedures of reinforcer exposure and reinforcer sampling should be used by the teacher to increase the range of available events which may serve as reinforcers.

These motivational characteristics of children with severe learning and behavior difficulties emphasize the critical need to identify reinforcing events which do work with each child with developmental difficulties and to initiate a systematic program of creating new sources of positive reinforcement.

CHAPTER 5

Other Methods of
Influencing Behavior Patterns

The use of a reinforcement procedure to strengthen behavior obviously depends upon the initial occurrence of the desired behavior. Before the child can be reinforced for correctly labeling a picture or for correctly matching colors, certain responses must occur. Before a child can learn to label a blue color as "blue" when presented with the request, "What color is this?" he must be able to say "blue." If the child can verbalize the concept, the teaching task is to get the behavior to occur consistently under the right conditions, i.e., whenever a blue object is presented and he is asked to identify the color or to describe the object. But if the child is unable to say "blue," the most powerful reinforcing event would be of no value in teaching the child to label a blue crayon.

BEHAVIOR SHAPING

If the behavior in the desired form is not in the child's repertoire, a procedure mentioned earlier called *behavior shaping* would be used. In this procedure successive approximations of the desired behavior are reinforced. Responses which the child *does make* and which have some similarity to the behavior to be developed are reinforced in the presence of specific cues. The desired behavior is shaped gradually by successively reinforcing closer and closer approximations of this desired goal.

The successive changes may be slight in some cases. Keen

observation is required by the teacher to insure that these changes are provided reinforcement.

The initial approximations which are reinforced may be quite different from the final behavioral objective. But they must be reinforced, as these attempts form the basis for the strengthening of similar behaviors which represent improvements or closer approximations of the desired goal behavior. At each stage in the shaping procedure, the behaviors for which reinforcement will be provided are increasingly similar to the goal behavior. Behaviors which are not increasingly similar are not reinforced; those which show improvements are reinforced. The child with learning and behavior difficulties frequently fails to learn as the educational program requires too much behavioral change at a given time. The child is unable to make the transition from what he does presently to what the program is requiring. The child might be quite capable of learning new patterns of behavior or more complex combinations of present behaviors *if the learning tasks were presented in a sequential order in smaller steps.* The shaping procedure provides the teacher with a means of turning failure into success.

Larsen and Bricker (1968) described the shaping process used for a child with severe learning difficulties:

> . . . we usually teach him bit by bit. For example, if we wanted to teach him to work a puzzle, we wouldn't try to teach him to do the whole puzzle all at once. Instead, we would start with one piece and make sure that he knew where it went before going on to the second. We would continue this way until he knew all of the pieces. The same thing is true in teaching a retarded child to dress himself. We would not give him his pants and tell him to put them on. Instead we would start by putting them on his legs and pulling them almost all the way up, teaching him to just pull them up the last inch or so to start with. Gradually we would teach him to pull them up further and further, until he could pull them up from the floor. Then we would start teaching him to put on one leg of the pants, after we had already put the other one on for him. Finally, we would teach him to put on both legs and pull them up by himself. It is very important to notice here that we *always teach good behavior in small steps.* (p. 24)

More specifically, the procedure of behavior shaping consists of:

1. *Setting precise behavioral objectives.* Examples would include, "John will look at me when requested to do so." "Sue will sit quietly and work at her desk for ten minute periods." "Phil will

speak loudly enough for the teacher to understand his request." "Dan will say the word 'ball' when shown a ball and asked to name it." "Al will put his pants on when requested to do so." It is desirable to inform the child of the behavioral objectives, including what he will learn to do as well as the level of desired performance. Whenever appropriate, it is desirable for the child to participate with the teacher in deciding upon the new behavioral skills to be developed.

2. *Identifying present-related behaviors.* These are the skills or behaviors which the child presently engages in and which will provide the *initial starting point* from which to shape the goal behavior. "Sue will sit at the work table for a short period when the teacher stands or sits beside her." Sitting for longer periods of time, engaging in increasingly acceptable table work, and maintaining this behavior with less and less teacher prompting will be shaped gradually by successively reinforcing larger and larger segments of these behaviors. "Don will on occasion verbalize the sound 'be' when shown a ball and asked, 'What is this?'" This will form the basis for gradual shaping of the sounds comprising the word "ball."

3. *Specifying the reinforcing events to be used and the manner in which these will be provided.* Examples would include, "Al will be provided a piece of candy, nut, or cereal accompanied by animated social praise immediately following every occasion of the desired behavior." "Training in dressing will be held just prior to meals in order to optimize the value of food items which will be used to reinforce dressing behavior."

4. *Developing a tentative outline of the steps in the program.* Complex skills are described as a series of smaller intermediate steps. The behavioral objective may represent a rather circumscribed behavior such as saying the word "ball" when shown a ball and asked, "What is this?" In this case the program may move through a series of steps which represent closer verbal approximations of the desired pronunciation. The steps should be small enough to insure continuous success and at the same time large enough to insure efficient learning.

> **New behaviors may be developed by reinforcing successive approximations of the desired behaviors.**

In devising the steps of a shaping program these steps must be viewed as tentative as a specific child may be unable to move from one step to another in the manner initially outlined by the teacher. In some instances the steps may be too difficult and thus require restructuring into small steps. In other instances, the child may skip a number of steps as he begins to experience success.

After the shaping program has begun, it is important that the child experiences frequent success, that he gains reinforcement for acceptable approximations described in each step. If the child is achieving success, movement to the next step representing more complex behavior should be followed. As soon as the approximation occurs and is reinforced a more complex approximation should be required. If the behavioral criterion (approximation) is set too high and the child is unsuccessful, the teacher should return to a preceding easier step and reinforce this behavior a few more times. In some instances, it will be necessary to add new steps which represent less complex transitions. In any case, the teacher should attempt to move the child continuously from the starting behavior toward an increasingly similar approximation of the final goal behavior.

Johnston and her associates (1966) used a shaping procedure to strengthen vigorous play activity on a piece of climbing equipment in a young child who was physically inactive. Initially the child almost never used the climbing frame. The teachers began providing social reinforcement for successive approximations of the desired play activity. Whenever the child approached or walked by the climbing frame, a teacher would smile and speak to him. She terminated her attention when he moved away. The criteria for reinforcement was gradually changed to require closer and closer proximity. The child eventually touched the frame and was soon climbing on it. Following this activity, reinforcement was provided only for climbing and remaining for longer periods on the frame. Within a short period of time the child was engaging in typical vigorous play activity on the climbing frame. By skillful use of the shaping procedure, the teacher attained her desired goal without having to resort to other procedures involving persuading, convincing, pushing, or requiring him to engage in an activity that apparently was of little initial interest to him.

DEVELOPMENT OF COMPLEX BEHAVIOR PATTERNS

Other behavioral objectives may represent more complex behavior patterns. The desired behavior pattern may be comprised of a number of independent or discrete behaviors, some or all of which may be in the child's repertoire. These individual behavior units may have been taught the child through a shaping procedure. In this case the behavior management program seeks to *integrate* or *chain* the simpler segments together into a more complex pattern of behavior. The program is described in a series of steps or segments which increasingly approximate the final behavioral objective. These programs may be concerned with such objectives as following classroom routine, successfully engaging in language lessons requiring a variety of separate skills, developing independence in lunch time activities (sitting, eating, cleaning table, remaining at table until teacher dismisses), and following directions involving use of various separate skills. These examples emphasize that any desired behavior pattern can be translated into behavior shaping and chaining programs.

A child may know how to sit in a chair, to work on a puzzle, to sit and begin work when requested to do so, to put his completed tasks away, and to remain at his work desk until requested to dress for outdoor play. However, considerable teacher monitoring is required to get each of these behaviors to occur and to insure smooth progression from beginning to end. The child has all the behavior components in his repertoire but these have not developed into an independent integrated pattern.

> **Separate behaviors may be integrated into more complex patterns by a procedure of chaining.**

BEGINNING WITH THE FINAL LINK IN THE CHAIN

In integrating behavior components into a more complex pattern, the goal is to bring more behavior segments under the influence of a final reinforcing consequence. Learning is frequently facilitated by beginning with the behavior that immediately precedes the final reinforcing consequence. This process is called *backward chaining*. As this final behavior segment is strengthened, longer and more complex sequences of behaviors are gradually added prior to the final behavior segment which results in the desired consequence. In a picture puzzle with six parts, the puzzle is presented to the child with the final piece removed. As the child is able to place this piece successfully and receive reinforcement on a few occasions, two pieces are removed. Following successful completion of these two pieces, the child is presented the puzzle with three, then four, then five, and finally six pieces removed. The reinforcing consequence presented following correct placement of the final piece serves to strengthen the entire sequence from beginning to end.

In a similar fashion, the last bead in a string pattern, the last part of a picture to be colored, the last segment of a figure to be drawn, or the last toy to be put into the toy shelf may be presented to the child initially. As he is able to complete these final steps of the more complex behavior pattern, he is provided an increasingly larger number of steps to complete prior to receiving reinforcement. Each step serves as a signal for the next steps which eventually result in the reinforcer. Of course, it may not be possible or feasible to begin with the final behavior component in some instances. The teacher would begin with the first behavior segment and add others from beginning to end. In other behavior patterns, the teacher may use a combination of backward and forward chaining.

The following is an illustration of a more complex behavior pattern which was developed by initial reinforcement of less complex segments and gradual integration into the desired goal:

Behavioral objective: The child will sit at his desk when work time is announced, will attend to instructions provided the group, will complete the ten perceptual–motor tasks presented, and will bring his completed work to the teacher.

Reinforcement procedure: The child will be provided a "smiling face" sticker on his completed work and social reinforcement of praise from the teacher. Five "smiling faces" may be exchanged for a variety of activities such as listening to music, looking at a slide viewer, taking a Polaroid picture, finger painting.

Step 1. The child is given one task and as teacher stands watching he completes it correctly. He is praised immediately and given a "smiling face" sticker. He is given a second and then a third, fourth, and fifth task while teacher is standing near by. She reinforces each as it is finished. As the child receives the fifth sticker and thus fills his sticker card, the teacher takes him to the reinforcement area and permits him to select the activity which he desires in exchange for the filled card. She verbalizes the the relationship between the good work, the "smiling faces," and the desired consequences.

Step 2. The child completes two problems prior to receiving a sticker. He now raises his hand when he is finished and the teacher comes to his desk. The number of problems required for each "smiling face" is shifted to three, four, and then five.

99

Step 3.   The child completes five problems and then brings them to the teacher's desk prior to reinforcement.

Step 4.   The child sits at his desk at work time and attends to group instruction. He completes the five problems, brings these to the teacher's desk, and receives a "smiling face" consequence.

Step 5.   The number of problems required prior to reinforcement is gradually shifted to 10.

Step 6.   The child now sits at his desk when work time is announced, attends to group instructions, completes his task, and takes it to the teacher's desk upon completion.

The entire sequence of behavior is being maintained by the final reinforcing consequences provided by the teacher. By gradually increasing the requirements, the final reinforcing event comes to influence and maintain more and more behavior. Once the behavioral objective has been reached, reinforcement should be continued for a sufficient period of time to insure that the behavior will be maintained.

In using behavior shaping and integration procedures, the teacher should:

> **Require as much behavior as the child is able to perform prior to reinforcement.**

and

> **Increase behavioral requirements prior to reinforcement as rapidly as possible.**

If difficulty is experienced in using these procedures, the teacher should ask the following:

1.   *Have I set the standard for reinforcement too high?* If so, the child is unable to demonstrate the behavior required for reinforcement. He quickly loses interest in the program.
2.   *Am I moving from one step to another too rapidly?* If so, the preceding behavior has not been reinforced sufficiently to develop adequate strength. The child soon forgets the behavior which was once demonstrated.

3. *Am I requiring too great a behavioral improvement as I move from one step to another?* If so, the child will make little progress and will become highly frustrated over his lack of success.
4. *Are my steps too simple?* If so, the program is inefficient and the child may become bored with the program and refuse to participate.

PROMPTING PROCEDURES

A desired behavior or an approximation of it may be in the child's repertoire but may occur only infrequently at the right time or place. In other instances the child may be able to make a desired response if shown or told what to do. There is no necessity in such cases for shaping by reinforcing successive approximations of the desired behavior. The tactic in these cases is to arrange the prompting and reinforcing components of the environment to insure that the behavior will occur and will be reinforced (strengthened) under appropriate conditions.

In these cases, as well as in those previously discussed instances in which some initial approximation of the desired behavior is needed, various techniques are available to get the child to engage in the behavior which then can be reinforced under the right cue conditions. These prompting procedures include

—visual modeling and other types of visual cueing.
—verbal instruction, verbal modeling, and other types of auditory cueing.
—physical guidance.
—precise environmental arrangements.

> **Whenever possible use prompting procedures to get the desired behavior to occur.**

and

> **As the desired behavior occurs following prompting, reinforce it immediately.**

These initial prompting stimulus events needed to get the desired behavior to occur are used in addition to the usual or natural discriminative events which eventually will come to control the behavior. In using any one or combination of these prompting procedures, an effort is made to get the desired response to occur in order to strengthen its relationship to specific discriminative conditions. As the behavior gains strength under these desired conditions, the prompts become redundant and unnecessary and are gradually removed.

Visual Prompts

Children can learn a behavior pattern more quickly if they can be guided in a manner that insures few errors. Practice does not make for effective or efficient learning if excessive errors are being made. Prompts can be used to facilitate desired behavior and then gradually removed as the child is able to behave appropriately in the presence of more natural cues. For example, while teaching a child to write letters or to draw geometric forms, considerable visual and mechanical prompts may be provided initially and gradually removed as the skills develop. In teaching a child to color within the lines of a drawing, heavy thread may be used as an outline of the picture. The size of the thread can be progressively reduced as the child learns to color within the lines.

Auditory Prompting

For any particular child, those prompting procedures are selected which hold greatest promise of facilitating the occurrence of the desired behavior under desired stimulus conditions. Some children are able to follow verbal directions and can produce the desired behavior patterns after these are described to them. "John, when the bell rings, bring your paper to me." The teacher then rings the bell and reinforces John as he hands the paper to her. The prompting verbal instruction is no longer needed as John learns that when the bell rings he is to hand his paper to the teacher. As another example, Tammy is asked to label a red ball but is unable to do so. The teacher then provides the prompt "Tammy say 'red ball,' " as she places a red ball on the table. As the child says "red ball" when the red ball is presented, the teacher smiles warmly and exclaims "That's great, Tammy."

Herman and Tramontana (1971) used precise verbal instructions to get young children with high rates of disruptive behavior to engage in appropriate behavior during a rest period.

The verbal instructions and the reinforcement provided following the occurrence of the instructed behavior resulted in a rapid increase in the rate of the desired behavior.   To emphasize the necessity for reinforcement once the behavior does occur, these teachers provided instruction without reinforcement.   The disruptive behavior quickly reappeared.

Physical Guidance

In other instances various forms of *physical guidance* may prove valuable.   The teacher may take the child's hand and move him through a cutting, coloring, or drawing task as the appropriate stimulus is provided.   The physical guidance is gradually removed as the child's behavior begins to occur in the presence of the verbal request to engage in these behaviors.

To elaborate upon the example (presented in Chapter 3, p. 43) of teaching Sue to look at the teacher when requested to do so, the procedures outlined on page 104 may be attempted.

Visual and Auditory Modeling

It is frequently valuable for the teacher or peer to *demonstrate* or *model* the desired behavior as the child observes.   This exposure to the desired behavior should also include a demonstration of the consequences of the desired behavior as it occurs.   Immediately following observation, the child should be prompted to engage in the desired behavior and be reinforced immediately.   The modeling procedure may be supplemented by other prompting tactics such as verbal or gestural instructions and physical guidance.

Lahey (1971) modeled the use of descriptive adjectives to young disadvantaged children and found a marked increase in the frequency of this aspect of speech.   The immediate increase in the use of descriptive adjectives other than the specific ones used by the teacher suggested that the children already knew the words but did not frequently use them.

Precise Environmental Arrangement

A related procedure for increasing the likelihood of occurrence of a desired response is to restrict the likelihood of occurrence of behaviors which may compete with the desired behavior.   The development of skills of attending to and persisting at a task may be facilitated by placing the child in a highly restricted environ-

Appropriate Cue Condition	Prompt	Behavior	Consequence
Cue (1) "Sue, look at me."		Sue continues play and does not look at teacher.	No teacher provided consequences
Cue (2) "Sue, look at me," is accompanied by the prompt.	Teacher gently places her hand under Sue's chin and moves her face toward eye contact with teacher.	Child momentarily looks at teacher under these prompting conditions.	Teacher immediately places candy in child's mouth, smiles at her, and exclaims, "Good girl, Sue."

(3) This sequence is repeated a few times. With each succeeding request the amount of physical guidance is reduced.

(4) In order to increase the likelihood of eye contact during the physical guidance prompt, the teacher begins to hold the candy close to and directly in front of her own eyes. As the child looks toward the candy, eye contact is made and the child is reinforced immediately.

(5) This visual prompt is gradually removed as the child begins to look at the teacher's face, including eye contact, when requested to do so.

(6) The final behavioral objective of Sue looking at teacher when requested to do so is maintained by frequent social reinforcement and occasional food reinforcement.

ment which removes distracting auditory and visual stimulation. The child may be placed in a small training booth with a teacher or a small screen may be placed around the child's desk during times when he is working on table tasks. Prompting procedures for producing the desired behavior may then become effective due to the reduced stimulation and related inappropriate response possibilities. As the desired behavior gains some strength and as the prompts are gradually removed, the child may move slowly through a series of environments which increasingly represent closer similarity to the natural classroom one.

Gradual Removal of Prompts

It has been emphasized that as the desired behavior gains in strength in the presence of the desired stimulus conditions, the prompting should be removed. The goal is to have behaviors occur spontaneously under natural cue conditions without supportive or additional prompts. The child should hang his coat on the coat rack when he comes into the classroom without an additional prompt from the teacher.

Excessive verbal prompting (the teacher saying *blue* and later *bl* and then *b* as the prompts for the child to label the blue color), gestural cueing (the teacher drawing an imaginary circle as a prompt following the assignment to "draw a circle"), physical guidance (the teacher holding the child's hand as he colors inside the boundary of the picture), or whatever combinations are being used, should become less conclusive and less frequent as the behavior becomes stronger. During this *fading* phase, other stimulus components which are more natural to the behavior and to the environment in which it is to occur will assume the cueing function. The picture, the desk, the blue color, the verbal request, or entering the classroom with a coat on will begin to cue or control the desired behavior. The teacher's request to "keep working," "watch those lines," "put your coat up," "do it this way," will no longer be needed as these prompts become excessive or redundant. The natural components of the environment will be sufficient.

Bricker and Bricker (1970) provide an excellent description of a shaping program used in teaching generalized motor-imitation skills in the young severely language-handicapped child. The use of various combinations of prompts and their gradual removal are described:

> A consistent stimulus, such as "Do this," should be used with the motor imitation training so that it becomes a discriminative signal for an imitative response from the child. Following the command of "Do this," the trainer should execute the behavior to be imitated, such as placing his hands on his head and leaving them there, while an assistant standing behind the child physically prompts the child to imitate the response. The assistant prompts the behavior by taking the child's hands and placing them on the child's head and then slowly removes his own hands from the child's. When the child keeps his hands in the correct position without the prompt, the assistant quickly reinforces the child. The procedure is recycled but with the assistant using fewer prompts on each trial. The child's behavior is closely observed and when it is apparent that the child is ready to spontaneously imitate a part of the response, the prompt for that part is withheld. . . . Prompt-

ing and fading are continued until the child imitates the response spontaneously and does so in the presence of the discriminative signal "Do this," followed by the modeled movement. (p. 107)

Care should be taken to insure that prompts are not maintained for an excessive length of time as the child may come to depend too much upon them. The general rule is to remove the prompts as quickly as possible. At the same time, care must be taken not to remove the prompts suddenly as the behavior may stop.

> **Prompts for desired behavior should be removed as quickly as possible.**

Finally, the teacher must be sensitive to individual differences. Children will acquire new behaviors at different rates, will need different types of prompts for optimal learning, will require prompts for varying lengths of time, and as emphasized, will respond differently to reinforcing events. It also must be emphasized that improvement, even though minor, must be reinforced. The teacher must be sensitive to minor changes in behavior which are in the direction of a previously-set behavior goal. The early education program constantly must require new behavior patterns that represent more complex forms and combinations of behavior patterns which the child presently does exhibit.

INFLUENCING CONSISTENCY OF BEHAVIOR

As suggested above, certain environmental events provide the child with information about the appropriateness and inappropriateness of various behaviors. These *cues* or *discriminative stimuli* mark the time, place, and other conditions under which specific behaviors are appropriate. Cues inform the child that specific behaviors will result in positive consequences. These cues which precede behavior account for the consistency in a child's behavior. Once a child learns new behavior patterns, these begin to appear only under certain cue conditions. The behavior occurs under conditions similar to past conditions in which the behavior has resulted in reinforcement. Examples would include:

—Sing in the music room, not during nap time.
—Play on the playground, not during class period.
—Color on paper; do not color on desk.
—Urinate in the toilet, not on the floor.
—Cry when hurt; do not cry following minor bumps or bruises.

These discriminations are acquired by differential reinforcement as follows:

	CUE	CHILD BEHAVIOR	CONSEQUENCE
A.	classroom	sitting attentively	positive reinforcement: teacher praise
B.	classroom	talking loudly	punishment: scolding from teacher
A.	"Show me the red ball."	pointing to the *red* ball	positive reinforcement: token
B.	"Show me the red ball."	pointing to the *blue* ball	no reinforcement: "That is *not* red."

After these relationships among cue ———→ behavior ———→ consequence are repeated on numerous occasions, the child begins to behave more selectively in the classroom environment.

A child does not randomly repeat his name once he has learned to pronounce it. Rather, he replies, "My name is John Jones," when someone requests this information. The reply under most other conditions would not be reinforced by the social environment. The goal of an early education program for children with learning and behavior difficulties is concerned both with influencing more complex and varied behavior patterns and also with insuring that these behaviors occur consistently under specific cue conditions.

Those cues that are present consistently when behavior results either in positive consequences or the removal of unpleasant consequences will gain some discriminative influence over the behavior. If the behavior is reinforced a number of times in the presence of these cues and not reinforced when the cues are absent, the cues come to control the occurrence of the behavior. The presentation of the discriminative stimulus or cue denotes that a given behavior pattern is likely to result in specific consequences. The reinforcement adds to this association between cues and behavior. To repeat, a particular cue, signal, or stimulus gains discriminative control over behavior as a result of its consistent association with the behavior and its subsequent positive or negative reinforcement. The cue conditions that should gain influence over specific behavior patterns at times may be most complex and difficult for a young child. The teacher thus must provide obvious cues in a consistent manner and on numerous occasions if they are to acquire reliable influence over specific behaviors.

> **Cues which are paired with behavior that results in reinforcement will gain control over that behavior.**

Young children frequently know what to do and further may intend to behave in a desired manner, but end up misbehaving. "I know he is a good child but he just will not do what he knows is expected," is a frequently heard comment. The child, for example, "knows" that he should sit and work but the sound of laughter across the room encourages him to leave his work unfinished and join in the play activity. Too many competing cues are present. Too many other events control behaviors that are contrary to that expected by the teacher. This problem could be avoided in many instances by more careful arrangement of cues and subsequent consequences for appropriate behavior. A child should not be "tempted" by competing cues until the appropriate behavior has acquired sufficient strength to overcome the temptation. As the appropriate behavior becomes attached to the desired discriminative cues through consistent reinforcement, these cues will become more effective in controlling the behavior. Other cues for behaviors which are inappropriate will become less influential and thus less likely to produce competing behaviors.

In arranging learning experiences for the development of adequate discriminations, the teacher should plan to correct inappropriate behaviors which occur in the presence of the desired cue. If the child makes the wrong response, he should engage immediately in the appropriate behavior in the presence of the desired cue and the subsequent reinforcer. If the child forgets to hang his coat as he enters the room, he should put his coat on again, go out of the room, and re-enter. As he enters the room insure that he hangs his coat and is reinforced promptly. After a number of experiences of this nature, the cues associated with entering the room will come to remind the child to hang his coat.

Children with developmental difficulties frequently display various attentional, perceptual, and cognitive difficulties which interfere with development of adequate discriminations. The child may tend to become confused because he does not recognize the appropriate cues. He does not know what behavior is being requested since the cues are too indistinct or too complex for him.

In some cases, auditory or visual memory difficulties interfere with adequate discriminations. The child may initiate an activity appropriately, but soon forget what he is to do. The teacher may request "Jim, put this book on my desk and bring me the box of crayons." The child starts toward the desk but soon forgets. The auditory cues provided by the teacher are not sufficient to keep the behavior going to completion. In this case, the child requires more frequent cueing. The teacher may repeat the cues in various phases of the activity. The child may repeat the directions aloud as he engages in the activity. The child may be given visual cues such as a figure drawing which depicts different steps in the activity which the child can check off as he completes. These redundant prompts can be reduced gradually as the child gains proficiency in responding to the more natural cues associated with the activity.

Provide Distinctive Cues

In arranging a behavior management program, it is essential that attention be given to arranging the cues which will provide the child with precise information about how he should behave. In teaching discriminations to the child, the teacher provides distinctive and perhaps even redundant cues initially. As the desired behavior becomes more consistent the redundant cues are gradually removed. The use of distinctive cues is essential in complex and difficult behavior patterns. The longer the time required to complete an activity and the more numerous the separate components involved in the activity the more the need for distinct and frequent cueing. These training prompts (i.e., those that will be faded out as an entire behavior pattern becomes stronger) should be provided at those times when the child's behavior is likely to "break down."

Children who are described as having short attention spans, as being distractible, or as being unable to persist at a specific activity require especially consistent, distinct, and frequent cueing for appropriate behavior. In these cases and especially in the early stages of learning new behaviors, it is also highly important to reduce to a minimum cues which control competing behaviors.   It is most important to remember that cues become effective in influencing desired behaviors only if these are followed consistently and frequently with reinforcing consequences.

A child who has difficulty in acquiring adequate discriminations may be requested to describe what he is to do in specific future situations.   Or the teacher may anticipate difficult situations by reviewing with children the desired behavior.   "Remember, as soon as the bell rings, we will put the toys on the shelf. What will we do when the bell rings?   When will we put the toys away?"   Such a procedure serves to emphasize the relationship between cues and associated behaviors.

The teacher should heed a word of caution: Neither nagging nor criticizing is effective cueing.   Becoming aggravated and punishing the child in one way or another after he fails to behave in a discriminating manner does not assist the child.   If the child is not responding appropriately to the cues that are being presented, the behavior management program is not appropriate. The cue-behavior-consequences should be examined and modified to insure more appropriate learning.

Behaviors frequently do not acquire the *specificity* desired in terms of the stimulus events under which the behavior occurs. Generalization occurs across similar stimulus conditions.   The differences across situations may be quite minimal and difficult for the child to discern.   The child responds in the same manner in situations which require different modes of behavior.   The child may label all circular objects (eggs, grapefruits, and apples) with the verbal response "ball."   Or he may not understand why he cannot play with the teacher and peers in the classroom when he can play with them on the playground.   A more specific discrimination will develop as the teacher provides specific *discrimination training*.   As an approach to the discrimination difficulty with circular objects, the child is reinforced for labeling a ball correctly and not reinforced for labeling as "ball" any other object.   Behavior occurring in the presence of certain specific cues is provided reinforcement.   That same behavior occurring in the presence of other cues, even though similar, is not reinforced.   In this manner highly similar situations can come to mark the occasion for highly different behavior.

TYPES OF AVERSIVE EVENTS

As a basis for the following discussion of negative reinforcement and the later presentation in Chapter 6 of the topic of punishment, the types of events which are aversive or unpleasant and the manner in which events may acquire aversive characteristics will be discussed.

Some events are naturally unpleasant to the child at birth. These include, for example, extreme states of deprivation of food, water, or air, painful stimulation such as a slap on the hand, loud noises, and extremes in temperature. These are *primary* aversive events in the sense that the child without benefit of prior learning naturally seeks to *terminate or to avoid* these unpleasant conditions.

A wide range of other neutral events may acquire some of the aversive qualities of these primary events. These neutral events like a frown, threat, gesture, presence of an authority figure, or a furry animal may have little or no unpleasantness associated with them initially. However, these once neutral events may become unpleasant events if frequently associated with the occurrence of other events which already are aversive to the child.

These events may become aversive to the child as they signal reduction in frequency or amount of positive reinforcers. Others become aversive as they coincide with or precede and signal the occurrence of other unpleasant events. Scolding, yelling, criticizing, and reprimanding by the teacher may become aversive events as they mark the occasion for a reduction in positive reinforcement. The teacher is much less likely after reprimanding a child to provide positive social comments or to grant privileges such as free-play or telling a favorite story. A threat by the teacher may become aversive; it has been associated with various aversive consequences such as being spanked or of being denied access to a TV show or to the music room. A peer's scream and angry face may become quite aversive; in the past these have coincided with previous painful physical attacks. The child learns to avoid, dislike, or to terminate these unpleasant events as soon as possible.

These *secondary* or *learned* aversive events become most significant in the life of the young child with developmental difficulties. It is not unusual for an excessively large number of events in the child's environment to acquire aversive qualities. His difficulties in learning along with other behavioral characteristics such as hyperactivity frequently result in failure to meet the expectations of family members and later of the educational staff. Except in a carefully designed behavior management environment, the child's failures result in numerous unpleasant consequences which gradually become attached to many aspects of his life.

> Neutral events may become aversive events if paired frequently with other events which have aversive qualities.

and

> Neutral events may become aversive events if these frequently precede the removal of positive reinforcers.

NEGATIVE REINFORCEMENT

In addition to learning new behaviors through immediate and frequent positive reinforcement, the child also may acquire behaviors which result in complete removal or in a noticeable reduction in the intensity of an unpleasant condition. Negative reinforcement may also serve to maintain behavior which already is in the child's repertoire. As noted earlier, the termination or removal of these unpleasant or aversive events has the effect of making stronger those behaviors which produced the removal or reduction. The strengthening of behavior through removal of unpleasant events is called *negative reinforcement*. A child may tell the teacher that he has a headache when asked to perform for the class. The teacher sends him to the nurse's room and he is given medication and permitted to lie down and rest. Assuming that the activity of performing for the class is unpleasant for the child, his behavior of reporting a headache to the teacher under these conditions would be strengthened. Under similar conditions in the future the same or similar behavior is likely to be repeated.

Behavior thus may become stronger both through positive and negative reinforcement procedures. Positive reinforcement works through *presentation* of a pleasant event following the desired behavior and negative reinforcement works through *removal* of an unpleasant condition. Negative reinforcement thus depends upon the presence of some unpleasant condition which the behavior may reduce or terminate.

Both desired and undesired behavior patterns may be

strengthened and maintained by negative reinforcement. A teacher may inform a child that he may join his peers on the playground after he stops crying and cleans off his desk. The teacher imposed an unpleasant condition which is promptly removed as the desired behavior occurs. Behaviors other than crying in combination with the cleaning behavior are strengthened as these remove the unpleasantness of confinement to the classroom. Other examples include: "After you get a smile on your face and talk in a normal voice, you may join the group," "You may play the music as soon as you stop being noisy." Those behaviors that resulted in the removal of the unpleasant restrictions would be strengthened.* In these instances the teacher is focusing on the relationship between the desired behaviors and a positive consequence. The child is placed in a choice situation. He gains experience in terminating undesired behavior. He learns to control himself. He decides when to remove the unpleasant conditions by engaging in appropriate behavior. He decides later to avoid the unpleasant conditions altogether by behaving appropriately.

In a similar manner a child may acquire a pattern of disruptive behavior if it removes him from a social group of a classroom experience which he finds unpleasant. Another child may learn to say, "I can't do that" or "I don't feel good, my stomach hurts" if these behavior patterns remove him from task requirements or social relationships which are unpleasant. Still another child may learn to be physically aggressive since such behavior results in the termination of unpleasant teasing or ridicule on the part of other children.

By the same principle, a teacher or parent may learn to yell or to threaten children in a harsh manner if that behavior produces a temporary reduction in disruptive, noisy, and other unpleasant behaviors on the part of the children in her class or home setting. A child engages in whining behavior as the parent turns the TV off and instructs the child to pick up his toys. The adult yells at the child and threatens to send him up to his room. The child stops his whining temporarily. The parent's yelling behavior is strengthened since it results in the termination of the obnoxious, unpleasant whining, even though the toys may still be ignored by the child. A teacher sends a disruptive child out of the classroom. Because she has removed a source of irritation, she is more likely to repeat this tactic in the future whenever a child becomes dis-

---

* In these examples, the teacher is using a *punishment procedure* when she imposes unpleasant conditions following the child's undesired behavior. She does this to discourage the preceding undesired behavior and to create the conditions for using a procedure of negative reinforcement to strengthen more appropriate behaviors.

ruptive. The adult may slowly acquire poor child-management practices.

> **Behavior which results in the removal of unpleasant conditions will be strengthened.**

and

> **Both appropriate and inappropriate behavior may be strengthened by negative reinforcement.**

Because negative reinforcement depends upon the presence of some aversive conditions, the procedure has limited usefulness for the teacher. However, the teacher must be sensitive to the rule of negative reinforcement as it is involved in strengthening and in maintaining considerable inappropriate behavior among children with developmental difficulties. As the process of learning new behaviors and of engaging in appropriate behaviors under desired conditions is a difficult one, many situations will represent unpleasantness to these children. Any behaviors that will remove this unpleasantness will be strengthened.

INSURING DESIRED BEHAVIOR MAINTENANCE

A child's behavior requires reinforcement not only as it is learned initially but also for it to be *maintained* over time. Behavior, regardless of its strength at any specific time following a training program, requires reinforcement on occasion for the child to continue the behavior. An important consideration is to insure that behavior will continue to occur in future situations in which reinforcement may be of a different kind and be less frequent and consistent than was present in the initial training program. The teacher is concerned both that the behavior is maintained in the original training environment and that the behavior which relates to situations other than the training one be maintained in these new settings.   The procedures for facilitating generalization of behavior change from the training situation to other settings will be discussed in the following section.   The present discussion will be concerned with procedures for insuring maintenance of the behavior once it does occur with some regularity in any setting.

Even in a highly structured behavior management program, it is not feasible to continue to provide reinforcement indefinitely every time a behavior occurs.   It is obvious that reinforcement in the natural environment is not continuous. Typically, the more complex and social the behavior, the less likely it is that reinforcement will be provided continuously once the child is removed from a special reinforcement program.

Problems can be created if a child is moved from one environment to a new one in which reinforcement for specific behaviors is provided less frequently.   A sudden change in the frequency of reinforcement can produce disruptive emotional reactions along with a disappearance of the previously reinforced behavior.

Kit, a five-year-old child with severe learning problems, was reinforced quite frequently by a mother who attempted to make him as happy as possible by immediate compliance to his request. Upon entering the child development program Kit discovered that many of his requests were not fulfilled.   He engaged in frequent emotional outbursts and quickly isolated himself from the other children.   He did not know how to function in an environment that failed to respond to his every request.

While it is true that behavior is strengthened initially most effectively by continuous reinforcement, it is also found that following a history of continuous reinforcement behavior disappears or becomes less likely to occur most rapidly when reinforcement is discontinued or significantly reduced.   Patterns of *intermittent* or *partial reinforcement*, which are more practical to implement, also result in behavior which is more durable, resistant to extinction, or which is maintained in strength over periods of time where reduction or elimination of reinforcement will take place.   Under these patterns, reinforcement is provided some of the time following the desired behavior, but not on every occasion.   When Jill complies with teacher requests, a behavior which has been acquired recently, the teacher begins to reinforce her socially sometimes but not at other times.   After experience with this time-to-time schedule of receiving reinforcement, the behavior will continue to occur for increasingly longer periods of time in which reinforcement is not provided.   This does not imply, of course, that the behavior will continue indefinitely under periods of nonreinforcement. Regardless of its reinforcement history behavior must still be reinforced on occasion if it is to continue to occur in a reliable fashion.

The procedure of gradual reduction of the frequency of reinforcement after a behavioral pattern has been acquired was followed in the previously mentioned program of Johnston and associates (1966). After using continuous social reinforcement to strengthen vigorous physical activity in a child, the teacher gradually shifted to a less frequent schedule of reinforcement. The teacher reduced both the number of times that she attended to the child's climbing behavior as well as the amount of attention she would provide on any one occasion.

It is also true that after experience with partial reinforcement, a given number of reinforcers will become more efficient. The child is less likely to become satiated with any specific reinforcing event as he receives fewer reinforcers. Fewer reinforcers will be required to keep the behavior occurring in a reliable manner at appropriate times. The child will complete more puzzles, make more polite responses, persist longer at a task, and play for longer periods prior to seeking adult attention as he gains experience with a schedule of less frequent reinforcement.

> **After a child learns a new behavior, reinforcement should be provided less frequently.**

and a related rule,

> **Although less reinforcement is required to maintain behavior after experience with an infrequent schedule, behavior still must be reinforced on occasion.**

How to Reduce Reinforcement

These relationships between patterns (schedules) of reinforcement and persistence of behavior over periods of infrequent reinforcement could be translated into classroom procedures. As new behaviors are being acquired reinforcing consequences should be provided on every occasion. After the behavior begins to occur with some consistency, the behavior should be reinforced less and less frequently. The reinforcement should be provided in an irregular fashion if persistence of a behavior pattern is desired. If an attempt is being made to increase the number of simple tasks completed by a child prior to his becoming disruptive, reinforcement may be provided after two completed tasks, then after three, then after one, after four, after two, after five, after one, after three, after six, and after two. This random pattern of reinforcement results in the most durable behavior. In this manner the child does not know when reinforcement is forthcoming and is more likely to work steadily and to persist for longer periods without looking for the reinforcing consequence. Reinforcing on a predictable schedule of every five minutes or after ten correct responses creates conditions which may produce problem behaviors. The child may behave appropriately (attending, studying, completing tasks, as examples) only when reinforcement is likely to occur. Also, the child learns to expect reinforcement at a given time and if it is not provided, the child is likely to engage in frustration behavior.

> **If persistence and a steady rate of behavior are desired, use an unpredictable pattern of providing reinforcement.**

The Rate of Reinforcement Reduction

There is no hard and fast rule relating to the absolute amount of reduction in reinforcement. It may be reduced from 100 percent to 90, then to 80, to 74, to 70, to 50, and finally to 30 percent of the time the behavior occurs. This reduction should be gradual. If reinforcement is changed from continuous to less frequent and the child begins to make too many errors, takes too long in responding, or behaves infrequently it is evident that the change in schedule of reinforcement has been too severe. In these cases, the frequency of reinforcement should be increased again for a while and, after consistency is regained and practiced, a second attempt at gradual reduction in reinforcement frequency should be initiated.

> **New behaviors will persist if provided frequent intermittent reinforcement.**

and

> **Well-established behaviors are likely to persist if provided random and infrequent reinforcement.**

In view of this relationship between the pattern of reinforcement and the persistence of behavior during periods of time in which no reinforcement is provided, the parent and teacher must be attentive to the occasional reinforcement of undesired behaviors which the child exhibits. This occasional reinforcement can produce patterns that are quite persistent. If a teacher who does not feel well or is in a hurry "gives in" on occasion to a child's misbehavior (because the surrender terminates the whining or demanding) she may well be creating a condition which renders this undesired behavior most resistant to elimination. The child learns that whining and demanding eventually pay off.

The parent and teacher must also be wary of following punishment on occasion with excessive reinforcement. The parent may become angry with the child, punish him, and then on occasion provide him with excessive attention, tangible reinforcers, or privileges. The child learns the behavior pattern which results in the punishment and the following reinforcing events and may appear to enjoy punishment. Other bothersome patterns such as "lying," "cheating," or "stealing" may become rather strong as a result of reinforcing consequences which, albeit infrequent, are nevertheless provided. Such behaviors produce an occasional reinforcing consequence. Lying and cheating behavior, for example, may remove the child from an unpleasant situation, even though punishment on occasion may be provided such behavior at a later time. Recall, however, the rule that behavior is influenced by immediate consequences. If the cheating or lying behavior results on occasion in immediate removal of unpleasant conditions, it is likely to reoccur under similar conditions in the future.

> **Partial reinforcement maintains inappropriate as well as appropriate behaviors.**

Summary

In summary, although frequent and immediate reinforcement may be required initially to teach new behaviors or to strengten existing ones, it is possible to maintain well-established behaviors by less frequent reinforcement. Also, the type of reinforcer used to strengthen the behavior initially may not be necessary to maintain it. A child may require primary reinforcers when first learning a new behavior pattern, but tangible and social events which the teacher provides may gradually replace the primary reinforcement. In many instances naturally-provided consequences may gradually replace the teacher-provided ones. A child may require teacher-provided primary and secondary reinforcers to interact appropriately with other children. After experience with this new behavior pattern, the attention which other children provide the child as he interacts with them is quite reinforcing and sufficient to maintain the behavior. The teacher-provided reinforcers can be withdrawn. Thus the teacher will constantly be shifting the types and frequency of reinforcing events which she provides. As one behavior is acquired, reinforcers can be faded as this behavior becomes self-maintaining by naturally occurring consequences. The teaching program can shift to another goal.

GENERALIZATION OF BEHAVIOR CHANGE

The major goal of an early education program is to teach new behaviors which will occur and be maintained in numerous other settings. However, it is true that once behaviors are acquired by a child, whether these be appropriate or inappropriate, they do not always spontaneously occur at other times or in other situations. A child may learn to be highly negativistic at meal time, during perceptual-motor activities, or under such conditions as "when a female adult" is present. At other times or under other conditions, the same child may be quite cooperative and successful. Likewise, a child may learn new behaviors under one set of conditions (at school) but not demonstrate these newly acquired behaviors in other settings (at home). It is rather commonplace to hear teachers report: "He has developed good skills of attention in the therapy room with Ms. Schroeter but I have considerable problems holding his attention." "His self-care and grooming skills are quite good at school but his mother reports that he seldom shows them at home." "He uses words quite freely with the speech therapists but I do not hear them in class." "He will talk at home but not at school." The behavior is acquired under the discriminative and reinforcement conditions present in one situation and may not generalize to other settings if these differ greatly in these critical aspects.

It is not unusual to find that the discriminative cues which come to control newly acquired behaviors are highly specific to those which were present in the initial training setting. The specific teacher, the time of day, the physical characteristics of the room such as lighting, furniture, and other similar types of events may come to exert strong control over the behavior. As the child moves to other dissimilar settings, the behavior disappears or becomes rather erratic. This observation emphasizes the value of modifying a problem behavior in the environmental setting in which the desired behavior is expected to occur. If the child is removed from the classroom and provided "special therapy" elsewhere, a problem of generalization of any newly acquired behavior to the classroom setting is created. It is not being suggested that behaviors acquired in one setting never generalize to other settings; on the contrary, many behaviors do generalize. However, sufficient problems of generalization of behavior from a training setting to other settings are encountered in work with young children with developmental difficulties to justify the teacher's attention to procedures of facilitating generalization. She should not take generalization for granted. She should actively program for generalization.

Herman and Tramontana (1971) were able to get appropriate rest-time behavior to occur in four boys with high rates of disruptive behavior under token-reinforcement conditions in a special therapy room. However, this appropriate rest behavior did not occur in the regular classroom. Wahler (1969a) describes the absence of spontaneous generalization of behavior change from a child's home to the school setting. A behavior management program was initiated in the home of a five-year-old boy who displayed a general pattern of stubborn and disruptive behavior in both home and school settings. Although this behavior reduced significantly as new behaviors of cooperation were reinforced by the parents at home, the more appropriate mode of interaction did not generalize to the school setting. At school he remained a stubborn and disruptive child. This behavior did change in the school when the teachers initiated a similar behavior management program in that setting. Another child described as having low motivation for school work in both school and home setting was provided a behavior management program in the home. Under the new reinforcement conditions followed by the parents, the child soon showed appropriate interest in school work at home. But this new behavior did not demonstrate itself in the school setting until the teachers began a similar reinforcement program.

To avoid or reduce some of these difficulties of generalization of behavior across different settings and conditions, the teacher should attempt to:

1. *Increase the similarity between the training setting and other settings in which the behavior is expected to occur.* This similarity dimension includes both the discriminative events which will serve to signal the occurrence of the behavior as well as the reinforcement conditions which will serve to maintain the desired behavior.

The teacher should attempt to arrange the training setting to be as similar as possible to other settings in which the behavior is expected to generalize. If the school (classroom, therapy room, special training room) environments are distinctly different in numerous aspects from other settings, a specific transfer or generalization program should be devised to facilitate the transition from one setting to the other. After the desired behavior acquired in the training setting has gained some initial strength, discriminative cues and reinforcement conditions from other settings should be introduced gradually. As they gain cue control over the behavior, the specific training-setting cues should be faded and eventually removed if possible.

As an example of transfer training, Ms. Steele was able to teach seven-year-old Josh to respond verbally to many pictures, questions, and other cues in the language-therapy room. However, none of this verbal responsiveness generalized to the classroom setting. In this setting, Josh would attend to his teacher and peers, would comply with various requests, would communicate with them in terms of physical gestures, but would not do so verbally. To facilitate generalization to the classroom setting, the teacher-assistant began to attend the individual language sessions with Ms. Steele and Josh. Gradually, the teacher-assistant began to present various components of the language lesson to Josh. After he began to respond consistently to her, the classroom teacher sat in on some of the lessons. Ms. Steele would initiate the lesson but then would assume an inactive role. She began to leave the room for longer periods of time as the teacher-assistant and teacher took over the lesson. The next step consisted of bringing first one, then two, and finally three of Josh's peers into the language lesson. After Josh was able to communicate verbally under these cue conditions, the final step was taken to move the lesson into the classroom setting. Effective generalization had been accomplished.

This example illustrates the necessity to plan for the gradual and systematic transfer of behaviors from one set of cues to other environments. If effective generalization of behavior does not occur, the teacher must arrange a set of experiences in which the discriminative control is gradually shifted from the training setting to other appropriate ones.

In many instances it will be necessary to match the reinforcement conditions of the training setting to those present in other settings. A child may acquire new skills in a reinforcement program which provides frequent immediate token reinforcers which are exchanged at frequent intervals for high-preference activities and objects. The new behaviors may drop out quickly, however, if the child is placed in a classroom that uses only infrequent social reinforcement. The training environment in this instance would gradually diminish the frequent token reinforcers and provide social reinforcement on a less frequent schedule.

2. *Practice the new behavior in numerous settings.* Risley and Wolf (1967), in shaping appropriate speech in children who mechanically repeat what they hear others say emphasize that generalization of speech from the training setting to natural settings is enhanced by practicing the speech with adequate reinforcing consequences in a wide range of places and under various conditions. Different people—family members, peers, teacher, neighbors—should cue and reinforce speech in a variety of locations—school, store, bus, church, home. This rule is applicable to any newly-acquired behavior which is expected to occur in numerous situations outside of the training one.

3. *Train people in the natural environments in which the child lives to use discriminative and reinforcing events in a manner similar to the training procedures.* It may be necessary for teachers and parents to use behavior management procedures similar to those used in the training setting. In the previously described Wahler (1969a) program, teachers were trained to use the same procedures in the classroom which parents had used in the home to increase the cooperative and study behaviors of their children. Patterson and Brodsky (1966) used various behavior management procedures in a clinic setting to produce desired behavior change in a five-year-old boy who exhibited numerous problem behaviors. Temper tantrums, which showed a pronounced reduction in frequency and duration in a clinic training

setting, quickly disappeared in the kindergarten class setting following the initiation by adults in this school setting of appropriate training procedures.

4. *Teach the child to manage his own behavior.* Behavior may generalize from one setting to another if the child can be taught to cue and to reinforce himself. This is accomplished by teaching him adequate verbal labels which he uses as discriminative cues to control certain of his behaviors in choice situations. He also may be taught to reinforce himself by labeling his appropriate behavior with such comments as "good job," "that's great," or "you finished that hard one."

> **Generalization of newly acquired behavior from training to other settings will occur if appropriate procedures are followed.**

CONCURRENT BEHAVIOR CHANGE

Although behavior management programs are designed to influence specific problem behavior areas, it is not uncommon to find desirable changes in other behaviors which were provided no apparent attention. Examples of behavior management programs are described briefly to illustrate this finding. Buell and her associates (1968) worked with a young preschool child who showed no cooperative play with peers, never used their names, seldom spoke to them or touched them, and showed only a low rate of parallel play as her major form of social interaction. She rarely used the outdoor play equipment. Although she interacted frequently with the teachers, this behavior was of a dependent and immature baby-like nature.

The focus of the behavior management program was on increasing the child's use of outdoor play equipment. It was reasoned that if her rate of using the play equipment was increased and maintained, she would have considerable opportunity for a variety of interactions with peers. These new experiences should contribute to her social development.

A behavior-shaping program was implemented using physical guidance as a prompt and social reinforcement of successive approximations of appropriate and prolonged play behavior. Consistent, continuous social reinforcement was provided for all forms of equipment play.

Use of outdoor play equipment during times when it was available to the child rose from approximately 2 percent prior to the behavior shaping program to a near 70 percent rate by the end of the two-month program. Other behaviors which were primarily child-oriented showed a collateral change. The child began to touch other children, to use their names, and to play cooperatively with them. At the same time the baby behavior disappeared.

A second illustration of concurrent behavior change provides an interesting finding (Nordquist, 1971). A five-year-old boy was the subject of a behavior management program designed to change his oppositional behavior. The boy was disruptive, often refusing to comply with adult requests and had an average of one tantrum per day. A long history of bed-wetting was reported. The program consisted of socially reinforcing the boy for appropriate compliance and other social behaviors and of isolating him in his room if he exhibited oppositional behavior. The boy's parents ignored his bed-wetting.

Cooperative behavior improved greatly and oppositional behavior reduced to a minimum following initiation of the program. The bed-wetting also was eliminated completely even though it was not provided any direct attention. These behavior changes remained stable over a continuous eighteen-month observation period.

In a highly similar program Wahler and associates (1970) used social reinforcement and brief isolation periods to control oppositional behavior in a young boy who stuttered frequently. It was found that the rate of stuttering was lower as the child began to develop improved skills of cooperation, although no direct program attention had been given to the stuttering.

Finally, Twardosz and Sajwaj (1972) reinforced sitting behavior in a hyperactive four-year-old boy who attended an early education program with seven other children with learning and behavior difficulties. He had poorly developed social skills, did not spontaneously talk to anyone, responded echolalically to questions, rarely played with toys, and spent most of his time either lying on the floor in unusual squirming postures or in walking around the room. After being reinforced with tokens and praise for sitting at a table during playtime in which table toys were provided, the boy showed a dramatic increase in time spent in sitting at the table. This new behavior resulted in an equally significant reduction in his inappropriate posturing behavior, and a most desirable increase in the amount of time playing with toys and in being in close proximity to other children.

The results of these behavior management programs lend support to the observation that no single or group of a child's behaviors exist in isolation. Changes in any behavior will result potentially in changes in the likelihood of occurrence of other behaviors. First, if the child engages frequently in inappropriate behavior, he has less opportunity to learn more desired ways of behaving. A reduction in or elimination of the inappropriate behavior will give the child more time to attend to and interact with learning programs which the teacher may present. Risley (1968) was successful in increasing the amount of eye contact and the imitation behavior of a six-year-old child after successful elimination of various stereotyped behaviors which the child previously had engaged in at a very high rate. Prior to the elimination of the inappropriate behavior, Risley was unable to encourage the child to engage in the socially desirable behaviors. Thus, one possible beneficial side effect of eliminating strongly disruptive behavior is that the child is more available for involvement in a program designed to teach appropriate ways of behaving.

Second, a child has a number of responses in his repertoire at any time. If some of these are occurring at a frequent rate others cannot be occurring. If a child engages in frequent temper tantrums, he cannot be smiling and playing with other children even though these skills are in his repertoire. Thus, a second beneficial side-effect of reduction in, or elimination of, inappropriate behaviors is the increasing likelihood that appropriate behaviors will occur. Carlson and her associates (1968) observed after reduction of temper tantrum behavior in a young child that ". . . during periods when no tantrums occurred she looked noticeably happier. She began to play and take part in group activities with the girls on the playground." (p. 118)

Third, changes in inappropriate behavior will result potentially in changes in the child's social environment which may have a beneficial effect on other behaviors. A child with highly aggressive behaviors may well frighten other children away from him. Elimination of these aggressive behaviors will open new modes of social interaction and reinforcement.

Fourth, increase in strength of any particular response, whether appropriate or inappropriate, may result in increase in strength of other similar behaviors. Behavior management programs concerned with the development of imitation skills in young children illustrate this beneficial side effect (Garcia et al., 1971). After reinforcing the child for imitating various motor responses, the child begins to imitate new behaviors which previously had never been reinforced. He acquires a generalized pattern of imitation. In a similar manner a child who has been reinforced for approaching and interacting with peers in his class will play new games with children even though he has never been reinforced specifically for playing these games. Thus, in reinforcing any new behavior, a behavior management program is frequently contributing to the development of more general behavior patterns.

> **Change in one behavior frequently leads to changes in other related behaviors.**

INFLUENCING BEHAVIOR BY PROVIDING MODELS

As noted earlier, parents and teachers make use of modeling or demonstration in (1) promoting new response patterns and (2) increasing the likelihood that desired behavior which the child has in his repertoire will occur. Experience with the use of modeling has demonstrated that a wide range of deficit and excessive behavior patterns may be influenced. Aggression, study behavior, avoidance behavior, social withdrawal, and fear reactions, to mention a few, have all been successfully influenced.

In teaching new behaviors, the adult shows the child how to complete certain tasks, how to pronounce a word, how to draw a circle, how to tie a bow, and how to engage in literally hundreds of other behavior patterns during the child's early years. Speech, for example, could not be acquired without imitation of models. Children soon learn to imitate what they hear and see others do. In fact, a child without imitation skills has an extremely difficult time acquiring any but the most basic of behaviors. As many young children with developmental difficulties have poorly developed skills of imitation, it becomes essential that these skills be taught. An illustrated teaching program will be presented in Chapter 11.

> **A child may learn new ways of behaving by observing others engaging in this behavior.**

Most effective learning occurs whenever the child imitates immediately what he sees or hears others do. At the same time, there is evidence that a child may be influenced by what he observes even though he may not be engaged in the behavior until a later time. In either event, the child is more likely to imitate an observed behavior if he also observes the model receiving reinforcing consequences. Further, it is likely that maximum effects of exposure to a model will be realized if the consequences provided the model's behavior are events which are highly reinforcing to the child who is observing. Of course, for the imitated behavior to become an established and reliable aspect of the child's repertoire, it must be reinforced as he engages in it.

The teacher may also find film presentation of models engaging in desired behavior to be effective in influencing the occurrence of this behavior in the child who observes the film. An experience of O'Connor (1969) illustrates the potential usefulness of this mode of presentation. Children with relatively severe deficits in social behavior attending nursery school classes were shown films projected through a large TV console. The sound-color film lasting some twenty-three minutes

> . . . portrayed a sequence of 11 scenes in which children interacted in a nursery school setting. In each of these episodes, a child is shown first observing the interaction of others and then joining in the social activities, with reinforcing consequences ensuing. The other children, for example, offer him play materials, talk to him, smile and generally respond in a positive manner to his advances into the activity. The scenes were graduated on a dimension of threat in terms of the vigor of the social activity and the size of the group. The initial scenes involve very calm activities such as sharing a book or toy while two children are seated at a table. In the terminal scenes, as many as six children are shown gleefully tossing play equipment around the room. (p. 18)

Children who had observed the filmed presentation showed a significant increase in social responsiveness. Other socially withdrawn children who did not see the filmed presentation of peer interactions remained socially withdrawn.

Characteristics of Models

Children are more likely to imitate the behavior of those teachers, parents, siblings, peers, and others whom they like—those who are major sources of reinforcement for them. The child may imitate inappropriate behavior just as he may imitate desirable ways of behaving. Peers, especially those of the same sex, frequently become the most influential models. Peers who are leaders or otherwise enjoy some status in the observer's eyes, close friends, someone with characteristics similar to those of the observer, or even peers whose behavior frequently does result in reinforcers are most likely to be attended to and imitated. The model may even be a stranger who has characteristics which the child likes. Cartoon figures, TV figures, or puppets can be used frequently to model various behaviors which the child will imitate. On the other hand, behavior that is modeled by a teacher or peer who is of neutral or negative value to a child will be imitated less frequently.

It is also likely that children will be more influenced by observation of multiple models engaging in the behavior to be imitated than would be found if observation is made of a single model. If modeling is used to increase the social interaction of a child who is socially withdrawn, it would be best to have him observe a number of different peers approaching other children and engaging in various types of social interaction in various situations.

If placed in an environment with peers who exhibit an excessive number of inappropriate behavior patterns, it is highly likely that the child will imitate some of these behaviors. This is especially true if the inappropriate behavior is reinforced. He will be more likely to imitate behavior which he sees resulting in desired reinforcers than he would be to imitate behavior that does not result in reinforcement as he observes it. Peer attention is highly reinforcing to many young children. A child may imitate another child who engages in excessive swearing, loud disruptive talk, or clowning behaviors as these actions may gain prompt attention from peers. The teacher may be attempting to ignore these behaviors but they may remain at high strength due to peer reinforcement. This observation emphasizes the need to place a child with various difficulties in an environment with peers who can provide good behavior models. If this is not possible, the teacher should at least attempt to remove any obvious reinforcement for inappropriate behaviors in order to reduce the likelihood that children who observe the behavior will imitate it.

> **Inappropriate as well as appropriate behavior may be imitated.**

Imitation of Complex Behavior

It is probably true that many of the more desirable and complex behavior patterns which children should acquire depend to a large extent on literally hundreds of observations of the patterns being modeled by significant others. Patterns of behavior which may be labeled as patience, calmness, or kindness would most likely develop only in a social environment in which significant people consistently demonstrated these behaviors. Children frequently behave precisely as the teacher behaves. If she is loud and punitive the child may well learn this orientation. If she is calm and pleasant the child is likely to develop these behavior patterns.

Insured Observation

In providing a model for the child to imitate, it should be insured that the child is in fact attending to the various components of the demonstrated behavior. This may necessitate such cues as, "Look how I hold this" or "Look, I put the big red one in first and then the little blue one in last." The child should be encouraged to rehearse the behavior immediately for best results. "Now you try it," with appropriate correction and reinforcement provided. The classroom peers may be used to model desired behavior. "Watch John find the *red square*. Good, John, you found it." In using a peer model, best results will be obtained if highly-preferred peers are used. Under this condition, the observer is more likely to attend to critical discriminative cues, the precise form of the behavior, and to the related consequences of the behavior.

Use Procedure of Successive Approximation

In using modeling for the young children with developmental handicaps as a means of facilitating acquisition of new behaviors, it frequently becomes necessary to use a procedure of modeling and of reinforcing successive approximations of the desired behavior. Complex patterns of behavior must be reduced to smaller subunits which are strengthened through modeling and reinforcement and later put together in more complex combinations or patterns.

The modeling of new behaviors which the teacher desires the child to engage in has an additional effect for many children with developmental difficulties. Most children with such problems have experienced difficulty and frequent failure with new tasks. As a result many children actively avoid becoming involved in learning new behavior due to the unpleasantness associated with previous involvement. Demonstration of new behaviors by a person with whom the child does have some positive relationship removes some of the uncertainty associated with attempting new behaviors.

Additional Effects of Observation

In addition to facilitating the acquisition of new behavior patterns, exposure to the behavior of a model may have other effects. First, there is evidence to suggest that a child may be less likely to engage in those observed behaviors which result in punishment to the model. Second, the child may be more likely to engage in undesired behavior which typically is under control if he observes this behavior in others. This effect is even more likely if the observed undesired behavior is rewarded or produces no aversive consequences. Third, the observation of desired behavior of others may serve as a cue for occurrence of these behaviors. A child may know how to work quietly but does so less frequently than desired. Exposure to a child who is working quietly may serve to increase the likelihood of this same behavior on the part of the observing child.

The teacher may make use of the rules of observational learning in the manner in which she deals with inappropriate behavior. If a child is overly aggressive toward peers the teacher may ignore the aggressive child and provide special attention to the peers. This will demonstrate to the child that his aggressive behavior produces nothing for him from the teacher and also that the teacher attends to other types of behaviors.

Allen and her associates (1970) used this tactic in successfully eliminating the aggressive and disruptive behaviors (hitting and kicking children, spitting, running off with other children's toys) of a 4½-year-old boy:

> On the first day of modification the teachers were instructed to give their undivided attention to the child who had been assaulted, while keeping their backs to Townsend. Nine episodes of aggressive behavior were tallied on this day. During the next 11 sessions, there was a marked decrease (an average of three per session). During the twelfth session, there was an upswing to seven episodes, then a gradual decrease until finally, no more grossly aggressive and disruptive acts occurred. (p. 122)

In another example, if a child who has the required skills refuses to cooperate or to participate in an activity, the teacher may publicly reinforce participating children with high preference reinforcers while the noncooperative child is observing. In so doing the teacher may remark loudly enough for the noncooperative child to hear, "Jill, I am pleased with the way you are working with Sue" or whatever comment is appropriate to the behaviors that are being reinforced. Such tactics may well be rather ineffective with children characterized by generalized isolated-behavior patterns or

130

with limited social-participation skills. In these instances modeling should be combined with a more structured behavior-shaping program.

BEHAVIOR REHEARSAL

New patterns of behavior may be effected more often by having the child rehearse these behaviors under simulated or highly structured conditions. A child who is highly aggressive may not know how to be polite or cooperative. Prompting the child to rehearse more appropriate ways of interacting with peers in a play-acting or role-playing setting may provide him with these behavioral skills. As these behaviors gain in strength, the similarity to the natural situations in which aggressive behavior previously occurred can be increased gradually.

Behavior rehearsal is also quite valuable in preparing for new situations or for situations in which inappropriate behavior has a high likelihood of occurring. Under highly-structured conditions, children can "walk through" the appropriate behavior patterns and can be provided cues and reinforcers which increase the likelihood of occurrence of these behaviors under future conditions. A child who is most likely to misbehave may be asked to demonstrate the appropriate behavior to the peer group. With sufficient prompting from the teacher, the child will be able to model the desired behavior and receive the social approval of teacher and peers.

HOW CHILDREN TRAIN ADULTS

Children can influence the behavior of parents and teachers in the same manner that they are influenced by the adults. In using certain approaches, if the teacher is successful in influencing the behavior patterns which she desired in her pupils, these approaches will be strengthened. These specific behaviors will be reinforced by the positive effects these have had on the child. Under similar circumstances in the future, the teacher will be more likely to use these approaches.

In like manner the teacher can develop inappropriate teaching habits in terms of the effects which these produce. A harsh threat may indeed result in a temporary reduction in bothersome behavior of a child. This teacher behavior is strengthened as it produces an immediate removal (albeit temporary) of an un-

131

pleasant condition. This was illustrated in a recent observation. A group of four- and five-year-old retarded children were seated in a semi-circle around a teacher and were asked to sit quietly as she presented each of them with individually prepared table tasks. Sue, sitting at one end of the table, began making a clucking sound as the teacher was presenting materials to children on the opposite end of the table. The teacher turned suddenly, shook her finger at Sue and said "No." Sue immediately broke out in a big smile and replied, "Hi." The teacher turned again to the other children. The sequence was repeated two additional times. After each reprimand, Sue sat quietly for a few seconds prior to beginning her disruptive clucking. After the teacher turned away following the third reprimand, Sue next stood up and reached for the work materials which were on the table in front of the teacher. This brought an immediate "No" from the teacher followed by the teacher grasping Sue's hand and firmly returning the child to her chair. This procedure was followed two additional times before the teacher gave Sue her table work. Following this, Sue became quite absorbed in her coloring task and created no more difficulty for the teacher during the period.

In analyzing this interaction pattern between Sue and the teacher, it becomes clear that Sue's disruptive behavior was being strengthened and maintained by the rather immediate and consistent attention which it produced from the teacher. At the same time, the teacher's behavior of finger shaking, frowning at the child, and verbalizing "No" were also being maintained as these produced an immediate, albeit temporary, termination of the disturbing activity. In this interactional pattern the teacher was maintaining the child's disruptive behavior just as the child was maintaining the teacher's ineffective reprimanding behavior. It is apparent that the suppressive effects of the reprimand were so temporary that the tactic should have been discarded by the teacher as an ineffective approach to influencing the child's behavior. The example does illustrate, nonetheless, how behavior can be influenced by events with little awareness by the teacher.

CHAPTER 6

Reducing or Eliminating
Behavior Patterns

Children acquire a range of inappropriate behavior patterns during the early years which can be highly disturbing to the child's environment. Tom's constant interruptions when the teacher is talking with other children and his tendency to refuse to fulfill classroom assignments are disturbing behaviors that require attention. Other patterns are acceptable under certain conditions but not under others. Sue's whining behavior when her older sister does not give in to her may be quite acceptable to her parents "because Sue is so handicapped." This same behavior at school would be viewed as unacceptable by the teacher and peers.

Some children become hyperactive, noncooperative, disruptive, noncompliant, nonattentive, or dependent. In almost every instance, these inappropriate behavior patterns have been strengthened by the consequences which these behaviors have produced from other people. The child who is aggressive and noncompliant is not intentionally naughty. He does not behave in these ways because he is mentally retarded, emotionally disturbed, or physically handicapped. He engages in these behaviors because people in his social environment (mother, father, siblings, relatives, neighbors, friends, teachers) have taught him to behave in this manner. In most instances the social environment does not intend to strengthen inappropriate behaviors. In fact, those in the social environment who interact with the child are seldom even aware of the role which their reactions to the child may assume in influencing the development of undesirable behavior patterns. Regardless of the intent or awareness of the father, mother, sibling, teacher, or other social agents, the manner in which the social environment reacts as the child behaves produces an immediate effect which influences the strength of this behavior.

It is true, as mentioned earlier, that children with various types of learning and behavior difficulties have a greater likelihood than usual of developing inappropriate behavior patterns. But these ways of behaving are seldom a direct or sole result of neurological, sensory, or other physical conditions. Later chapters will deal with the particular combination of learning experiences which may be involved in the development of specific patterns of problem behavior.

As the previous chapter emphasized, both inappropriate and appropriate behaviors may be strengthened by consequences which follow the behavior. If whining behavior results in the child "doing as he wishes to," the behavior of whining under the same and similar situations is more likely to reoccur. If the child's compliance behavior results in mother's approval, the child is more likely to fulfill mother's requests in the future.

Just as there are procedures which when followed will strengthen behavior patterns, there are also procedures which may be used to control, decrease in strength, or eliminate a child's behavior patterns. The procedures which result in (1) *reinforcing alternative behaviors*, (2) *extinction*, (3) *satiation*, (4) *stimulus change*, and (5) *punishment* are available for this task. Punishment may involve either the *presentation* following behavior of some aversive consequences or the *removal* of various positive consequences as a result of specific behaviors engaged in by a child. It should be emphasized prior to a discussion of each that the strength of appropriate as well as inappropriate behaviors may be reduced by these procedures. Desired behavior may be eliminated from a child's repertoire, for example, if reinforcing consequences no longer follow the behavior. Or a child who is taken advantage of by other children when he attempts to be cooperative soon ceases to be cooperative.

REINFORCING COMPETING BEHAVIORS

The major focus of behavior management program efforts should be on strengthening those desirable behaviors which will compete with and eventually replace undesirable patterns of behaving. Whenever possible, it is helpful to reinforce that behavior which is actually physically incompatible with the undesired behavior. In this instance, if the child is engaging in the desired behavior, he cannot be engaging in the undesired one at the same time. Rude behavior could be ignored and polite behavior reinforced in a systematic manner. A child who is out of his chair excessively could be reinforced for remaining seated and for engaging in an assigned task. Such planned reinforcement of remaining-in-chair and other task-related behaviors would render unnecessary other less desired procedures involving punishment. Punishing the child for getting out of his chair at designated times only demonstrates to the child what he should *not* do, and not what he *should* do. Such punishment would be generally inconsistent with a goal of developing positive emotional characteristics and other behaviors of competency.

On other occasions, although physically incompatible behavior cannot be strengthened through positive reinforcement, it would be possible to teach more appropriate behaviors which gradually would replace the undesired one. Positive reinforcement of incompatible behavior or of competing behaviors which will replace the undesired one, in contrast to punishment procedures, informs the child precisely what he can do to obtain positive reinforcement and to avoid or terminate aversive consequences. Again, punishment for "not doing" some required behavior does not increase the strength of doing the right thing, although on occasion it may render the appropriate behavior more likely by suppressing other behaviors which may interfere with the desired one.

Providing positive reinforcement for desired behaviors which will replace inappropriate ones was used successfully in a program described by Hamblin and his associates (1971). The children were described as "five extraordinarily aggressive four-year-old boys" who had been diagnosed by psychiatrists as hyperactive and who had not responded to drug therapy. Hamblin noted that the classroom teacher

> ". . . was, variously, strict disciplinarian, wise counselor, clever arbitrator and sweet peacemaker. In each role, however, she failed miserably. After the eighth day, the average of the children was 150 sequences of aggression per day! . . . Wild? Very. These were barbarous little boys who enjoyed battle. Miss Sally did her best but they were just more clever than she, and they *always* won. Whether she wanted to or not, they could always drag her into the fray, and just go at it harder and harder until she capitulated. She was finally driven to their level, trading a kick for a kick and a spit in the face for a spit in the face." (p. 101–102)

The teacher initiated a procedure providing token reinforcement for cooperative behavior (compliance with another's request or spontaneously helping the teacher or another boy) and turning her back on an aggressor. After a few weeks of this new procedure, the frequency of aggression went down to a near normal level and cooperation increased to a level which exceeded that found in the typical preschool classroom.

Desired behaviors which will compete with and eventually replace inappropriate behaviors may be strengthened by procedures involving negative as well as positive reinforcement. A child who engages in rude behavior may be required to sit in isolation following rude behavior. He may be permitted to shorten his confinement by being polite to the teacher. Polite behavior may also be reinforced positively by peers and teacher at a later time as he is polite to them in appropriate circumstances. Thus a general behavioral pattern of being polite to others is strengthened as it results in the removal of unpleasant conditions associated with isolation (negative reinforcement) and also produces, at other times, pleasant consequences (positive reinforcement).

It is easy to punish inappropriate behavior as it occurs; it is more difficult to identify and to provide systematic reinforcement for appropriate competing modes of responding. The major question should be, "What should the child be doing at the time he is behaving inappropriately?" Once this is established and demonstrated to the child, such behaviors or reasonable alternatives can more easily be strengthened through reinforcement. It may be helpful to encourage the child to rehearse the alternative behaviors and then to provide whatever guidance is necessary to insure that this behavior will occur at the appropriate time and place.

In preparation for initiating a procedure of reinforcing alternative behaviors, it will be helpful to list acceptable alternatives to undesired behaviors.

In considering alternative behaviors which will be rein-

Undesired Behavior	Alternative Desired Behavior
1. Crying	1. Smiling
2. Wandering around room	2. Sitting at table, completing table tasks
3. Hitting and pushing other children; teasing, annoying, threatening, and disparaging other children	3. Playing cooperatively with peers
4. Sitting passively	4. Coloring, cutting, looking at pictures
5. Engaging in stereotyped hand-waving	5. Using hands in appropriate motor activity such as throwing a ball, drawing, or cutting

forced, select those which will be most beneficial for the individual child. A child who is aggressive toward younger peers could be taught to stay away from these peers. However, this alternative behavior pattern would not reflect constructive social skills. Instead, the alternative behavior pattern to replace the aggressive one should consist of skills like playing and working cooperatively with younger peers. These competing behavior patterns, as suggested, should be rehearsed by the child and reinforced by the teacher in the situations in which the undesired behavior occurs. Such rehearsal usually increases the likelihood that such behaviors will occur in the future. An attempt should be made to remove all reinforcement following the undesired behavior and to provide support following the alternative behaviors.

In reinforcing behaviors which will serve as acceptable alternatives to undesired ones, the teacher may follow various procedures. First, she may reinforce any and all other appropriate behaviors which occur under the conditions in which the inappropriate behavior occurs. The teacher may reinforce Tim, a boy who is hyperactive and distractible, for any behaviors that would compete with these modes of responding. She would reinforce him for persisting at a task, for attending to her verbal instruction, for remaining in his chair, for watching a slide presentation, for responding appropriately under distracting stimulation, and for staying on his cot for a designated period of time during rest period. If at all possible, she would not attend to his undesired behaviors. This procedure is called *differential reinforcement of other behaviors*. Again, the undesired behaviors are ignored and a range of other behaviors which are appropriate and which will compete with the undesired behaviors is provided positive reinforcement.

A study by Becker and his colleagues (1967) demonstrates the value of differential positive reinforcement of a range of desired behavior which replaced a variety of disruptive ones. A group of culturally deprived children attending elementary school classes were identified as exhibiting a high rate of disruptive behaviors judged to be incompatible with learning. These disruptive behaviors included such things as getting out of one's seat, walking around, rocking in one's chair, tapping a pencil or other objects, grabbing objects or work, destroying another's property, hitting, slapping, kicking, pulling hair, crying, answering teacher without being called on, ignoring teacher's request, and making comments when no question is asked. Through a set of explicit rules the classroom teacher initially reminded the children about those behaviors which were expected. Then she began ignoring the inappropriate behavior whenever possible and praising any behavior which facilitated learning. Statements of praise and recognition were used: "Good job; you are doing fine," "I like the way you are working quietly," and "I see Johnny is ready to work." After a few weeks of providing this social reinforcement for appropriate behaviors, many of which directly competed with the child's unruly behavior, there was a significant reduction in those behaviors which were incompatible with effective classroom learning. Seven-year-old Albert had been described as a noisy child who fought with others, would not stay in his seat, blurted out, did little required work, sulked, and responded negatively to everything. These behaviors showed a dramatic reduction following the initiation and consistent use of the "ignore and praise" technique. After a few weeks the teacher described him as a "delightful child and an enthusiastic member of class."

As another example of differential reinforcement of incompatible behaviors, Brown and Elliott (1965) describe their experience with a group of young children attending a nursery school program. Behaviors of physical and verbal aggression were ignored and cooperative and nonaggressive behaviors were provided immediate and frequent social attention from the teachers. Within a few days following the initiation of this procedure, there was a significant reduction in both physical and verbal aggressive behaviors.

As a second tactic for reinforcing competing behaviors, the teacher may select a single specific behavior to reinforce which will replace the inappropriate behavior. A child who eats with his fingers may be reinforced specifically for using a spoon. A child who is out of his seat excessively may be reinforced specifically for remaining in his chair.

Finally, the teacher may reinforce the child for engaging less frequently in the undesired behavior. This procedure, called *differential reinforcement of low-rate responding,* would be used typically in combination with the previous procedures. The child would be reinforced for alternative behaviors and for decreasing occurrence of the undesired behaviors. This procedure was used effectively to eliminate a child's excessive scratching behavior (Allen and Harris, 1966). In this behavior management program, a five-year-old child was provided with both tangible and social reinforcement following periods of time in which the scratching behavior did not occur. Whenever the scratching did occur, it was ignored. At the initiation of the program, the child would scratch herself until she bled. The scratching over the past year had resulted in large sores and scabs on her forehead, nose, cheeks, chin, and one arm and leg. Pediatric and psychiatric consultation had failed to eliminate the behavior or to identify a medical basis for it. Within a few weeks of reinforcing the child for increasingly longer periods in which no scratching had occurred, the excessive scratching behavior was eliminated.

When using a procedure of reinforcing alternative behaviors, the possibility of reoccurrence of the inappropriate behavior remains. The undesired behavior remains in the child's repertoire; it occurs with less frequency and may even eventually disappear as other behaviors become relatively stronger. The inappropriate behaviors may reappear, however, if the alternative behaviors are not maintained through positive reinforcement. Many behavior management programs which use a procedure of reinforcing alternative behaviors fail because the school and home environments are not consistent in the continuing reinforcement of the desired behaviors for a sufficient period of time.

> **Inappropriate behavior patterns may be eliminated by reinforcing alternative appropriate behaviors.**

EXTINCTION

It is possible to decrease the strength of both appropriate and inappropriate behavior patterns by removing the reinforcing events which serve to maintain the behaviors. Under these revised conditions, a particular behavior is no longer followed by reinforcing consequences. John, a five-year-old nonverbal child with Down's Syndrome, had learned to forcefully take toys and books away from his younger brother. This aggressive behavior pattern had been learned and continued to occur because of the reinforcing consequences that it produced—obtaining the toys and books. Mother, although inconsistent in her response to this behavior, generally thought that John's behavior was acceptable because "John can't talk and has no other means of making his wishes known." She rationalized that "His younger brother doesn't mind, though, because he knows John is retarded and can't help himself," even though the sibling frequently cried when John took things from him. When John entered a developmental education program he attempted the same behavior on numerous occasions. However, he discovered that such behavior did not work as the other children would not give in to John's aggressiveness. The behavior gradually disappeared in this new setting, even though John was quite upset in the beginning. The behavior served no purpose in the school setting. The other children were as strong and big as John and would not permit him to take their possessions. Extinction occurred; the behavior disappeared in the school setting because it was not reinforced as it had been previously. John continued his aggressive behavior at home, nonetheless, as it still worked. If the home environment were to consistently follow this extinction procedure, it would be expected that the previously reinforced aggressive behavior would eventually disappear in this setting also, especially if the parents gradually shaped desired alternative means of obtaining objects from others.

In a similar case, four-year-old Terry engaged in frequent disruptive whining and shouting in the home (Hall *et al.*, 1972). Both parents, after determining that these episodes occurred on an average of ten times daily, immediately turned away from the boy when he whined or shouted. They engaged in other activities and later attended to him when he was behaving appropriately. Following consistent use of this extinction procedure for about a month, the obnoxious whining and shouting behavior decreased to a daily level of two or so occurrences.

Undesired behavior may be eliminated by removing the reinforcing consequences which the behavior previously has produced.

Since extinction can be most useful in a behavior management program designed to reduce or virtually eliminate the occurrence of problem behaviors, the teacher should be aware of the following characteristics to maximize its usefulness.

Reinforcing Events May be Difficult to Identify and Remove

An extinction procedure will be useful only if the reinforcing events which are maintaining the behavior can be identified and removed. This is sometimes difficult, especially for behavior which has been present for a long period of time. It is not unusual for a specific behavior pattern to be maintained by multiple sources of reinforcement: peer attention, occasional teacher attention, and occasional assistance in removing the child from an unpleasant situation. It is not unusual for the behavior itself to have secondary reinforcing characteristics, when it has been associated frequently with other sources of reinforcement. The behavior would be maintained for a period of time independent of other sources of reinforcement. The elimination of the disruptive behavior by following an extinction procedure would require removal of the positive reinforcement associated with peer and teacher attention as well as the negative reinforcement associated with the contingent termination of unpleasant conditions. To be effective, it would also be necessary to continue withholding the reinforcing events for a sufficient length of time to insure that the reinforcement associated with the behavior itself is eliminated.

Behavior May Show Temporary Increase

In following an extinction procedure, there may be an initial increase in the frequency or intensity of the behavior which no longer is being reinforced. If for example, Jane had previously received the teacher's attention whenever she yelled at her peers, her yelling may well become more frequent and louder for a short period of time after the teacher initiates an extinction procedure of ignoring her yelling in those instances.

The experiences of Hawkins and his associates (1966) and of Allen and her colleagues (1970) in using extinction to eliminate temper tantrum behavior support this observation. In both programs, extremes of tantrumming were noted in young children after this behavior was put on extinction. In one instance, a child whose tantrums averaged five minutes prior to extinction continued in tantrum behavior for 27 minutes on the first occasion of nonreinforcement. *Thus the problem behavior put on extinction may intensify or get worse before it gets better.* This period of intensified behavior may last for numerous hours or even for many days, depending upon the type and pattern of previous reinforcement. Behaviors that have resulted previously in highly valued reinforcing events on frequent occasions are more likely to become more frequent and intense following initiation of an extinction procedure that would be seen whenever relatively unimportant reinforcing events have been provided on a less frequent basis.

The teacher must exercise care to avoid reinforcing this more intense behavior as it occurs. If reinforcement is withheld successfully until the behavior becomes worse, this more aggravating behavior may be strengthened and thus may be difficult to eliminate. The teacher in these instances will end up with a more difficult problem. In summary, it must be reemphasized that a temporary increase in the difficulty of the behavior is a predictable result of extinction. The resurgent behavior will subside if consistent nonreinforcement is implemented.

Aggressive and Emotional Behaviors May Occur

It is not unusual for young children to display a range of disruptive emotional behaviors under those extinction conditions in which valuable positive consequences are no longer forthcoming. They may whine, cry, scream, become violent, attack others, or engage in self-abusive behavior. Such children are sometimes described as having a low frustration tolerance. They have not developed skills pursuing alternative ways of attaining the same or equally desirable reinforcers. As an example, four-year-old Ann had learned that Mother would let her continue playing if she whined loudly when asked to stop playing and get ready for bed. Her whining had been reinforced by the longer play period which it produced. Mother decided to ignore Ann's whining and she began to persist in her request for the child to stop playing. Under the new conditions, the whining no longer produced the positive consequences of an extended play period. The child initially engaged in more intense and vigorous emotional outbursts which involved crying, screaming, and shouting, "let me play; I don't want to go to bed." Mother remained calm and required, and then reinforced, compliance with praise. The emotional outburst, including the initial whining behavior, gradually became less frequent and intense and eventually disappeared.

Slow Reduction in Behavior Strength

An extinction procedure typically results in a slow but steady decline in the nonreinforced behavior. It may take one or two weeks or longer before any decline is noted. The number of times a given behavior pattern will occur after reinforcing consequences have been withdrawn is related to: (1) the number of times the behavior has been reinforced prior to the beginning of extinction, (2) the type and magnitude of previous reinforcing experiences, (3) the pattern of reinforcement previously provided, (4) the availability of alternative means of behaving which will produce the same or equally appealing reinforcers, (5) the relative state of deprivation for the reinforcer at the time extinction is initiated, and (6) the difficulty level of the behavior. A behavior that is more difficult for the person to engage in will disappear more quickly when no longer reinforced than will a behavior requiring less effort. As noted in the previous chapter, behavior that has gained its strength through being reinforced frequently and then in an intermittent manner is more likely to persist longer after reinforcement has been removed than will those behavior patterns which have been acquired and maintained through continuous reinforcement. If inconsistent in nonreinforcement during extinction the teacher may even produce a behavior that becomes even more difficult to eliminate.

A behavior with a limited history of reinforcement will disappear sooner than one with a more extensive history of reinforcement. The more times the behavior has previously resulted in positive consequences, the more it will persist following the termination of reinforcing consequences. At the same time, the more continuously the behavior has been reinforced in the past, the more likely disruptive emotional reactions will be prompted when reinforcement is no longer provided. A behavior which has been strengthened and maintained by highly valuable reinforcers will be more difficult to eliminate than one which has resulted in less valuable consequences.

Avoiding Occasional Reinforcement

The relationship between persistence of behavior over periods of no reinforcement and the previous patterns by which this behavior has been strengthened and maintained suggests that the teacher must be prepared to withstand a period of withholding reinforcement following inappropriate behavior. Too often the teacher is prone to give up after a few times of not reinforcing the undesired behavior, especially when she sees the behavior pattern and related emotional reactions increase in intensity. As suggested, this increase is predictable and will disappear if the teacher does persist in the procedure. It is most important that the undesired behavior is not reinforced during the extinction period. Even a single contingent reinforcement prior to complete elimination of the behavior may result in its reappearance at renewed strength.

Strengthening Competing Behaviors

When removing the reinforcing event, it is desirable whenever possible to use this positive consequence to strengthen new alternative behavior patterns. An experience reported by Hart and her associates (1964) illustrates this strategy. A four-year-old boy attending a nursery program frequently burst into crying episodes whenever confronted with the least amount of frustration. An average of eight crying outbursts was observed during the morning session. This high rate was virtually eliminated within ten days during which the teachers ignored the crying episodes but did attend to the boy whenever he showed any appropriate response to frustration. Social attention which the teachers had provided initially whenever crying occurred apparently was maintaining the crying behavior. This same consequence was used to strengthen appropriate behavior.

Other Undesired Behaviors May Appear

It is not unusual after a problem behavior has been eliminated by extinction to find that other problem behaviors may begin to occur in the same situation. This may happen because a number of behaviors may be under the influence of a single or a group of similar reinforcing consequences. If one behavior (in a group of related behaviors which make up a response class) no longer results in the desired consequence, other behaviors may be tried by the child. Some of these other behaviors may be socially appropriate and some may be as undesirable as the initial behavior which was extinguished.

Ullman and Krasner (1965) report an interesting experience with a child who exhibited a long succession of maladaptive behaviors following initiation of an extinction procedure. The child's camp counselor ceased attending to him when he engaged in various self-punishment behaviors such as hitting, slapping, or biting himself. The child engaged in rather intense temper tantrums; after these brought no social attention, he began to remove his clothes in public. Next, he stole food from other children's plates. Following the appearance and extinction of other inappropriate behaviors, the child finally began to engage in appropriate behaviors which produced the counselor's social attention.

This example emphasizes the interrelationship among behaviors. The teacher should be neither surprised nor discouraged when a child demonstrates a sequence of inappropriate behaviors. The previous social learning experiences apparently had selectively reinforced these more frequently than the more appropriate patterns of behavior.

Other Undesired Behaviors Should not be Strengthened

The teacher also must be careful that other undesired behaviors are not strengthened during an extinction period. If teacher attention has been the reinforcing event for certain behavior patterns caution must be exercised to insure that teacher attention is not provided except following appropriate behaviors. A child had learned that by waving his arm during class he could get the teacher's attention. When this became too frequent, the teacher decided she would extinguish this by ignoring it.   After a few experiences of arm waving without getting the teacher's attention, the child began to stand in his chair and to wave his arm rapidly. The teacher, becoming aggravated at this new display of unwanted behavior, would reprimand him on occasion and at other infrequent times would instruct the child to come to her desk. The teacher's attention following this behavior was quite pleasing to the child.   In attending to the child at this time, the teacher inadvertently taught the child to engage in a more disturbing behavior pattern than was initially present.

Desirable Behavior May Be Eliminated

It should be emphasized again that desirable as well as undesirable behaviors may decrease in strength or be eliminated by extinction conditions.   Once acquired, desirable behaviors must be reinforced on occasion if they are to be maintained.   The young child who has acquired new skills, eating without spilling or putting the toys away after playing, for example, must be reinforced on occasion for these actions or else the behaviors will become less frequent. Even well-established behaviors will not continue to occur if reinforcement is not provided on occasion.   If behavior has recently been acquired and is of less than maximum strength, it is even more essential that reinforcement be provided if extinction is to be avoided.

Use in Combination with Reinforcing Alternative Behavior

It must be reemphasized that a procedure of extinction should seldom be used in isolation.   Such a procedure does not strengthen desired behaviors which should replace the extinguished one.   In some cases, the temporary increase in behavior strength associated with extinction would be more than the child's social environment could tolerate if there was no plan to strengthen acceptable competing behaviors.   Reinforcement of appropriate alternative behavior should be an integral part of the behavior management program which uses an extinction procedure.   Madsen and associates (1968) found that disruptive behavior of young children in elementary classes did not show improvement when a procedure ignoring the misbehavior was initiated.   After an added feature of socially reinforcing appropriate behavior was used, however, a significant reduction in disruptive behavior followed.

145

Behavior May Reappear

Using an extinction procedure to eliminate undesired behavior patterns, the teacher should not assume that once the behavior no longer occurs it is removed completely from the child's repertoire. It is a common observation that the behavior reappears at some later time following its initial disappearance under extinction conditions. This phenomenon known as *spontaneous recovery* should not discourage the teacher. Continued persistence in using the extinction procedure in those instances will result in the total disappearance of the behavior.

In addition to the likelihood of spontaneous recovery, it is always possible that the behavior will occur at some later time after extinction. If reinforcement is provided as the behavior reoccurs, it may quickly regain its original strength, especially if other more appropriate behaviors do not result in the desired reinforcing events. This observation reemphasizes the necessity of insuring that alternative behaviors are reinforced which become useful to the child in producing positive consequences.

A Final Comment on Extinction

The teacher using extinction should avoid a sudden generalized reduction in the total positive reinforcement that a child receives. When observing many problem children, it is not unusual to discover that most social attention is provided for inappropriate behaviors. Appropriate behavior may be ignored or, if it occurs infrequently, it may be reinforced much less than undesired behavior. If a strategy of extinction is suddenly implemented in which no social attention is provided for inappropriate behaviors, the child may suddenly be left with little social reinforcement. In this case, it is best to select a limited number of problems for extinction and to attempt to replace these quickly with more appropriate behaviors which will provide the child with the needed social attention.

SATIATION

A valuable procedure in selected cases is *satiation,* a process which encourages the child to engage in a bothersome behavior over and over again until he tires of it. Tim may hum or talk to himself when requested to work quietly. This behavior is distracting to the other children and appears to be maintained by the attention which is provided on occasion by his peers. Mrs. Kinlock may interrupt the class activity and state "Tim likes to hum and talk to himself. Let's all stop our work and listen while Tim does this. Now Tim, continue with your humming and talking." If Tim stops, the teacher would encourage him to continue until he appears to be quite tired of the behavior.

The effects of a satiation procedure may be somewhat temporary, especially if the behavior has been in the child's repertoire for an extended period of time. The teacher can increase the likelihood that the satiated behavior will not reappear by insuring that in the interim period in which the behavior is absent or of low strength, other more appropriate behaviors are reinforced which will replace the undesired pattern.

CHANGING THE STIMULUS ENVIRONMENT

Problem behaviors may be controlled on a temporary basis by changing the stimulus conditions which influence these behaviors. A classroom with a water fountain was a convenient excuse for John's frequent trips to drink water. Under these conditions he seldom completed his work. The teacher announced that the fountain would be turned off during desk work and further that those who completed their work could have free access to the fountain during the afternoon arts and crafts period. The problem was solved by removing the cues which controlled the excessive behavior.

In other instances, the teacher may identify stimulus situations in which inappropriate behavior has a high likelihood of occurring. For example, Susan is likely to become overly emotional and hyperactive when she is unable to complete tasks assigned to her. The teacher could remove difficult tasks when it appears that Susan will experience difficulty, and then provide her with alternative easier ones.

Instead of removing the stimulus conditions which influence inappropriate behaviors, the teacher may find it useful to present cues which serve to inhibit the problem behavior. The teacher-aide may sit behind Elmer to discourage his aggravation of Sue and Jill. Kitty may be seated next to the teacher to reduce the likelihood that she will roam around the room.

Finally, the teacher may prompt desired behavior which will compete with problem behavior. She may request that Percy assist her in passing out toys or puzzles to his classmates at a time when he usually is taking possessions away from them.

These procedures removing discriminative events which

147

control problem behaviors, presenting cues which inhibit problem behaviors, and presenting cues which control behaviors which serve to compete with problem behaviors all produce temporary results. The teacher uses these procedures in order to increase the likelihood that desired behaviors may occur which can be reinforced. The goal is to strengthen desired behaviors to the point that they will replace the problem ones.

PUNISHMENT

Punishment is a rule of behavior which indicates that those behaviors resulting in unpleasant consequences will be less likely to be repeated. Such consequences inhibit the preceding behavior. Under similar circumstances in the future, the behavior is less likely to occur again. On the first day of school, if Tim approaches Simon and greets him with a friendly "Hello," he is less likely to engage in this social behavior if Simon reacts with a nasty reply or pokes him in the stomach.

The punishment rule refers both to:

—*the presentation of aversive (unpleasant) consequence following behavior,* for example: behavior produces physical pain, being yelled at, ridiculed, frowned at, or threatened, and
—*the removal or withdrawal following behavior of positive consequences which the child has or which are available to him,* for example: sitting child in corner and thus removing him from his peer group, reducing his play time, taking away his toys, losing a friend.

The latter may involve *time-out* or *response cost* procedures. Each will be described in the following sections.

> **Behavior which results in unpleasant consequences will be less likely to be repeated.**

These consequences may represent (1) naturally occurring unpleasant results of various behaviors or (2) unpleasant events which are arranged by others. The child eats too much candy and gets sick, the child takes his gloves off in the snow and his fingers hurt, the child touches a hot pot of coffee and is burned, the child steps on cinders and hurts his feet. The behaviors resulting in each of these unpleasant consequences will be less likely to be repeated. The rule of punishment in a sense is a rule of self-protection.

Unpleasant consequences following specific behaviors may also be arranged by the teacher or delivered by others to discourage the reoccurrence of these behaviors. Just as there are rules of nature which suggest that certain behaviors should be avoided (as examples, eating excessive candy, removing gloves when handling snow, touching a hot pot of coffee), there are also rules of social living which discourage various behaviors. The child hits a peer and gets hit in return. Another child is rude to his peers and they no longer play with him. While teaching these rules of social living to children, it is sometimes necessary for adults to arrange for unpleasant consequences to occur whenever the child ignores these rules. These rules and the resulting punishment for breaking the rules should not be arbitrary, nor should these be presented in a harsh, punitive, ridiculous, or derogatory fashion. The rules of social living and the resulting consequences should be logical and understandable to the child. In every case, the child should have a choice. Adherence to the rule of social living results in positive consequences; if the rule is not followed there will be specified logical consequences which are unpleasant to the child.

Each of the punishment procedures mentioned above should be viewed as a minor and infrequently used aspect of a behavior management program. The excessive use of punishment procedures can only result in aggressive outbursts and in excessively inhibited and overly emotional children. The teacher who uses punishment in a harsh, punitive, hostile, or aggressive manner when she is angry or aggravated provides an aggressive model which the child being punished and others who observe are likely to imitate. These children are more apt to use these same modes of behavior when they are angry or have control over someone else such as a younger peer or sibling. When used in skillful combination with procedures based on positive reinforcement, however, the selective use of punishment procedures may contribute to the positive behavior development of young children. The potential usefulness as well as the potential dangers and limitations of punishment procedures will be discussed.

Presentation of Aversive Consequences (PAC)

The presentation of unpleasant consequences following undesired behaviors may result in temporary suppression or relatively permanent control of these behaviors depending upon the intensity of the punishment. A temporary reduction or control of the behavior may be most useful to the teacher as she is able to use this period of time to teach and strengthen more appropriate means of behaving. A PAC procedure also provides other children with information about the consequences of specific types of behaviors. This observation may assist the children to inhibit such behavior on their part and to select more desired modes of responding. Finally, mild punishment may assist a child in making a discrimination between correct-incorrect or appropriate-inappropriate behavior. There are, however, other effects to be considered.

Does not teach desired behavior. As noted, a PAC procedure does not teach the child what he should do. It suppresses or controls behavior, but when used in isolation the procedure does not provide a more appropriate mode of behavior as a replacement. It merely serves to reduce (typically on a rather temporary basis) the likelihood that the punished behavior will be repeated under similar circumstances. In addition, the child should be taught what to do and how best to do it under the conditions in which the punished behavior has occurred.

The limitations of a punishment approach when used in isolation are illustrated by the following experience with Kit, a five-year-old socially isolated boy. Kit was creating considerable problems with his female peers in a child development center by frequently pulling their hair. The teacher, under the supposition that if Kit could experience the pain associated with hair-pulling he would refrain from pulling the hair of others, initiated a procedure for pulling Kit's hair immediately whenever he engaged in this behavior. The procedure was indeed effective in reducing his hair-pulling behavior, but since the child had only poorly developed skills of interacting with other children, he was rather isolated from them. Now he just sat and engaged in no peer interactions. The teacher was pleased with her strategy because it worked in terminating the bothersome behavior, but the punishment did not teach Kit any appropriate ways of interacting with his peers. A PAC procedure thus represents only one aspect of an appropriate behavior management program. The program also must provide for alternative desirable behaviors which produce positive consequences. As punishment is provided to render the inappropriate behavior less likely, positive consequences should be used to increase the strength of alternative appropriate behaviors. The desired competing behaviors will replace the inappropriate behavior.

Effects of mild PAC highly specific. When PAC is used in isolation and when the aversive event is not too intense, it is not unusual for the effects of punishment to be restricted to highly specific conditions. The influence which punishment may have over the undesired behavior may be effective only as long as the possibility is great that the behavior will result in unpleasant consequences.

A teacher may reduce the likelihood that certain disruptive behaviors may occur with a rule that unpleasant consequences will follow such behavior. This punishment control of the disruptive behavior will make behaviors which are acceptable to the teacher more attractive. Unless the teacher provides consistent positive consequences for these other behaviors, however, they may occur only as long as the likelihood is great that punishment would follow the disruptive behavior. Under conditions in which the behavior is under punishment control, a reduction in the likelihood of punishment may result in a sudden reappearance of the disruptive behavior. A substitute teacher who does not represent the punishment control may find the child to be highly disruptive even though the regular teacher has "well-behaved" children. A child may learn not to hit another child in Mrs. Gill's classroom because of previous punishment in this setting. He may continue, however, hitting children on the playground when Mrs. Gill is absent.

A PAC procedure not only fails to teach the child what he should do, it may serve to suppress inappropriate behaviors only under highly specific conditions. As these conditions are removed or changed, the punished behavior may reoccur.

Effects of mild and of intense aversive consequences. The inhibiting effects of a PAC procedure are frequently temporary if the aversive consequence is mild. The punished behavior may not occur for a short period of time following the aversive consequence, but unless alternative behaviors are strengthened the behavior may reappear. The behavior frequently is not eliminated; it is merely inhibited for a period of time.

It is true, in contrast, that extremely intense aversive consequences may decrease the punished behavior for long periods of time. But the possible negative effects are too great to justify the use of such procedures. The child may become highly emotional, engage in explosive aggressive outbursts, or become generally inhibited and withdrawn. He may become fearful and nonresponsive to many aspects of his environment in addition to those associated directly with the intense punishment.

Teachers should be aware of the behavioral effects of intense and frequent punishment, for some children may exhibit symptoms of such a conditioning history. In these cases, care must be taken to avoid the use of even a mild form of punishment if it can be avoided. For children with such histories, even mild punishment can provoke intense emotional reactions and related avoidance behaviors.

Negative side effects to frequent mild punishment. The negative effects of using intense aversive consequences may also be observed when mildly aversive consequences are used too frequently in an effort to influence a child's behavior. A child whose behavior frequently results in unpleasant consequences may reduce his general interaction with his environment. Behaviors other than those punished may be inhibited. The child may become shy and nonresponsive. If the child is criticized frequently for his clumsy motor behavior when playing group games, he will soon begin to avoid the playground or group activities. These become unpleasant places and activities.

Further, persons who are associated with the punishment may become unpleasant to the child. The child may develop a distinct dislike for the teacher who punishes too much, and will tend to avoid her. The teacher becomes a cue for unpleasant emotional reactions. She alienates herself. The child does not seek to please her, to attend to her, or to imitate her behavior (except through fear of noncompliance) as the teacher does not represent a positive social reinforcing agent.

A child who is punished too frequently by parents and teachers may begin to feel uncomfortable around all adults, or around those adults who resemble in one way or another the teacher who provides aversive consequences. In a similar manner, such cues as time, place, or activity may become associated with the unpleasant emotional reactions which accompany punishment. The child may begin to avoid those situations in which punishment is a likelihood.

It is true also that frequent mild punishment may produce aggressive behavioral reactions, disruptive emotionality, and temper tantrums. These behaviors may be directed toward the person associated with the punishment or displaced toward an innocent person or object. It is not unusual for excessively punished children to engage in such behaviors as destruction of school property, excessive fighting, and intense emotional outburst at minimal provocation. Under these circumstances, the teacher may feel that she must increase her punishment because "she cannot let the child get away with such bad behavior." The teacher runs the risk of increasing the likelihood of the inappropriate behavior. She also places herself in a position of greatly decreasing her effectiveness as a person concerned with influencing appropriate behavior patterns.

A teacher who uses the rule of punishment too frequently

or who provides highly unpleasant consequences will most likely invite fear, anxiety, and dislike from her children. The teacher who is harsh or who threatens or punishes too frequently is likely to produce a variety of disruptive or other undesirable behavior patterns. The shy, uninvolved child, for example, avoids becoming involved in these situations that have resulted in punishment too frequently in the past. Another child may be harsh and aggressive to other children by imitating the aggressive behavior patterns of the teacher.

In view of these possible negative effects, a PAC procedure arranged by the teacher should be used sparingly, and even in these instances only after careful planning. In order to be most effective as a teacher of young children with learning and behavior difficulties, procedures involving positive reinforcement must far outnumber those having unpleasant consequences. Through frequent association with the delivery of positive consequences the teacher will acquire some of the desirable reinforcing characteristics of these events. The child will like her and will acquire new behaviors in order to obtain her approval, attention, affection, or praise.

PAC may not be effective. It is not unusual to observe that a child will persist in behavior which results in consequences that appear to be unpleasant to the teacher. Parents or teachers may report, "He seems to enjoy being punished because he will insist on doing those things that he knows will lead to unpleasant consequences." A child may engage in a certain behavior "to see if he can get away with it." On occasion he does "get away with it"—he is reinforced—and at other times the child is punished. This unique combination of reinforcement, punishment, and extinction has taught the child, "Sometimes I get reinforced for the behavior. At other times I don't. On occasion, I get punished." The child does not persist in inappropriate behavior because he is devilish or naughty. He does not become "sneakish" because he wishes to be dishonest. He behaves in this manner because his experiences with those directing his environment have taught him these behaviors. The occasional positive reinforcement following the behavior apparently is sufficiently influential to override the unpleasant consequences of punishment.

It is also true that aversive consequences may signal the occurrence of reinforcing events. The adult may be considerably more attentive, more positive, and more available immediately after punishing the child than at other times. Thus those behaviors which produce the unpleasant consequences are strengthened by the subsequent positive reinforcement. Finally, the social attention that is provided as punishment is administered may be more reinforcing than the unpleasant consequence is aversive. Under these conditions the preceding behavior would be strengthened or maintained, and not inhibited as expected.

PAC procedure unpleasant to teachers.   When a PAC procedure is used excessively, it becomes highly difficult to manage.   Excessive use is quite inefficient because it must be provided immediately and consistently or else the punished behavior will reappear.   It is also true that most teachers do not enjoy using a PAC procedure. Presenting aversive consequences is emotionally disquieting to the teacher.   Additionally, an emotional climate is created that disrupts children other than the child being punished.   Such an environment makes children more likely to be passive and fearful or negativistic and noncooperative.

Removal of Pleasant Consequences

Even though the child's behaviors may on occasion produce physical pain from peers or natural events (for example, fast running on occasion results in falling and pain; staying outside in subfreezing weather results in ears, nose, and fingers hurting; biting a peer results in being bitten in return), punishment procedures involving inflicting physical pain or other derogatory consequences such as yelling, being harsh, or threatening should be avoided whenever possible by the teacher of young children.   The teacher is left with the procedures of *time-out* and *response-cost* as means of discouraging undesired behavior patterns.

Time-out from Positive Reinforcement (TO)

Time-out (TO) is a procedure temporarily removing the child from a reinforcing situation following inappropriate behavior and placing him in a location in which reinforcement is minimal or unlikely to occur.   In the school setting, the child who persists in disruptive behavior may be removed from the presence of teacher and peers and placed in an isolated or quiet room or location which contains a minimal number of objects, little or no social stimulation, and minimal opportunity for interesting activities.   In this setting the child has little opportunity to receive positive reinforcement.   Following a designated period of time (usually less than ten minutes) the child is given the choice to return to the classroom.

In other instances the source of reinforcement is removed following inappropriate behavior.   Following John's rude behavior the teacher may turn away from him and ignore him for a period of time.   Another child who begins to be messy in his self-feeding may lose his lunch tray for a short period of time.   A child who becomes distractible or acts silly during individual language therapy may be ignored by the teacher until he once again pays attention.   Watson (1972) terminated all training activities at the moment a 4½-year-old "autistic" child began to cry or whine. After the child terminated this negativistic behavior the teacher resumed interaction with the child.   This behavior was virtually eliminated within a few training sessions following initiation of the TO procedure.

The use of a TO procedure involving the removal of the child from a reinforcing environment is illustrated in the writer's experience with Lisa, a 39-month-old child attending a nursery school (Briskin and Gardner, 1968).   This child was described as hyperactive, disruptive, and difficult to control in the school setting.   Specific inappropriate behaviors included screaming and throwing things in fits of anger, crying or whining when not getting her way, not waiting her turn to engage in art projects and physical activities, hitting, biting, grabbing, rough pushing, not responding to verbal instructions, and leaving the room, group or activity without reason or permission.   After an observational period revealed the average frequency of these behaviors in structured and unstructured activity periods throughout the school day, a TO procedure was initiated.   Whenever any of these behaviors occurred during the three structured periods, Lisa was immediately removed from the classroom and seated outside for a two-minute period.   The only verbal interaction during the TO consisted of a short statement informing Lisa why she was taken from the classroom ("You pushed Jill.   You must sit in the chair." "You are whining.   Sit in the chair.").   Following the two-minute period she was returned to the classroom.

In order to strengthen behaviors which were desirable and which should replace the inappropriate ones, an additional procedure was used providing prompt teacher praise and other forms of social interaction following the occurrence of appropriate behaviors.   Although Lisa voiced her objections to being placed in TO during the first few experiences, she soon accepted the action as an unpleasant consequence which she produced by certain disruptive behaviors.   Within a few days inappropriate behavior was reduced from an average of 31 percent to 2 percent of the time at school.   There was a concurrent increase in appropriate behavior which was maintained over a follow-up period.   It is interesting to note that the improvement in Lisa's behavior had a pronounced positive effect on the teacher, aides, other children, and on Lisa's mother.   All interacted more readily with Lisa and provided her with the social attention which was apparently quite valuable to her.

This experience with Lisa emphasizes both the importance of social attention to children and the highly critical significance of providing social attention for appropriate behaviors and not primarily as a reaction to disruptive behaviors. Observation of Lisa prior to initiation of the program revealed that the adults in the school environment were giving Lisa almost constant attention for her disruptive behaviors. She was seldom provided attention when she did behave appropriately. Thus, attention which appeared necessary to control her inappropriate behavior patterns was apparently having the effect of strengthening and maintaining it. The initiation of a TO procedure for unacceptable behavior and providing the child with an enriched amount of social reinforcement only following desired behavior resulted in a happier, more enjoyable, and accepted child.

A TO procedure may be effective in eliminating bothersome behavior even in those children with severe developmental difficulties who appear to be relatively unresponsive to social reinforcement. Watson (1972) describes the successful use of a combined TO and extinction procedure in modifying the temper tantrums in a six-year-old described as "a profoundly retarded psychotic child." Following the beginning of a temper tantrum, he was completely ignored by everyone in his environment for five minutes. The weekly frequency dropped from a high of 50 to a level of infrequent occurrence within approximately three weeks.

In using a TO procedure the teacher should:

Administer it in a matter-of-fact nonemotional manner. Scolding, reprimanding, or otherwise rejecting the child is not the procedure. The teacher is merely being instrumental in removing the child on a temporary basis from a source of positive reinforcement.

Insure that removal from a situation or location is in fact unpleasant to the child. The situation from which the child is removed must contain sources of reinforcement which are pleasant to the child. In the case of Lisa, even though she was in frequent conflict with teachers and peers, she remained close to them. Their presence apparently was reinforcing to Lisa as she easily could have isolated herself and avoided them. It was speculated that temporary removal from their presence would be unpleasant and thus would serve to inhibit the inappropriate behavior. If the situation from which the child is removed is in fact aversive to the child, the preceding behaviors may actually be strengthened (negative reinforcement) rather than being inhibited.

Be consistent in the TO procedure. The teacher should remain with the procedure until sufficient time has elapsed to evaluate its

effectiveness.   If the child gets away with misbehavior which
produces reinforcement only on occasion, this reinforcement may
well offset the effects of more frequent TOs.

*The physical location of the TO period must be evaluated carefully
to insure that the TO area is rather void of sources of positive
reinforcement.*   Placing the child in a hallway, sending him to the
nurse's office, or sitting him in a supply closet may be quite reinforcing due to the opportunity for new sources of attention or
activities.   Under these conditions, the behavior pattern which
resulted in his being placed in these settings may well be strengthened rather than weakened.

Keep the TO period relatively short.   Periods from one to ten
minutes have been found to be effective with many children.
Longer periods may be reinforcing to the teacher as the child
spends less time in the classroom, but a longer time-out period
does not contribute to eliminating the child's problematic behavior.
The earlier mentioned Briskin and Gardner (1968) program
found a two-minute TO period effective.   Sibley and her associates
(1969) used a five-minute period in a successful program designed to decrease the aggressive, negative attention-getting and
resisting behaviors of a five-year-old boy in a kindergarten setting.
White and his colleagues (1972) even found a one-minute TO
period effective in suppressing aggressive, tantrum, and self-
destructive behaviors in moderately and severely retarded
children.
        In many instances the child will begin to engage in disrup-
tive behaviors when first placed in TO.   He may scream, cry, kick,
attack the physical environment, and display similar frustration
behaviors.   The TO period should begin following the cessation of
these behaviors.   If the child is permitted to return to the environment from which he was removed as he is engaging in disruptive
behaviors, these behaviors may well be strengthened.   Thus the
TO procedure would only confound the child's difficulty.   Again,
the TO period should begin following the cessation of disruptive
behaviors.   The child is returned to his previous activity or environment when he is engaging in appropriate behavior.   This
behavior is likely to be strengthened since it precedes the removal
of the unpleasant TO period.

Reinforce alternative behaviors.   As is true in using a PAC approach, a TO procedure is designed to stop and to eliminate undesired behaviors; it does not teach the appropriate behavior.   Once
the TO procedure is no longer used, the punished behavior is likely

to reappear unless competing behaviors have been reinforced. This was evident in a program by Pendergrass (1972). A two-minute TO procedure was found to suppress persistent, high-rate misbehavior in two severely withdrawn children. The children were not provided positive reinforcement for behaviors which would replace the misbehavior. The misbehavior reappeared after the TO procedure was no longer used. Abbott (1969) describes a successful behavior management program in which a TO for inappropriate disruptive, resistant, and aggressive behaviors of a child in a kindergarten classroom was combined with a tactic of positive social reinforcement for alternative desirable behaviors. Following consistent reinforcement, the appropriate behaviors soon began to replace the inappropriate behaviors which were discouraged by the TO experiences.

Inform the child which behavior produces TO. At the time the child is provided a TO, he should be informed in a matter-of-fact manner the behavior which resulted in the TO. This emphasizes those behaviors which are unacceptable and also focuses on the relationship between these behaviors and the contingent unpleasant consequences.

Response Cost (RC)

Inappropriate behavior patterns may be discouraged while using a Response Cost procedure by requiring the child to give up some positive event which he has in his possession or which would be provided for him. His inappropriate behaviors cost him; he is fined for them. A certain number or amount of reinforcing events are removed from him. Following inappropriate behavior, for example, the child may lose recess privileges, may not have dessert for three meals, may lose his role as teacher assistant for a day. A child who takes an excessive amount of time in cleaning up his mess after play may lose some of the time which is available for watching cartoons. If watching cartoons is a highly desired activity, the child may be provided a set amount of time for cleaning up after play. Any time in excess of the allotted time will be subtracted from his cartoon-watching period.

This practice of removing positive reinforcers after inappropriate behavior is quite different from extinction procedures. Behavior that has been followed by reinforcers no longer produces those reinforcers in an extinction procedure. A response cost, in contrast, involves the removal of events or privileges which the child has available to him.

A wise use of an RC procedure frequently results in a rapid

reduction of the undesired behavior. However, there is considerable variation among young children in the nature and degree of
effect associated with this procedure. To be effective, the teacher
must initially identify, and then be in a position to remove,
reinforcing events which the child has. This assumes that the
child does have events in his possession which can be removed
such as dessert, snack time, free play time, and other privileges or
objects. An RC procedure is easy to manage whenever a token
system is in operation. This was illustrated in a program of
Perline and Levinsky (1968) who used an RC procedure in combination with a tactic of providing token reinforcers for behaviors
incompatible with a number of disruptive aggressive and hyperactive behaviors. Tokens were given to each of four severely
retarded children attending a preschool program whenever one
engaged in desired behaviors. Upon engaging in a maladaptive
behavior, a token was taken away from the child. An immediate
drop in the maladaptive behavior was obtained under these conditions.

As with any punishment procedure the RC approach must
be used somewhat infrequently. If used too much the child will
become discouraged. Also, the magnitude of the fines should be
within reasonable limits. If the fine is excessive, discouragement
and frustration behaviors are likely to result.

The child may be provided an opportunity to regain reinforcing events following appropriate behavior. This strategy effectively combines a positive reinforcement procedure with the RC
one. This combined approach results in the strengthening of
appropriate behaviors which will compete with the undesired ones.
This is critical in a behavior management program as the RC
procedure only discourages specific behaviors from reoccurring.
As the bothersome behavior is reduced in strength, the likelihood
is increased that desired behavior may occur and, if reinforced, be
strengthened. The role of an RC procedure is to temporarily
control inappropriate behavior so that alternative appropriate behavior may occur and be strengthened.

The teacher using an RC procedure must insure that
the child understands the rules of behavior which will govern the
removal of the reinforcing events. Also, he must insure that the
child has alternative appropriate behaviors in his repertoire and is
aware of the rule for using these behaviors to avoid an RC. The
RC procedure under these conditions can be presented to the child
in a matter-of-fact manner. The child is provided with a choice.
A specified number or amount of reinforcing events will be removed from the child following inappropriate behavior. Following
appropriate behavior, positive events will be provided.

A behavior management program described by Sulzbacher

and Houser (1968) provides an illustration of the effective use of an RC procedure with a group of children. Mildly retarded children attending a primary level class were causing considerable disruption in the classroom procedure by frequently using the "naughty finger" (raised fist with middle finger extended). The teacher awarded the class a special ten-minute recess at the end of the day. However, if any member of the class made the naughty finger gesture, or if other children made reference to it, one minute of the ten was lost by the entire class. The RC procedure resulted in an immediate reduction in the undesirable behaviors—from an average of 16 occurrences prior to the RC procedure to an average of two occurrences after the RC was used.

THE TIMING OF PUNISHMENT

To achieve maximum effects in controlling behavior, unpleasant consequences should immediately follow the inappropriate behavior. There is evidence to suggest that effects are greater when punishment is provided at the time the child initiates an inappropriate behavior than would be evident if the child is punished after the misbehavior (Walters, Parke, and Cane, 1965). If the teacher wishes to punish a child for removing materials from the supply cabinet, she should attempt to reprimand or otherwise punish the child as he reaches for the materials rather than doing so later after he has the materials and has used them. Or, if punishment is provided a child who forcefully takes possessions from his smaller peers, it is best to observe him and administer the punishment as he reaches for and begins to pull a toy away from his peer. If he is punished only after he has gained possession of the toy and has played with it, the behavior already has been reinforced. Punishment at that time is less likely to have a suppressive effect on the likelihood of his behavior occurring in the future.

Waiting until a later time to present unpleasant consequences may result in punishment for the wrong behavior. If the teacher suggests to the child after some inappropriate behavior, "Mother will hear about this when she comes to take you home. I'm sure she will be upset," such a threat may create a state of emotionality as the child dreads mother's arrival. If the mother does punish the child for earlier misbehavior, she is inadvertently punishing responses which immediately precede the unpleasant consequences. Also, mother's appearance may acquire aversive properties and her son may hesitate to approach her. If this sequence is repeated frequently, the son may actively avoid mother when she does appear.

HOW UNPLEASANT CONSEQUENCES SHOULD BE ARRANGED

The manner in which the rule of punishment is used becomes critical. The natural world of the child requires that he learn to choose between certain forms of behavior which result in pleasant consequences and other forms of behavior which result in unpleasant consequences. To protect the child from all naturally occurring unpleasant consequences obviously would be unjust to a child. As noted earlier, a child learns that touching a hot stove produces unpleasant consequences. The rule of punishment indicates that such behavior would be unlikely to be repeated.

A child learns that he cannot take toys away from his peers when such behavior results in unpleasant consequences like being hit by them or of losing their friendship. The rule of punishment would indicate that this behavior would be less likely to be repeated in the future. Thus a child development program should teach a child to choose between behaviors which produce pleasant consequences and those which produce unpleasant ones. This is done by providing certain rules of social living which guide behavior. On many occasions the child can learn to understand or appreciate the rules only by experiencing the unpleasant consequences of noncompliance. At the same time, it is essential that the child does experience far more positive consequences than negative ones. The school experiences must be arranged to insure that the child is protected from excessive aversive consequences. Choices involving negative consequences for inappropriate behavior must be gradually introduced in the child's experiences and not suddenly imposed on him.

Vicarious Experiences with Consequences

On occasion the child may be provided the background experience in making choices between appropriate and inappropriate behaviors and their related consequences through various activities and games which demonstrate these relationships. Puppet play, animated stories, cartoons, and role-playing activities may be used to good advantage to demonstrate to the child that certain behaviors result in desired consequences and other behaviors produce unpleasant results.

Emphasis on Choice

In arranging the learning environment both pleasant and unpleasant consequences should be as naturally and logically related as

161

possible to the behaviors which produce them. For example, the teacher may have a rule that a child must remain seated at the table throughout snack and lunch time. The positive consequences of this behavior are eating food and enjoying the company of his peers. The unpleasant consequence of leaving the table prior to completion of the meal—an application of the punishment rule—is a logical one: once the child leaves the table without teacher permission, he may not return to finish his meal. In this instance, the child has a choice. The punishment—losing the remainder of the meal—is not a harsh, punitive result delivered by an angry adult. It is the logical consequence of not following the rule demonstrated previously to the child. The child makes a choice and experiences the related consequence.

The rule of punishment provides the child with an opportunity to make decisions about his own behavior when used in this manner. The adult is not angry, rejecting or otherwise negative. She responds to his choice in a matter of fact fashion. "I see, John, you decided not to eat your food today." The child's behavior produced the unpleasant consequences.

WHEN PUNISHMENT SHOULD BE USED

On occasion it may be helpful to use mild punishment to assist the child who is making a discrimination between acceptable and unacceptable behavior. The teacher can show and inform a child what to do but on occasion inappropriate behaviors are strengthened by previous reinforcement. Permitting the child to experience unpleasant consequences in a contingent fashion and at the same time insuring that he experiences frequent pleasant consequences for alternative appropriate behavior may serve to facilitate positive behavior development. Punishment may be used on occasion to hasten the elimination of inappropriate behavior and to increase the likelihood of other alternative acceptable behavior.

In other cases, disruptive behavior may be too intense to be ignored and the teacher may be unable to direct the child to behave in a more acceptable manner. The teacher may also be unable to control all sources of reinforcement associated with disruptive behavior. Peers frequently maintain inappropriate behaviors by the social attention they provide each other. As frequently occurring inappropriate behavior is likely to be imitated by observing peers, punishment may be needed to terminate the spread of this behavior. Punishment of one child may serve to decrease the behavior in the punished child as well as in other children who observe the punishment. Experience has demonstrated that children who observe others being punished for a certain behavior are less likely to engage in that behavior themselves for a time (Walters, Parke and Cane, 1965). Punishment of one child may be useful as a temporary measure to inhibit bothersome behavior in a number of observers and to provide an opportunity for acceptable behaviors to occur and to be strengthened through reinforcement.

In a few cases, inappropriate behavior may be of such strength that the likelihood is quite low that alternative appropriate behaviors will occur. At times a crisis is reached between the teacher and child which can be resolved only by a rather immediate reduction in inappropriate behavior. The teacher may feel that she no longer can tolerate highly disruptive behaviors. Temporary management of the child's behavior by means of punishment procedures may offer a solution. A reduction in the problem behaviors may result in the child remaining in the class and thus provide an opportunity for the strengthening of competing appropriate behavior.

Carlson and her associates (1968) describe such a situation. A young child in an elementary classroom was creating considerable difficulty by her frequent and intense tantrum behaviors. These behaviors included profane screaming, running wildly from place to place, picking up chairs, throwing them, and attacking other children. She was described as having poor social relationships with her peers and obvious learning difficulties. Sending the child to the school office at the initiation of a tantrum had no beneficial effect due to the excessive attention which this tactic attracted. As no suitable time-out facility was available, a procedure was initiated to hold the child in her chair while she was engaging in her tantrums. The chair was placed in the back of the classroom. Such a tactic was deemed to be aversive as she resented being touched or held. Her peers were reinforced with a candy treat whenever they refrained from looking at the child during the time the tantrum control procedure was being used. The child was reinforced for periods of time in which tantrum behavior did not occur. This skillful combination of punishment following tantrum behavior and positive reinforcement for appropriate competing behaviors resulted in a rapid reduction of the tantrum behavior. After the tantrum behavior disappeared, the child began to engage in a range of academic and social behaviors which resulted in positive attention from teacher and peers.

Finally, in some selected instances, a child may reside in a family setting in which aversive control through punishment and threat is the major mode of behavior influence. If the child is placed suddenly in a school environment which attempts only to reinforce appropriate behavior and to ignore inappropriate modes

163

of responding, he may be excessively disruptive and uncontrolled. In these unusual instances, it may be necessary to remove the threat of punishment gradually as the effects of positive reinforcement begin to gain influence over appropriate behavior.

GUIDELINES FOR THE USE OF PUNISHMENT PROCEDURES

While using the rules of punishment, attention to the following guidelines will produce the most desirable behavioral effects and the smallest number of negative side-effects:

1. *Punishment must be used infrequently.* The person (teacher/teacher-assistant) who administers the punishment should provide a large amount of positive reinforcers at frequent times for varied behaviors in different situations. In this manner the adult will be associated predominantly with positive experiences and will be a cue to the child for positive emotional reactions. It is also true that punishment, if used too frequently, will either lose its value as the child adapts to it or will result in generalized avoidance behavior. The inappropriate behavior may no longer occur, but the child may begin to interact less with all aspects of the situations in which punishment has been used excessively.

2. *The inappropriate behavior, the conditions under which it occurs, and its strength must be precisely defined.*

3. *The punishment procedure to be used should be well-articulated.*

4. *The circumstances in which punishment will be used must be explicit.*

5. *Alternative behaviors which will replace the punished one and the reinforcement procedures to be used to strengthen them should be readily identifiable.*

6. *Time-out or response cost should be used whenever possible rather than a procedure involving the presentation of aversive events.*

7. *The child should be informed in a clear and precise manner about those behaviors which will produce positive consequences and those that will result in negative consequences.* If necessary, demonstration of these relationships should be provided. The child may observe others or he may be "walked through" the sequence. A rule of punishment should not be presented unless it will be implemented. Empty threats only serve to teach the child to ignore rules. When punishment is used, the

child must understand why he is being punished and what he can do to avoid it in the future.

8. *Rules regarding punishment should be implemented consistently and immediately.* The behavior must be punished as it begins if possible; the child cannot be allowed to avoid the consequences. If the child's behavior produces unpleasant consequences after he chooses to ignore a rule of social living he should not receive sympathy or relief. The teacher must aim to be objective and controlled. It is desirable to label for the child the specific behaviors which have produced the unpleasant consequences. Emotional involvement should be avoided when implementing various punishment procedures. Extra attention, affection, or other positive reinforcers should not be provided at the time punishment occurs. As emphasized, the child should be provided with these positive consequences at frequent other times in his daily life following appropriate behaviors. If positive consequences closely follow punishment the child may learn to misbehave in order to receive punishment and the resulting greater magnitude of positive reinforcement.

The punishment can not be postponed. The policy of "Your father will spank you when he gets home" is unlikely to influence the misbehavior. In fact, if father is the designated adult to punish children they may learn to avoid him on his arrival at home. Father's homecoming may become an unpleasant experience.

9. *The teacher should always provide alternative behavioral possibilities.* There must be a choice between desired behavior and positive consequences and inappropriate behavior and unpleasant consequences. Whenever possible, reinforcing events associated with inappropriate behavior should become contingent on desired alternative behaviors.

In fulfilling this requirement, the child *must have appropriate alternative behaviors in his repertoire* and the environmental control over inappropriate behavior must not be excessively strong. The sole purpose of punishment is to facilitate the strengthening of appropriate behavior patterns by reducing the likelihood of competing inappropriate behavior patterns.

10. *Maximum intensity of the aversive event must be present from the beginning.* If the intensity of the punishment is gradually increased, the child may learn to adapt to each succeeding increment.

The intensity of the negative consequence should match the strength of the behavior. A well-established behavior will require aversive consequences of greater intensity or amount for inhibition than would a behavior of low strength.

11. *When using a punishment procedure, care must be exercised to insure that the consequences are in fact unpleasant to the child.* Those consequences which the teacher or parent may view as punishing may not be so to the child. A verbal reprimand or threat may actually serve a reinforcing function and strengthen that behavior which produces it. Sending the child out of the classroom may actually be reinforcing as aspects of the room environment (teacher, activities, groups) are unpleasant to the child. He finds that being out of the room is more pleasant than being in the room. Of course, in such cases, being out of the room may be the lesser of two evils. Being out of the room may be unpleasant, but not as much as being in the room.

12. *The unpleasantness of the aversive consequences must be stronger than the positive consequences associated with the undesired behavior.* It is not infrequent for a teacher or parent to exclaim, "I can't understand it. He keeps on fighting with Joe even though he is punished every time." Apparently the reinforcing consequences associated with the fighting behavior have a maintaining effect which is greater than the suppressive effects of the punishment. In such cases, it is foolish to continue punishing the child. Other tactics should be added including reduction or removal of these reinforcing events along with strengthening alternative behaviors.

13. *After the punishment rule has been presented to the child, routine use of a threat or warning that his behavior will produce unpleasant consequences if he does not stop (or following the next time the inappropriate behavior occurs) is to be discouraged.* Nagging and punishment when the teacher is emotionally upset are likely to result in harsh or inappropriate punishment. Such behaviors as "Stop that or I'll send you out of the room," "John, sit down this instant or you will not listen to the music" are inappropriate. These demands, intended to inhibit these behaviors, may actually facilitate them. Also, if the child is warned, or threatened, he may learn that his behavior will result in punishment only after the warning and not at times when no warning is provided. On the other hand, it may be helpful on occasions in which the likelihood is great that he will engage in inappropriate behavior that the teacher remind the child of the appropriate behavior before he responds, and of the consequences of inappropriate behavior: "Sue, remember to finish your work," "John, you have almost finished your peas. After you finish we shall have dessert," "Tim, remember to remain in your chair until we have finished."

14. *When reprimand is used as a punishment procedure with a child, it should be presented so that it does not attract the attention of other children.* Studies by O'Leary and Becker

(1968) and by O'Leary, Kaufman, Kass, and Drabman (1970) suggest that a loud reprimand directed toward a single child which could be heard by the other children in the group will have less effect on reducing the strength of disruptive behavior than when the reprimand is presented in a soft manner heard only by the child being punished. It is possible that the loud reprimand provides the disruptive child with peer attention which merely seems to further strengthen the disruptive behavior. A loud reprimand would also serve to distract other children from their work activities.

A soft, rather than a loud, procedure of reprimanding children in selected instances could also be justified from the position that punishment should be a private matter between the teacher and the specific child. Presenting a reprimand which is heard only by the child whose behavior is inappropriate informs him of the undesired behavior and of the disappointment of the teacher in relation to this specific behavior. It avoids placing the child in an embarrassing or demeaning position in the eyes of his peers as is possible when the teacher's reprimand is heard by other peers in the class.

CHAPTER 7

Influencing Emotional Behavior

A child learns to be anxious, fearful, happy, sad, and to engage in a variety of other specific and general emotional and attitudinal behavior patterns. The emotional behaviors of the young child with learning and behavior difficulties are influenced by the teacher and others in the school setting even though they may be quite unaware of *what* specifically is being influenced or even *how* emotional behavior is influenced. The basic rules which may be used in an educational program of influencing the strength of emotional behaviors will be described and illustrated.

The behavior management program designed for each child should reflect a keen sensitivity to the child and his specific emotional characteristics. A child's learning difficulties can be reduced in many instances by careful attention to the manner in which competing disruptive emotional behavior may be controlled or eliminated. Children with developmental difficulties frequently experience considerable problems in emotional expression and control. They may respond emotionally too frequently and intensely to many aspects of their school environment. Other children are apt to be emotionally bland and to show an insufficient amount and variety of emotional responsiveness. These characteristics interfere with the acquisition of new cognitive and social behaviors which help the child to avoid experiences which will result in even more undesirable emotional behaviors.

But the child can acquire more appropriate and enhancing patterns of emotional responsiveness. He can do so by being exposed to an emotionally expressive teacher and provided with carefully designed program experiences which produce plentiful sources of positive reinforcement. Social experiences in a structured environment that insures successful interpersonal contacts and systematically reduces the negative emotional impact of previous frightening and unpleasant consequences will reduce the general adjustment difficulties of young children with developmental problems. A child who is able to approach and interact with his school environment in a relaxed and trusting manner is a child who is free to learn and to be enthusiastic about learning. These general response patterns result from numerous experiences which provide consistent and predictable positive consequences.

UNLEARNED EMOTIONAL RESPONSES

At a basic level certain stimulus events presented to the child automatically produce various emotional reactions. These reactions are unlearned or reflexive. These occur naturally without the benefit of previous learning experiences whenever certain stimulus events are presented. A diaper pin sticking the child, wet diapers, hunger, thirst, extremes in temperature, and intense light or noise produce certain reflexive motor and other muscular and glandular *respondent* or *emotional* behaviors. Whenever these stimulus conditions are present, the child is described as feeling uncomfortable, being unhappy, or as being distressed or in pain. These are events which the child dislikes and which he avoids if possible. The infant has only a few reflexive behaviors which serve to remove these painful events. The child soon learns many behaviors which remove or avoid these events which result in unpleasant emotional or feeling states.

Other events presented to the child produce emotional conditions of relaxation or pleasure. Providing food to the hungry child, liquid to the thirsty child, warmth to the child who is cold; physical stroking (cuddling), removing physical irritants (for example, wet diapers)—these actions produce feelings of pleasure, delight, or satisfaction. The child likes these events and behaves in whatever manner will produce them.

Thus there are primary events which when presented or removed will produce or coincide with various primitive or basic emotional conditions. These emotional states may be described as variations of feelings of pleasure or delight and of pain or distress.

BASIC RULE OF EMOTIONAL (RESPONDENT) LEARNING

As the child gains new experiences interacting with his physical and social environments, two important changes in his emotional

169

responsiveness occur. First, the rather undifferentiated emotional reactions of distress and delight elaborate into a range of other reactions such as joy, anxiety, affection, glee, disgust, guilt, happiness, jealousy, anger, and sadness.

Second, a number of events other than the initial primary ones will come to influence the occurrence of these emotional reactions. A mother's smile can result in positive feelings for the child. The sight of a dog can cause the child to be fearful. The child can become anxious when he is left by mother. He may become gleefully excited when he is promised a new toy. These new associations between events in the child's environment and emotional behaviors are developed through a process of emotional (respondent) conditioning or learning. The basic rule of emotional learning is:

> When a neutral event is paired frequently with any other event which produces an emotional reaction, this neutral event presented alone will begin to produce the emotional response.

The procedure to follow in applying this rule would be to:

Step 1.   Identify an event that produces an emotional response.
Step 2.   Identify a neutral event which should produce this emotional response.
Step 3.   Arrange for the simultaneous occurrence (pairing) of these two events on a number of occasions. As a result of these pairings the neutral stimulus when presented alone will begin to produce the emotional response.

An event is viewed as neutral if prior to learning it does not produce the emotional reaction which it later comes to influence. This neutral event may be any aspect of the child's experience: words, sounds, a classroom setting, a person, tone of a person's voice, or an activity such as listening to music or coloring with water colors.

A mother's smile and her soothing tone of voice, when presented while the child is enjoying his food or his warm bath water, will soon begin to influence the comforting emotional feelings of pleasure, relaxation, or delight. In this instance the food or warm water represents an unlearned or *unconditioned stimulus event* (US). The emotional state of relaxation or delight represents the unlearned or *unconditioned response*. After a number of temporal associations of unconditioned and neutral events during which learning occurs, the neutral events of mother's smile and tone of voice will begin to produce the positive feelings; these become *conditioned or learned stimulus events* (CS). This conditioning process is depicted here.

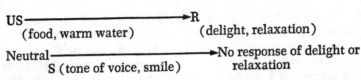

US————————————————————►R
  (food, warm water)   (delight, relaxation)

Neutral—————————————————►No response of delight or
        S (tone of voice, smile)   relaxation

After numerous pairings of the unconditioned events with the neutral events, learning occurs and the neutral events become conditioned events. The conditioned stimuli when presented alone as depicted below produce emotional responses (called *conditioned responses*) that are similar to the original *unconditioned responses:*

CS————————————————————►R
  (tone of voice, smile)   (delight, relaxation)

In this manner various emotional responses may become attached to a wide range of preceding stimulus events.

A mother who frowns at her child, yells "No" and "Bad boy" as she slaps his hand will soon find that the frown alone, or the frown and "No" or "Bad" will produce the uncomfortable and disruptive emotional reactions produced initially only by the hand slap. In this instance of learning, the slap represents the unconditioned stimulus (US/slap) which produced the unconditioned emotional reaction of distress (R/distress). The frown, "No" and "Bad," all neutral stimuli initially, after a number of pairings with the slap, become conditioned events (CS/No, Bad) which produce the conditioned emotional reaction of distress (R/distress) in the absence of the slap.

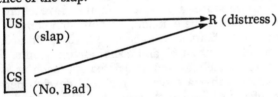

US ———————————————►R (distress)
  (slap)

CS
  (No, Bad)

The critical factor in the learning is the temporal pairing of the US and the previously neutral events. After a few such pairings the neutral events become conditioned stimulus events. Again, any neutral cue which is present at the time the child engages in an emotional reaction may come to produce that reaction. The conditioned emotional response is highly similar to the initial unconditioned emotional reaction.

This basic rule of emotional learning underlies the development of the specific and generalized emotional patterns of young children. A teacher who shows disappointment with, reprimands, or otherwise frequently punishes the children in her class will become a conditioned cue for fear and related negative emotional reactions in her children. In fact, many of the specific cues present as she punishes the children may come to produce the disruptive emotional reactions. These include such events as the teacher's voice quality and tone, the type of clothes that she wears, the classroom activities occurring as punishment is provided, and the time of day.

If the child consistently has difficulty with specific types of assignments, for example, these tasks can become conditioned cues for negative emotional reactions. He begins to dislike these tasks. Behaviors which will either avoid these or which will remove these once presented to him will be strengthened through negative reinforcement. In extreme cases, the entire physical characteristics of the classroom environment can become conditioned stimuli for such conditioned emotional responses as fear, anxiety and distress. The child will become uncomfortable whenever in the classroom and will strive to get away from it whenever possible.

In like manner, the teacher who is calm, relaxed, and who reinforces children with positive events will come to produce desirable emotional reactions in children. They will feel good about being with the teacher, about being in school, and about engaging in the variety of activities which the teacher presents to them. Those events which are present on numerous occasions at the time positive reinforcers are presented to the child, while initially neutral, will become conditioned events which will produce positive emotional reactions.

In summary, cues which are associated a number of times with events which produce a type of emotional reaction will gradually begin to produce the emotion. A child can come to like or dislike, to enjoy or be fearful of, to become involved in or avoid numerous aspects of his physical and social environments. The specific combination of feelings and associated approach or avoidance behavior patterns that a specific child will develop depends upon the nature of the emotional experiences which become associated with various people, places, things, and activities.

> **Neutral events come to control emotional reactions, both pleasant and unpleasant, after being associated on numerous occasions with other events which produce those reactions.**

CONDITIONED EVENTS AS SECONDARY REINFORCING AND AVERSIVE EVENTS

Secondary Reinforcing Events

The basic rule of emotional learning can be recognized as the rule which was described in Chapter 4 in the discussion of the procedure for developing secondary reinforcing events (p. 65). It becomes apparent that conditioned events for positive emotional responses also become secondary reinforcing events. As such these events act both to produce positive emotional reactions and to reinforce or strengthen any immediately preceding operant behavior. Every time a secondary reinforcer is presented to a child, it not only strengthens the preceding behavior but also produces a positive emotional reaction. Emotional learning occurs since any new event which is present at the time of the positive emotional response may become a new conditioned stimulus for this reaction. Thus, the child reports that he feels good about or likes those of his activities which produce or provide positive reinforcers. The child may be described as demonstrating positive attitudes in relation to specific activities or toward a wide range of related activities. This is a reflection of his experiences with these activities, the resulting positive reinforcers provided, and the related positive emotional reactions which are produced by these positive reinforcing events. The mere anticipation of activities and events can produce positive emotional reactions of enthusiasm and delight which facilitate the child's approach and involvement in these experiences.

> Secondary reinforcers serve as conditioned cues which produce positive emotional reactions.

Secondary Aversive Events

The basic rule of emotional learning is the same as that described in Chapter 5 (p. 111) as involved in the development of secondary aversive events. Those events which acquire aversive qualities through learning are conditioned events for negative emotional responses. As such these events act both to produce negative emotional reactions and to influence operant behavior through negative reinforcement and punishment. The child reports a dislike for these events and engages in whatever behavior will reduce, terminate, or avoid these events. A child may become upset just by thinking about or hearing about a future activity, place, person, or event. The symbolic representation of the future experience is a conditioned event for negative emotional reactions. The child can become quite upset even before he is confronted directly with an unpleasant situation.

> **Aversive events serve as conditioned cues which produce negative emotional reactions.**

HIGHER-ORDER CONDITIONING

As implied in the preceding discussion of the basic rule of emotional learning, neutral events which are paired with well-established conditioned events may also gain influence over emotional reactions. Emotional responses can be controlled by neutral events which are associated with conditioned stimulus events. This represents the rule of *higher-order conditioning* of emotional responses. A child may receive attention and praise from the teacher when he correctly identifies the primary colors. Assuming that praise is a conditioned cue which produces a positive emotional response, the activity of successful color identification can become a conditioned event for a positive emotional response. After a number of associations the child may appear to be pleased or satisfied with his successful color identification, even when the teacher is not present or when she does not provide praise. Attending to the teacher as she presents a language lesson may be a pleasurable activity for a child as this attending behavior has been previously associated with other events which produce positive emotional reactions.

The same rule of higher-order conditioning is involved in the development of more general emotional and attitudinal behavior patterns. A child who has been reinforced positively on numerous occasions for a range of different activities may acquire a general pattern of being pleased or satisfied with being involved in or with successfully completing activities or tasks. He may be described as having a positive attitude toward work, and may develop what has been called achievement motivation. Aspects of initiating activities, persisting at activities, solving difficult tasks, and task completion have become conditioned events for positive emotional reactions. These events have acquired secondary reinforcing qualities through numerous previous associations with other positive consequences.

Just as numerous aspects of the child's environment may become conditioned events for positive emotional reactions, other events may also come through higher-order conditioning to control negative emotionality. Due to visual-perceptual and related eye-hand coordination difficulties, Sue Ellen may experience considerable problems with such relatively simple nursery tasks as stringing beads, coloring, and cutting. The teacher, believing that the child can learn if she would exert sufficient effort and patience, requires Sue to remain with these tasks even after she becomes highly frustrated. The child often becomes highly disorganized and even begins to cry on occasion. The teacher becomes a conditioned event for negative emotionality. The child begins to show a dislike for other activities with which the teacher is associated. These activities become conditioned events for negative emotional reactions through higher-order conditioning.

If the child is unsuccessful in most of his school activities, many cues in the school environment can become conditioned events for negative emotionality. The child will become generally unhappy or perhaps even fearful over many of his experiences.

WHAT INFLUENCES THE INTENSITY OF LEARNED EMOTIONALITY

Intense emotional responses can become conditioned to new stimulus events in a single or small number of associations. The more intense the initial stimulus event the more intense the emotional reaction. A minor frightening experience will produce a mild emotional reaction. A frightening traumatic experience will produce a strong and intense emotional reaction. Conditioned stimuli associated with these will influence similar reactions.

> *The more intense the emotional reaction, the fewer the number of pairings required for the development of a new conditioned cue which will produce the emotional reaction.*

A dog may attack a child and produce intense fearfulness in the child. In the future, the sight of the dog and his bark serve as conditioned events which will provide intense emotionality. If the dog had created only mild apprehension, a larger number of such experiences with the dog would have been required before the dog would have become a reliable conditioned cue which consistently produced the mild apprehension.

In the same manner, a conditioned event which has been associated with events which produce highly intense positive and satisfying emotional reactions will come to influence similar highly positive emotional reactions after a few associations. A teacher who becomes associated with events which produce only mild positive emotional reactions will become, after a larger number of associations, a conditioned event for similar mild emotional responses.

> The larger the number of associations between an emotionally provoking event and an initial neutral event, the stronger the relationship becomes between the new conditioned event and the emotional response.

A teacher who reinforces a child on numerous occasions will become a strong conditioned cue for positive emotional reactions. The teacher who only infrequently provides reinforcing events will become a less reliable conditioned cue for positive emotional reactions. However, the number of associations does interact with the intensity of the emotional reaction to determine the actual strength of a conditioned stimulus at any given time. This suggests that a conditioned stimulus which has been associated with a large number of events producing intense emotional reactions will persist in its influence over the emotional behavior longer than will a conditioned event which has been paired less frequently with an emotional reaction of equal intensity.

GENERALIZATION OF CONTROLLING EVENTS

> Emotional reactions can be controlled by new cues which have never been associated directly with the occurrence of these reactions.

In this case of *stimulus generalization*, cues which are most similar to other events which do influence emotional responses are more likely to become conditioned events than are less similar events. The child on the first day of school may be fearful of the teacher simply because she is a strange adult. The child's previous experiences with strange adults have been unpleasant ones on numerous occasions. The teacher as a strange adult is a conditioned cue for a fearful emotional reaction.

Vernon (1972) reports an experience with a young girl who would not talk in the presence of her teachers even though she talked freely with her peers and with family members. A careful exploration of the child's school experiences failed to identify any negative emotional incidents which might account for this highly selective mutism. It was speculated, after examination of the child's previous home experiences, that generalization had occurred from an authoritative and dominating father to the teachers. The child had experienced considerable negative emotionality as a result of the father's rather harsh reprimanding tactics in relation to the child's speech. The teachers, with their rules, admonitions, and directions, behaved in a "father-type" manner. Thus the teacher, through stimulus generalization, produced negative emotionality in the child. The child was able to avoid being reprimanded by not talking to teachers.

A teacher may attempt to use a time-out procedure to control six-year-old Steve's disruptive behavior. The only space available to her in implementing this mildly aversive procedure is a small poorly-lighted observation booth which is attached to the classroom. Examination of his case file revealed that his foster parent had used corporal punishment following noncompliance and then would require him to sit in a small dark closet until he stopped crying. His intense negative emotionality associated with the closet generalized to the observation booth.

In a similar manner, involvement in a new task at school may produce negative emotionality because involvement with other new tasks at home and at school has resulted frequently in unpleasant consequences. The cues associated with initiating the new task, due to similarity to previous tasks, influence negative emotional reactions. The child may eventually develop a general attitude of disinterest or apathy. He refrains from entering into new tasks. Or, if forced to become involved, he may react in a most active and emotionally disruptive manner. Again, these behavior patterns may occur in a new situation in which the child has had no previous experience.

This rule concerning generalization of stimulus events which control emotionality may explain many baffling and apparently inexplicable emotional reactions: "I don't know why he doesn't like me. I've never been harsh to him," or "His intense emotional outburst after I reprimanded him is a mystery to me. I think this is the first time I have ever criticized him."

There also may be generalization across stimulus events which influence positive emotionality. A child may be enjoying a positive emotional relationship with his parents at the time of entrance into a developmental education program. The teacher and aide, whom the child has never met, may well be strong conditioned events for positive emotional reactions. In like manner, a child who begins to enjoy play and other school activities as a

177

result of consistent pleasant consequences is more likely to enjoy other similar situations or activities. The wider the range of positive experiences which result in the development of more conditioned events for positive emotionality, the greater the possibility of generalization to new situations. It is true also that the reduction in negative emotionality associated with a person, situation, or event frequently results in a discernible reduction in negative emotionality influenced by other similar events. A child may fear adults because of experiences with a harsh father. A reduction in the fearfulness associated with father as a result of a series of positive experiences with him may in turn result in a reduction in fearfulness toward other adults.

This rule concerning the generalization across events which influences emotional behavior emphasizes that no emotional experience can be viewed as an isolated incident. Any experience provided a child has a potentially broader effect on his behavior development and functioning.

REDUCING UNDESIRED EMOTIONAL BEHAVIOR

It has been suggested that a child may learn to be apprehensive, fearful, anxious, or sad in many situations due to previous associations of these situations with unpleasant experiences. The more intense and frequent the associations with unpleasant experiences, the greater the likelihood that the child will engage in excessive emotional behavior which disrupts and interferes with appropriate learning and with enjoyable social interactions. The basic rule which underlies the elimination of the influence which conditioned events have over these negative emotional responses is:

> *Repeated presentation of the Conditioned Stimulus which controls emotionality without pairing it with the Unconditioned Stimulus, or with the conditioned event in higher–order conditioning, will result in the gradual reduction and eventual elimination of the effectiveness of the conditioned stimulus in producing the emotional behavior.*

The conditioned stimulus thus loses its influence over the emotional behavior. This procedure is called *extinction*. The particular stimulus events, of course, can regain control over the emotional behavior through future additional pairings with the unconditioned stimulus or with one which serves as such in higher order conditioning.

The number of experiences required for extinction generally depends upon the level of previous learning. The more frequent and the more intense the previous pairings of unconditioned and conditioned events, the slower the rate of extinction. A teacher who has punished a child in a mild manner only a limited number of times will soon cease to create negative emotionality once she no longer punishes the child as she interacts with him. On the other hand, a school environment that contains strong conditioned cues for apprehension and anxiety will continue to produce these emotional reactions for an extended period of time even though no new negative consequences are presented.

The mere passage of time does not result in a reduction of the influence which conditioned events have over emotional reactions. The child may bring a fear reaction or a more general reaction of depression into the school setting even though these were learned some weeks or months prior to his enrollment in school. At an earlier time the fear may have been a realistic one attached to a potentially dangerous situation. The danger may, however, no longer exist. A conditioned event nonetheless may maintain its influence over the fear reaction for extended periods of time until new learning occurs. The teacher cannot assume "Oh, he'll get over it. Just give him time." The child must receive new experiences in the presence of the conditioned or similar events in which aversive consequences are no longer provided. This emphasizes the need for an active and systematic behavior management approach to influencing emotional behavior.

FACILITATING EXTINCTION OF UNDESIRED EMOTIONALITY

In addition to using an extinction procedure, excessive undesired emotionality may be reduced by exposing the child to situations which are likely to produce contrasting and incompatible emotional reactions. This procedure of *counterconditioning* may be used to speed up the elimination of conditioned stimulus control of undesirable emotional behavior. This procedure involves both the presentation of the conditioned stimulus in the absence of further pairing with other aversive events (an extinction procedure) and the added feature of presenting other stimulus events which produce more favorable emotional reactions. It emphasizes the presentation of events which produce uncomfortable emotional responses on those occasions in which the child is likely to be relaxed, comfortable, or otherwise experiencing positive feelings. These positive emotional reactions compete with the negative ones. A child cannot be relaxed and anxious or happy and sad at the same time.

A teacher who produces negative emotionality in a child may refrain from punishing the child who is fearful of her and at the same time may provide him with numerous positive reinforcers which produce pleasant emotional reactions. She interacts with him when he is eating, playing, enjoying music, resting, or otherwise having fun. After a number of such pairings, the teacher may lose her fear-provoking qualities and eventually will come to influence positive emotional responses. Under these new conditions the child may begin to like the teacher as she becomes a positive conditioned reinforcer.

If a child is afraid of pets due to previous negative experiences with dogs and cats, a rabbit may be introduced in the classroom during times when the child is relaxed and happy. This exposure should be quite gradual and every effort made to insure that the child is relaxed during the introduction of the pet. After a number of such exposures, the fear response to the rabbit will be reduced.

> Excessive fear* reactions may be reduced by exposing the child to the fear object at times when he is experiencing positive emotionality.

INFLUENCING EMOTIONAL BEHAVIOR THROUGH OBSERVATION OF OTHERS

Acquiring New Emotional Responses

> *"Scott is just like his mother. He's afraid of many things. I don't know why he gets so emotional. He has never had bad experiences that I know of." "We have trouble getting Jackie to ride the bus. She is just as afraid of riding the bus as is her mother. I don't know why she's afraid. Jackie has never been in a bus until she enrolled in school and she hasn't had any bad experiences on the bus."*

These and similar comments suggest that emotional reactions may be acquired without direct, emotionally arousing experiences. This learning may result from the child's emotional arousal as he observes others engaging in emotional behaviors. A parent who expresses a fear of darkness, of strangers, of bugs, or

---

* Other negative emotional reactions such as disgust, anxiety, discomfort, guilt, and apprehension may be substituted for fear. The rule remains the same.

thunderstorms, or who demonstrates obvious distaste for certain foods, people, clothing, or music is likely to instill similar fears and dislikes in her young child who on numerous occasions observes these emotional reactions.

Children may learn a wide range of positive and negative emotional behaviors if exposed to other people engaging in these behaviors in the presence of specific events. The basic rule of emotional learning accounts for this learning. The person being observed by the child engages in an emotional response which in turn arouses a similar emotional reaction in the child. Any stimulus events temporally associated with this arousal become conditioned events which, after a few associations, will begin to produce the emotional reaction. This learning occurs in the following pattern:

Step 1.   Child observes someone (peer, sibling, teacher, parent) engage in some emotional behavior.
Step 2.   The child becomes emotionally aroused as a result of this observation.
Step 3.   Neutral cues are temporally associated with the child's emotional arousal.
Step 4.   These neutral cues, after a few pairings, become conditioned events which produce the emotional arousal.

In such observational learning of emotional reactions, faster learning occurs in an observer who is intensely aroused. In addition, the larger the number of observations and subsequent emotional arousals the greater the strength of the conditioned emotional reaction.

Reduction of Emotional Behaviors

It is true also that emotional reactions to specific events can be reduced or eliminated through observational learning. Fears or other negative emotions may be extinguished by having a child observe others demonstrating positive emotional reactions in the presence of events which produce negative emotions.

The steps involved in using this rule to influence the reduction or elimination of emotional behavior are:

Step 1.   Identify conditioned events which produce negative emotionality in the child who is the observer.
Step 2.   Identify a model for which these events do not produce negative emotionality and toward which the model could behave in a positive manner.
Step 3.   Arrange for the model to approach and remain in the presence of the conditioned events.
Step 4.   Arrange for the child to observe the model interacting in a positive manner with the fear provoking event.

Step 5.   Repeat this observation on a number of occasions. The conditioned event will gradually lose its influence in producing the negative emotional reaction.

In using this procedure, steps must be taken to insure that the child actually observes the model approaching and remaining in the presence of the feared object. If the observation is too unpleasant, the child may quickly turn his attention to other aspects of his environment. Also, if the fear object produces an intense emotional reaction the child may become highly aroused as he observes a model interacting with the fear object. Under this condition, the fear response would not be reduced. In this case, the model should gradually approach the feared object. Each successive exposure will progressively approximate a natural presentation of the feared event. In each step, the model should display positive affect and related approach behavior in his interaction with the feared cues. If any apprehension is displayed by the model, even so mild, this will interfere with the extinction process.

The extinction process can be enhanced by using a model that the child views as a friend, someone he likes, has confidence in, and is likely to imitate. If the model is a stranger or differs greatly from the observer's own characteristics, the observer is less likely to be influenced by what he sees.

Bandura and his associates (1967; 1968) provide examples of the use of modeling procedures in successfully reducing the fear reactions which a group of young children exhibited toward dogs. These children observed a fearless peer model exhibit progressively more fear-provoking interactions with a dog. The physical restraint of the dog, the closeness and amount of contact with the dog, and the duration of interaction between the model and dog were varied. All of the model's experience with the dog was pleasant and fun-like in nature. Some children observed several different girls and boys of varying ages interacting positively with many dogs. The size and fearsomeness of the dogs increased with each successive observation experience. Exposure to either types of modeled experiences resulted in a significant reduction in the fear of dogs exhibited initially by the observer. Children, after observation of peers approaching and playing with dogs, were able to engage in this behavior themselves.

GENERALIZED EMOTIONAL CONDITIONS

Various patterns of emotional reactions, which may be called emotional states or moods, are of interest as these reactions serve as discriminative events and render more likely the occurrence of certain subsequent behaviors. A child who is angry is less likely to engage in cooperative and productive behaviors than would be true at other times when he was not so aroused. In contrast, a child who is smiling, relaxed, or otherwise in a positive emotional state is more likely to engage in behaviors of cooperation, concentration, or even persistence in the face of difficulty. The effective behavior management teacher will attempt to influence these positive emotional states.

It is not unusual for young children with learning and behavior problems to be described as "being in a bad mood," "being grouchy," or "down in the dumps." These descriptions imply that the child's emotional state influences his responsiveness to a variety of aspects of his environment. The teacher will find it necessary to attempt to identify and control the aspects of the child's world which produce such states. At the same time, she will attempt to counterbalance these by presenting other events which will produce a more appropriate emotional state. Verbal instructions, encouragement, charm, "turning on her own personality," and reminding the children of future positive consequences may all be used to create a more pleasant emotional mood in young children. "Let's settle down now and finish so that we can listen to our favorite record." "Let's all listen carefully and I shall tell a funny story before we begin our work today." "Remember that game of who can laugh the loudest? Let's see who can smile and laugh like Santa Claus. John, you go first." These tactics may set the stage for a relaxed emotional state and subsequent periods of concentrated productivity.

DEVELOPMENT AND ELIMINATION OF AVOIDANCE BEHAVIOR

A child learns to escape or to avoid unpleasant events. If a situation, activity, or person is one which the teacher wishes the child to avoid, she should pair it with stimulus events which produce negative emotionality. After sufficient temporal pairings, this event will become a conditioned aversive event which influences negative emotionality. Recall also that this same event will become a discriminative event for avoidance behavior. By escaping and staying away from these aversive events the child is able to remove the unpleasant emotionality. The avoidance behavior is reinforced negatively through this removal.

In this manner words and other symbols can acquire aversive characteristics and control certain behaviors. Words such as

"No," "Danger," and "Hot" become aversive events through an emotional conditioning procedure and result in those behaviors that will remove them from the child's immediate experience.

The teacher of children with learning and behavior difficulties will discover many patterns of avoidance behavior which she wishes to eliminate. As there are many conditioned aversive events associated with school activities, an excessive amount of the child's behavior is of an avoidance nature. The behavior management program must focus on the reduction of this non-adaptive avoidance behavior.

An example of avoidance behavior in a child will illustrate its development and possible procedures for its elimination. Kim, a moderately retarded child with severe visual difficulties, has begun to avoid other children in the classroom and prefers to play alone. When encouraged by the teacher to join her classmates in any type of activity, Kim displays an obvious negative emotional reaction. At times, when the teacher pressures her too much, she begins to cry and will run into the corner and hide her face in her lap.

Although the teacher was unable to provide any background information on the types of negative experiences that resulted in this fear and related avoidance behavior pattern, observation of Kim in the classroom does suggest that close proximity and the possibility of interaction with her peers have become aversive events which control negative emotionality. Being close to other children is a discriminative cue for avoidance behavior. This avoidance behavior apparently had been strengthened as it resulted in the removal of the aversive cues and related negative emotionality.

As the aversiveness associated with the presence of other children controls the avoidance behavior, the behavior management strategy which may be used with Kim would consist of: (1) a counterconditioning procedure to eliminate the aversive components of peers, and (2) a positive reinforcement procedure to strengthen appropriate peer interaction. Peers would be associated with the presentation of numerous events which produce positive emotional responses in Kim. Additionally, Kim would be guided through a graduated and increasingly complex series of contacts with peers and provided high preference reinforcing events for any improvement in social interaction behaviors.

School phobias and related generalized withdrawal patterns may be viewed as avoidance reactions. Aspects of a general setting acquire aversive qualities which in turn produce escape and avoidance behavior. Patterson and Brodsky (1966) describe a successful behavior management program used to eliminate the intense fear reaction and related tantrum behavior exhibited by a five-year-old boy when his mother attempted to leave him at school. Various modeling and counterconditioning procedures were used to decrease the negative emotionality associated with being separated from the mother. Additionally, tangible and social reinforcers were provided for approaching and interacting with the school environment. The extensive avoidance behavior pattern diminished as the fear associated with separation from mother was eliminated and as aspects of the school environment (teacher, peers, activities) became stronger conditioned stimuli for positive emotionality.

A final example of a behavior management program designed to deal with a general avoidance pattern of behavior will be described in greater detail as it provides illustration of the combined use of a number of different procedures. The program was developed by Ross and her associates (1971) for a six-year-old boy enrolled in a preschool program whose entry into public school had been delayed because he exhibited extreme social withdrawal from peers. He would avoid looking at other children, withdrew from any possible physical proximity or tactual contact, ducked his head or turned away when a peer initiated verbal contact, abruptly left a solitary activity upon arrival of a peer, would run away when an adult advocated social interaction with peers, and would hide during large-group social interaction. When forced by peers into close physical proximity he exhibited intense fearfulness.

The behavior management program which was provided consisted of the following:

1. Initially, a male teacher whom the boy had not met established himself as a conditioned event for positive emotional responses. He rewarded the child with a variety of tangible and social reinforcers for imitating many of his behaviors. This was done to insure that the child would become emotionally attached to the teacher. The teacher became an important source of secondary reinforcement and produced considerable positive emotionality in the child. The teacher could then require various behaviors from the child and could reinforce these with his approval and praise. A female adult was introduced and the child began to interact with this adult.

2. After the male teacher had established a good relationship with the child, a series of experiences was designed to eliminate the child's fear and avoidance behavior and to teach him social interaction, motor, and general game skills. Initially, the child was exposed to interactions between the teacher and other children. This was designed to permit the child to observe approach and interaction behaviors which produced no negative

consequences. The child hid his face in his hands and even cried on several occasions. When this happened the adult would describe the interaction to the child.

3. The child was given short presentations of pictures, stories, and movies. This allowed the teacher and the female adult to discuss aspects of the presentations while the child was present and to emphasize the reward value of young children.

4. The teacher, while the child was present, showed extreme reluctance about peer interactions and would ask the female adult specific and somewhat fearful questions. This allowed her to provide reassurance to the teacher about approach and interaction behavior. The boy was not drawn into these discussions. The purpose of this experience was to expose him to specific reassurances in the absence of fearful reactions.

5. The adults demonstrated appropriate social behavior within the context of prearranged arguments about humorous social interactions. The boy was drawn into these arguments to assist the teacher to win the argument with the other adult.

6. The teacher engaged in social interaction with other children with the boy accompanying him. The boy initially assisted the teacher by carrying materials. Gradually, he entered into more direct and active interactions. The teacher remained close by to ensure success for the boy.

7. The adults provided the boy with practice in general game skills, tricks, rituals, slang and other behaviors which would facilitate the boy's effective interaction in a peer group.

8. Finally, the boy was taken to a park area separate from the school and sent into a group of children (strangers) while one of the adults remained at a distance. He was gradually encouraged to engage in longer and closer social interactions. These experiences formed the basis for other role-playing and modeling sessions to give the child additional reinforced practice at social interaction.

The results of these modeling procedures with guided participation were highly positive. The boy was able to interact with his peer group without undue fear or avoidance. These newly acquired behaviors were maintained and generalized to other settings. In a two-month follow up in

> . . . playground settings that differed markedly from the protected preschool setting, the boy was able to join ongoing play groups, initiate verbal contacts, and sustain effective social interactions, all with children who were complete strangers to him. Furthermore, the boy accomplished these tasks competently, unhesitatingly, with obvious pleasure, and with no adult intervention whatsoever. (p. 277)

EMOTIONAL CHARACTERISTICS OF CHILDREN
WITH LEARNING AND BEHAVIOR PROBLEMS

In planning educational experiences for children with learning and behavior difficulties, the following events should be considered. These children have experienced numerous failures, and in many instances they have not developed the behavioral skills that produce positive consequences. They also have developed inappropriate behavioral characteristics that create an excessive number of negative consequences. As a result, in comparison with the child without a history of excessive failure:

1. *There are fewer conditioned stimulus events in the child's environment which produce positive emotional reactions.* The child has had fewer experiences being successful and reinforced with a range of tangible and social reinforcers. As a result less emotional learning involving positive feelings has occurred. There are fewer things that he likes, has fun with, approaches, or that make him feel good.

2. *There are more conditioned stimulus events in the child's environment which produce negative emotionality.* Many of these events are associated with typical school routine. Being asked to participate in certain activities may be a cue for considerable emotional discomfort. He is more likely to be in a bad mood and to object to advances made by others to get him involved.

3. *There is greater likelihood that the child will engage in intense and disorganizing episodes of negative emotionality.* There is also increased likelihood that the child will engage in episodes of aggressive behaviors. This may reflect a natural frustration reaction to being placed in a situation which produces extremely unpleasant emotions, and not being able to escape from it. The child may strike out in a blind or disorganized fashion. These behavioral reactions are more likely to occur among children with learning and behavior difficulties as more aspects of their environment produce unpleasant emotionality from which the child is unable to escape or avoid.

4. *The usual events which produce positive emotional responses in most children, or which are neutral, may in fact become cues for negative emotional reactions.* The teacher's smile or a display of affection would be a positive reinforcer for most children and would result in positive feelings on the part of the child. Some studies of children with behavior difficulties suggest, however, that such social stimulation may have a negative effect on some children. Thus the teacher who smiles at a child in expectation that such would be pleasing to him may be disappointed. She may find that the smile for some children is an aversive event

which produces a negative emotional response of anxiety or apprehension. The smile, in this case, would produce avoidance behavior. The child would engage in those behaviors that would terminate and, if possible, avoid the teacher's smile. For other children, being in the presence of people may be a cue for apprehension. Engaging in solitary activity may be more enjoyable to another child. Being left at school by mother, a neutral event for most children, may produce intense anxiety and related panic behavior.

5. *Minor sources of irritation or frustration may produce unusually strong emotional reactions.* When confronted with a task which is difficult, the child may engage in temper outburst or may become excessively negativistic. When confronted with conflict or other sources of frustration or disappointment he is likely to overrespond. The child may be described as having a low frustration tolerance. Minor signs of rejection may produce a general inhibition of social interaction.

6. *There are fewer positive self-referents depicting emotional reactions.* The child is less likely to report such feelings as "I like myself," "I feel good," "I am happy," "I am excited," "I am pleased." Labels depicting adequacy and positive emotional states are seldom applied to children with developmental difficulties. Labels such as pretty, sweet, good, great, fast, strong, skillful, smart, and quick, which become conditioned events for positive emotional reactions for most children, fail to gain this influence with children who experience excessive failure in learning and social interaction situations. Positive self-referents which produce healthy emotional responses are typically absent.

7. *There are more negative self-referents depicting emotional reactions.* The child is more likely to report such feelings as "I don't like myself," "I hate myself," "I don't feel good." Labels which reflect inadequacy have been applied to him. Such terms as slow, ugly, bad, stupid, poor, crippled, damaged, dumb, and weak become part of the child's self-referents. These are typically conditioned cues for negative emotional reactions. The child may be described as having excessive feelings of inadequacy or as reflecting poor self-concept behaviors. These negative self-referents and related negative emotional reactions arise out of literally hundreds of previous failure experiences. These create even greater difficulty as they serve as discriminative stimuli for avoidance behavior. If the child reports, "I can't do that," "I don't want to," "I don't like that" in relation to many aspects of the school environment, he is highly unlikely to attempt interaction with the school environment.

8. *There are more negative and fewer positive referents toward others and things depicting emotional reactions.* The child

is likely to report such feelings as "I don't like that," "I hate you," "I'm afraid of that."

9. *The child may have a more limited range of emotional reactions or he may demonstrate difficulty in discriminating the appropriateness of various emotional reactions.* He may laugh or cry at the wrong time, he may become sad or happy in response to inappropriate events, or he may express fear of events which represent no real danger to him. In other cases, a child may not have developed the usual emotional caution over potentially harmful events and therefore does not develop adaptive defensive behavior. He does not seem to be able to anticipate danger or aversive situations. These events are not conditioned events for negative emotional reactions.

IMPLICATIONS FOR BEHAVIOR MANAGEMENT PROGRAMS

In view of the above described characteristics of many children with learning and behavior difficulties, the behavior management program must be sensitive to these unusual emotional reactions and to the events or situations which influence them. If a child balks at engaging in a desired task, the teacher must not assume that the child is being willfully negativistic or stubborn. Aspects of the task situation may well control negative emotional reactions which underlie the avoidance behavior. Active program efforts must be directed toward the reduction of these and toward the development of more appropriate emotional behaviors.

The behavior management program would involve the following:

1. *Developing new conditioned events for both negative and positive emotional reactions.*

2. *Increasing the consistency of appropriate emotional responding.* As an example, a child may like school and various activities one day and dislike it the next. Experiences which produce a more stable acceptance and enthusiasm of school would be provided for the child.

3. *Increasing the intensity or magnitude of specific emotional responses.* The child may display a minimal fear reaction toward strange animals, for example, but is not sufficiently wary to avoid approaching any animal that is in his presence. The child thus is in danger of being harmed by an aggressive animal. Another child may express some minimal pleasure over peer interaction but not sufficient for an obvious display of enjoying other children.

4. *Teaching the appropriateness of emotional reactions.* A child should learn to be a little wary of a teacher who is displaying anger but not of the same teacher, or of other adults with some similar characteristics, when she is not angry.

5. *Decreasing the intensity of some emotional reactions.* Children who overrespond to minor sources of frustration and other children who demonstrate intense negative emotional reactions to events or people which represent no actual danger should be provided with extinction and counterconditioning experiences. As these crippling reactions are reduced or eliminated, the child is better able to explore and learn about his environment.

6. *Decreasing the number of conditioned events which influence various emotional reactions.* A child may be fearful of numerous aspects of his school environment due to previous experiences outside the school environment. As a result of generalization, the child's negative emotional reactions are influenced by similar conditioned events present in the school setting. An active program of extinction and discrimination training will be required to eliminate many of the nonadaptive and unrealistic emotional reactions.

The behavior management program obviously must reflect the individual deficit and excessive emotional behavior patterns of each child. The previously discussed rules of emotional learning will lend direction to the general and specific experiences to be designed to influence these emotional behaviors.

Generally, a child can become emotionally comfortable and less likely to engage in disruptive emotional responsiveness in a program that is structured and predictable. A program with routine and well-defined limits provides the consistency which results in security (freedom from excessive fear or apprehension) and enjoyment. The child in this environment is able to be successful. He can develop generalized positive emotional patterns. He can learn to tolerate increasing amounts of frustration and social conflict without resorting to intense and disruptive emotional outbursts. As the child acquires a wider range of positive emotional reactions through the success which a highly structured program brings, he can then be exposed gradually to less and less structure. He can be taught to make decisions and to accept the consequences of these decisions. This can be done through demonstration by the teacher, by guided practice of the observed behaviors, and by joint participation with the teacher and peers in successful completion of numerous social and nonsocial problems.

In providing a program for influencing the emotional behaviors of children, it is essential that the teacher and other significant adults in the child's life consistently demonstrate those emotional behaviors which they wish the child to acquire. If the child is to learn to be relaxed, enthusiastic, or cheerful the teacher must consistently model these reactions. She should also provide children with many opportunities to practice various emotional behaviors and to label or describe them. This can be done through role-playing experiences or as the child reacts to various social interactions and other situations throughout the school day.

To employ a role-playing procedure, the teacher may introduce a game to the children which requires them to show how a child would feel in various situations. A puppet may be used to enhance the attention and participation of the children. The puppet would be described as being in situations which would result in his being sad, happy, apprehensive, pleasantly surprised, pleased, contented, angry, and the like. The children would be guided into acting-out the various feelings depicted and encouraged to describe their feelings.

The teacher should utilize any experiences throughout the day in teaching the child to engage in and to describe various feelings. A teacher may express satisfaction to a child for the task that the child has just completed. "I feel good because you finished the task. It's fun to do things. I'm glad you did it. I'm going to do one of those puzzles and you tell me how you feel." She then finishes the puzzle and guides the child into expressing satisfaction. The teacher next gives the child another puzzle and then guides him into expressing pleasure over his own accomplishment.

In a similar manner, the teacher can assist the child in talking about his feelings when he is angry, sad, unhappy, or disappointed. She can help him to identify the relationship between the emotional reactions and environmental events which produce them. She also will be able, when appropriate, to provide the child with alternative positive emotional experiences.

In conclusion, children with learning and behavior problems are quite likely to exhibit a variety of difficulties in emotional responsiveness. The behavior management program must analyze the emotional characteristics of each child and provide him with specific and systematic experiences to offset the difficulties and to teach him alternative positive emotional behaviors. Every experience in the school environment potentially will result in emotional learning. The sensitive teacher will utilize these events to contribute positively to the child's emotional competency.

PART III

Development of Behavior Management Programs

CHAPTER 8

Defining and Measuring
Behavior

The home and school environments are constantly attempting to influence behavior change in the young child with learning and behavior difficulties. The child is encouraged to acquire new skills, to improve upon skills he has, to use present skills in a more discriminating manner, to maintain these skills for extended periods of time, and to reduce or eliminate ways of behaving that are viewed as inappropriate. This chapter will focus on procedures for describing and measuring the strength of behavior; Chapters 9 and 10 will consider the development of acceptable program goals defined as behavioral objectives and will outline the step-by-step procedures to follow in developing specific programs.

IDENTIFYING THE PROBLEM

The initial step in devising a program of changing a child's behavior is to decide that a problem exists. In taking this step, the adult recognizes that the child does not behave as expected or desired in some area or areas. The problem may involve behavioral deficits, excessive behavior patterns, or a combination of these difficulties. Deficit behavior problems usually represent concern with how a new behavior can be taught or how one can strengthen and improve the form of a *developmental* skill such as dressing, speaking, attending, coloring, or making visual discriminations. Any developmental area may be the target of concern. The program focus may be on developing general classroom behaviors like sitting, attending, persisting, and general compliance with teacher request. The program may involve improvement of skills of social interaction, emotional expression, self-care, or abilities of a pre-academic nature such as recognition of letters, colors, forms, and reproducing visually presented patterns. The concern may be with teaching a more complex or higher level skill than that presently existing. A focus on deficit behaviors of a developmental nature implies that the child will be able to develop more complex behavior patterns or a new behavior pattern. He is ready to learn the next stage or level in a developmental sequence of skills.

A focus on an excessive behavior pattern emphasizes that some *disruptive* behavior—biting, stereotyped activity, crying, pinching, excessive fearfulness, looking at irrelevant objects—requires change. All of these excessive behaviors disrupt or interfere with the successful acquisition or performance of more appropriate means of behaving.

DESCRIBING WHAT THE CHILD DOES DO

After recognizing that a problem exists, the next step is to describe what a child does do in situations which require a level or type of behavior which he does not demonstrate. The adult may expect the child to dress himself completely without assistance or to identify similar objects when presented one of a class of objects. The child may be only partially successful and not be able to demonstrate the level of behavior required. The adult may expect a certain type of behavior; for example, compliance to verbal requests. The child may engage in other types of behavior such as actively refusing, ignoring, or crying.

Focus on What Child Does

Although it is easy to focus on what a child *does not do* (for example, "He just will not sit still," "John is not interested," "He will not finish his work," "He won't remain quiet," "He will not dress himself"), a program can only be based on what a child *does do* in various specific situations which require behaviors other than those exhibited by the child. Describing the child in the manner, "He does not sit still" does not indicate what he does do. What does he do in a situation that requires him to sit still? Does he move about excessively while remaining in his chair? Does he move out of his chair? What does he do when away from the table?

What does the child do when "He will not dress himself?" Does he attempt to put his shirt on? Does he turn away and yell "No" when requested to dress? Does he push the clothes away and begin crying? Does he sit and stare at the clothes and make no attempt to reach for them?

Stating that a child is unable to label pictures of common objects, cannot identify basic colors or shapes, and cannot copy simple forms is equally as inadequate as descriptions of the child's behavioral skills. What does he do when presented with pictures of objects or with colors? Is he able to match pictures with objects or colors with objects of similar colors? Does he have the verbal labels for the objects and colors and does he use these, although inappropriately, when requested to label objects or colors?

These *does do* behaviors are the ones with which the teacher must begin in her program to teach more desirable or complex forms of behavior.

Behavior Described in Specific Terms

The description of what the child does that deviates from an expectation of what should be done must be presented in highly specific terms. Consider the following:

"Eudora is spoiled."
"John is disruptive."
"She is always teasing others."
"Pete has limited language skills."
"John is too naughty."
"Jim is too shy."
"Kathy has a poor self-concept."
"What an aggressive child she is!"

All of these categories are much too vague as described. Words like spoiled, naughty, limited, shy, disruptive, poor, and aggressive mean different things to different people. Two children described as aggressive may engage in quite different "aggressive" behaviors under different conditions. Sue may fight with her peers, but only when the teacher is not present. Jill, in contrast, will fight anyone whenever she is upset. These generalities must be translated into specific behaviors which make up the "spoiled," "disruptive," "limited," "naughty," "shy," "poor," or "aggressive" descriptions. The behavior management program will be based on what the child does do which creates parent or teacher concern. "John is disruptive" may refer to the following actions:

He pushes other children.
He forcefully takes toys away from his peers.
He screams when he is required to remain at the table after he finishes his lunch.
He talks too loudly during quiet time.

"Eudora is spoiled" may refer to:

She cries when she cannot be first.
She whines when required to clean up her mess.
She fusses when she is required to eat her meat before getting her dessert.

It may be helpful to provide more precise definitions of such behaviors as "cries," "whines," and "fusses." Hart and her associates (1964) successfully decreased the crying episodes of children by extinction and differential reinforcement of other behaviors. They defined a crying episode as a cry (1) loud enough to be heard at least 50 feet away and (2) of five seconds or more duration.

Adequate behavioral descriptions are stated in such a manner that an observer could know if these behaviors occurred or did not occur under defined conditions. These are the specific behaviors which will be the initial focus of a behavior management program. These are his *does do* behaviors which create difficulty: behaviors which deviate from what is desired or expected.

Behavior Described in Specific Situations

After an adequate objective description of the behavior has been made, the behavior should be described in relation to a set of conditions. "What does the child do in specific situations which creates difficulty or which is disappointing to the adult?" becomes a most meaningful question. Crying may not be inappropriate following an injury but may be quite inappropriate if it occurs whenever the child is only mildly frustrated.

Some behaviors occur only under highly specific situations and others may occur across seemingly different circumstances. John does not push other children all the time. Rather, it may be observed that he is likely to engage in inappropriate pushing behavior when other children approach him while he is playing with his favorite truck or when another child has arrived at school earlier than John and is playing with the truck when John arrives. In other situations he seldom pushes other children. Dan may begin crying when requested to complete a difficult visual-motor task. Kathy, in contrast, may cry on numerous occasions throughout the day. These examples emphasize the need to lodge behavior in a situation in order to provide a meaningul description of the behavior. In so doing, the environmental events which influence the behavior are identified.

DESCRIBING WHAT THE CHILD SHOULD DO

After a specific description of what the child does do, the next step is to describe in comparable specific terms the behaviors that are desired. These become the *should do* behaviors and serve as the *behavioral objectives* of the behavior management program. In considering the *should do* behaviors, attention is given to the qualitative aspects of the behavior as well as to a description of the conditions under which the behavior should occur. The child may be expected to develop skills of attention to teacher instruction. How long and under what conditions will he be expected to attend to the teacher? These questions of program objectives will be considered in detail in Chapter 10.

The *should do* behaviors which are set for each child are typically translated into both short-term or *target* behavioral objectives and more long-term or *terminal* behavioral objectives. The specific set of objectives developed for any child will evolve out of an assessment of that child. These *should do* behavioral objectives are viewed as tentative and as subject to change as the child is exposed to a behavior management program.

In developing a program for a child the specific target and terminal *should do* behavioral objectives which are devised are intimately related to how the child does perform in response to specific stimulation. If the general goal is to teach new dressing skills to the child, the adult must evaluate in specific detail what the child presently does when confronted with a task of dressing himself. These behaviors form the beginning steps in a program designed to teach more appropriate or skillful dressing. It may be that the child does have adequate self-dressing skills but that he uses them only infrequently. The assessment task in this instance is to identify those dressing and related skills that he does have so that a training program can be devised which uses these skills as a basis for developing new skills. These *does do* behaviors are the *entering behaviors* which he brings into a program designed to modify them. The more immediate and transitional target behavioral objectives as well as the long-term goals for this child are established and a program is designed to teach these "missing behaviors." This emphasizes that the specific teaching program for a child cannot be delineated until the *does do* and *should do* behaviors have been specified. The program begins with the *does do* and is designed to eliminate the gap between these and the *should do* behavioral objectives.

Assume a situation that requires six-year-old John to sit at a table and complete three picture puzzles without getting out of his seat or disrupting others. The teacher reports that he never finishes this assignment. As an initial step in devising a plan to teach John to complete this assignment, it will be necessary to describe what the boy *does do* when presented with the task. How long does he attend to the task? How many puzzles does he complete? When not attending to and working on the puzzles, what does he do? Does he leave his desk? Does he look at or talk to other children? As these types of questions are answered, program personnel will be able to evolve a behavior management plan that is suitable to the individual child and his specific behavioral characteristics.

With another child the problem may involve learning the names of the basic colors. In this case, it would be necessary to discover what the child does when presented with the colors. Can he color match correctly? Does he have the labels in his verbal repertoire? Does he correctly label the colors on occasion?

A form for use in recording the *does do* and *should do* behaviors of a child is included in Table 8.1. Note that the initial column refers to the situation or conditions in which the *does do* behavior occurs. Also remember that in describing what the child does, it is necessary to focus on how he actually behaves and not on what he does not do. "He did not name the color correctly" does not describe what the child did do under the conditions of being presented colors by the teacher with the request that he name them.

OBSERVATION AND MEASUREMENT OF CHILD BEHAVIOR

"What does the child do" can be answered only by observation of that child in relevant situations. A wide variety of procedures of assessment of what the child can do is available for teacher use. These include standardized tests, behavioral checklists, developmental inventories, and other similar guides to observing what the child does. The present discussion will focus on direct behavioral observation of the child's behavior as it occurs in natural settings. That is, what does the child do in the home and school settings in

Table 8.1: Recording Sheet for *Does Do* and *Should Do* Behaviors

Child: John Mack _____   Observer: W. March _____

Date: 8-9-73 _____

Physical and Social Situation (Under what conditions?)	Does Do Behaviors (What does the child do?)	Should Do Behaviors (What do you wish the child to do?)
1. In a classroom with five children sitting at a table, teacher presents colors and asks "What color is this?"	1. He looks at the colors, reaches for them, and shakes his head "no" when prompted to name them.	1. He correctly names the colors red, blue, green, yellow, black and white.
2. During lunchtime when seated with five children and teacher, he is asked to use his knife, fork and spoon in eating his food.	2. He uses his spoon and fork appropriately but spills food on the table when he attempts to cut meat with his knife.	2. He uses all eating utensils appropriately during mealtime.
3. At end of school day he is provided coat, overshoes, and gloves and requested to "Get ready for the bus."	3. He puts his coat on and attempts unsuccessfully to button it. He attempts unsuccessfully to get his overshoes on. He gets his gloves on the wrong hands.	3. He dresses himself completely and satisfactorily in preparation for going home at end of school day.
4. In classroom setting of six peers, a teacher, and a teacher aide, he sees a peer who requires some assistance.	4. He turns away from children in difficulty and will assist them only when instructed specifically to do so.	4. He approaches another child who is experiencing difficulty (e.g., in moving a table, in lifting a heavy box) and will offer to assist.

the presence of various types of stimulating conditions?   This description must denote *what* the child does under specified conditions as well as provide some indication of the strength of the behavior.   Does he engage in the behavior under designated conditions on every occasion, on most occasions, or only infrequently?   Once begun, how long does the behavior continue? How intense is the behavior?   This topic of behavior strength will be discussed briefly along with a description of various procedures for obtaining measures of behavior strength.

BEHAVIOR STRENGTH

Behavior may vary in terms of its (1) *frequency* of occurrence, (2) its *magnitude* or intensity, (3) its *duration* of occurrence once begun, and (4) in terms of the *latency* or time which elapses between being stimulated and responding. The specific measure of behavior strength which the teacher or parent may use will be dependent upon, as will be illustrated, the type of behavior which is of concern. As emphasized, measurement of behavior strength is needed as a means of evaluating the effectiveness of a behavior management program. Prior to the initiation of a specific program, some objective measure is needed of the strength of the behavior which the program is designed to influence. This initial measure of behavior strength is known as *baseline* recording and represents the *preprogram status* of the behavior. This is a measure of what the child does do prior to teacher initation of a program designed to change the behavior. This measure provides the teacher with an objective indication of his present behavior. Such a baseline procedure also provides a check on the adequacy of the definition of the problem behavior. Has the behavior been defined in terms that permit reliable counting? If so, the behavior is adequately defined.

Without such baseline information it frequently is difficult to determine if a specific behavior management program has had any effect on the deficit or excessive behavior problem. Additionally, a measure of initial behavior strength permits comparison of different children. A child who has an average of five temper outbursts during a daily 45-minute unstructured play period has a higher strength of temper tantrum behavior than does another child who engages in such behavior less than two times daily. It provides an objective basis for assignment of program priorities within a group of children.

In some cases it would not be desirable to obtain an adequate baseline recording of behavior strength due to the nature of the behavior. A child begins biting her peers; a behavior change program should be initiated immediately. In such cases, at a minimum, some procedure for measuring the strength of the behavior should be initiated as the behavior management program is begun. In this manner it is possible to get some impression about the effects of the program. If the initial program is unsuccessful, a baseline recording will thus be available for evaluating the effects of a modified program.

RATE OF BEHAVIOR

Event Recording

The measure of behavior strength that is most useful with a wide variety of behaviors and which typically is the most easily obtained by the classroom teacher or parent is the *frequency* of behavior. The frequency is translated into a *behavior rate* by expressing the frequency as the average number of times the behavior occurred in a given period of time. Kim is described as an over-active child who will not remain on her cot during rest period. To obtain a measure of her overactivity during rest period, the number of times that Kim gets up during rest period may be selected for baseline recording. The baseline data presented in Table 8.2 reveal that Kim got off her cot 40 times during a five-day period.

The total frequency of 40 could be divided by the number of observation periods—in this case five daily periods—and thus provide an average daily behavior rate of eight (Rate $= \frac{\text{no.}}{\text{time}}$; $\frac{40}{5} = 8$). During this observation period of one week, Kim got off her cot during rest time an average of 8 times daily. This type of behavior measurement is known as *event recording*.

Methods of recording events. In event recording, every occurrence of a certain behavior during a specified time period is tallied on a note pad on the teacher's desk, on masking tape wrapped around the teacher's wrist, on the chalkboard, or by any other mechanical means and transferred to the data sheet as detailed in

Table 8.2: Event Recording of Behavior Frequency

Child: Kim	Observer: Mrs. Jimi

Behavior: Getting off cot during rest period

Physical/social situation: Classroom rest period.

Fifteen minutes daily.

DATE	FREQUENCY	NUMBER
June 14	ЦЖ II	7
June 15	ЦЖ IIII	9
June 16	ЦЖ II	7
June 17	ЦЖ ЦЖ	11
June 18	ЦЖ I	6
	Total	40

Table 8.2. Such recording provides a cumulative frequency within a designated time period. The method of recording would depend upon the behavior that is being observed and the circumstances of observation.

Some teachers and parents have found a hand or wrist counter useful in recording behavior frequency. Lindsley (1968) has described an inexpensive but reliable golf counter which has been used successfully. This method is especially useful when measurement is taken of behaviors which have a high rate of occurrence. As it is worn on the wrist, it is available when needed without eliminating the use of one hand as would be the case with a hand counter. Also, such a simple procedure of recording frequency leaves the teacher relatively free to engage in her normal activities, especially if the behavior rate is low.

An alternative to the wrist counter is a hand counter which can be purchased in many styles. A simple grocery counter usually provides up to four digits and can be held easily. Manual counters found in school supply stores usually have a ring for secure holding and vary in the number of digits available. A harmonica-shaped manual counter (Mattos, 1968) has five separate three-digit display panels so that the observer can record up to five behavior categories of a single child or a single behavior category for up to five children using the fingers of only one hand. These tend to be cumbersome and difficult to manipulate if one needs the use of both hands for some other activity. Masking tape and pen, paper and pencil, or blackboard and chalk as well as any of the event-recording methods described above can be used for recording any behavior for which the teacher wishes a frequency count in a given period of time.

Event recording can become problematic if more than one or two behaviors are observed at the same time. A student teacher in a special classroom found that she made numerous recording errors when counting the number of verbal responses of five boys while trying to conduct an SRA language drill. An experienced teacher of deaf children rearranged her lesson plans for a week since she found that she could not conduct individual reading classes and record correct usage of manual communication (sign language, finger spelling) simultaneously. The reconciliation between behavioral measurement and other duties of the classroom teacher can be facilitated by the use of the most convenient event-recording technique and by recording either continuously through the day or only during designated periods of time.

This rate measure of behavior strength is valuable when observing such patterns as aggressive behavior, disruptive behavior, number of words or pages read, number of times a child cries during play period, number of spontaneous verbalizations, number of puzzles completed, or number of times a child initiates social interaction.

When should events be recorded? The daily time period during which observation is made may refer to the entire school day, the lunch period, play time, the initial 30 minutes of each day, or any other period during which a behavior of concern may occur. The length of each observation period as well as the time within the daily schedule during which behavior is measured would obviously depend upon the type of behavior being observed as well as its general frequency. If the behavior occurred quite frequently and did not appear to occur any more or less frequently in relation to different time periods or to different situations, measurement of frequency may occur for a short period of time each day.

If, on the other hand, the behavior has a rather infrequent rate of occurrence, continuous recording of each event throughout the day may be most appropriate. For example, the child may exhibit temper tantrums, may soil himself, may engage in crying episodes, or may hit or bite other children at a bothersome but not at a frequent rate. Thus relatively low-rate behaviors which are to be decreased in strength or eliminated are best recorded by continuous event recording as these have a high probability of escaping less frequent observation.

Recording and graphing data. To further illustrate the use of a frequency measure of behavior, rate data obtained on Susan will be presented. This five-year-old child attended a developmental education program with five other children. The teacher became quite distraught over Susan's aggressive behaviors and was almost at the point of dismissing her from the classroom.

As an initial step in devising a specific behavior management program to deal with the behaviors, the teacher defined the specific behaviors which she viewed as aggressive. She included the behaviors of biting, scratching, hitting, pushing, and pinching other children, pushing teacher, and pinching herself. After defining each of these categories, a teacher aide recorded the number of times these behaviors occurred throughout each of four 45-minute periods. The daily recording sheet used is presented in Table 8.3. Separate recordings were made for each of the four periods of the school day in order to determine any variation in these behaviors as activities and times change.

Recording was continued for five days in order to gain an impression about the daily fluctuation of the behaviors. These total daily frequency data were then represented in graph form as shown in Figure 8.1. Note that time is represented on the graph by the horizontal axis, with the vertical axis used to indicate the

Table 8.3: Recording Sheet for Frequency of Aggressive Behaviors

Child: Susan   Observer: Ms. Karan

Date: 3/9 (Day 1 of 5 day baseline)

Physical/social situation: Classroom and playground. Six children in a group.

Behaviors	Period I Language	Period II Music	Period III Play	Period IV Lunch	Total
Biting			11	1	3
Pushing Peers				1	1
Scratching				1	1
Hitting			11	0	2
Pinching Others		1			1
Pinching Self					0
Pushing Teacher			1		1
Total Frequency	0	1	5	3	9

frequency of the behavior. Figure 8.1 shows the total frequency of all seven behaviors for each of five days as well as a separate representation of the total number of times each day that Susan bit other children. The biting is represented separately in this case as this was the behavior that most upset the teacher and the other children in the classroom. Biting behavior over the five-day period had an average daily rate of three. The average daily rate of all aggressive behavior for the five-day period was 9.6. The strength of the biting behavior was consistently higher than any other specific category of the aggressive behaviors observed.

Figure 8.2 shows the total number of aggressive behaviors per day during each of the four class periods. The average occurrence or rate per class period for the five days was found to be as follows: (Total aggressive behavior for all 5 days ÷ 5 days)

Period 1 = .4
Period 2 = .6
Period 3 = 5.0
Period 4 = 3.6.

It can be seen that few aggressive behaviors occurred during the early morning structured class periods. The rate changed drastically later in the morning as the child entered unstructured play and lunch periods.

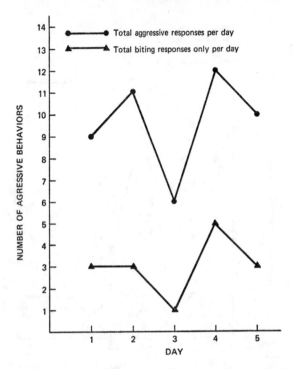

FIGURE 8.1:   *Total Number of Biting and Aggressive Responses*

Rate as a percentage of total events. In some instances it will be useful to express frequency data as a *percentage of times* that the defined behavior occurred under specific cue conditions. In obtaining a measure of the strength of compliance, it would be useful to divide the total number of times that a child complied with a teacher request by the total number of requests made. If the teacher presented 25 requests to Sammy (e.g., "Sit at your desk," "Put your toys on the shelf," "Bring your paper to me") and Sammy complied with 20 of these, he would have a compliance rate of 80 percent. If one child complies with teacher requests on an average of 92 percent of the time and another child has a percentage of 35 percent, the first child obviously has a stronger skill for fulfilling teacher requests. It may be said that his rate of compliance is higher or that he has a higher likelihood of complying with teacher requests than does the second child. Zeilberger and associates (1968) used this measure of behavior strength in evaluating the effects of a behavior management program on the compliance behavior of a young boy. During baseline the boy followed instructions given by mother in the home on an average of 30

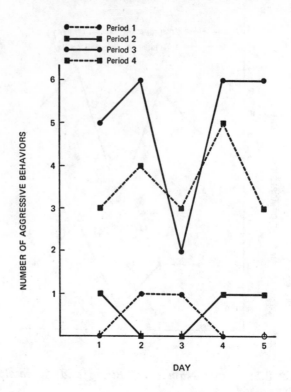

FIGURE 8.2: *Total Number of Aggressive Behaviors Per Each Daily 45-Minute Period*

percent. Following initiation of behavior management the child followed mother's instructions 78 percent of the time.

Such a percentage rate would be useful for discussing the strength of the following kinds of behavior: the percentage of a number of assigned puzzles which were completed, the percentage of total words read which were pronounced correctly, percentage of total class of children who dress themselves without assistance, the percentage of pictures correctly labeled, and the percentage of total number of social interactions which were aggressive in nature.

Rate as percentage of total time. A final rate measure of behavior strength refers to the percentage of a given period of time which is spent in a designated behavior. A child may be observed to spend only 20 percent of a 30-minute period in sitting at his work table. Another child may spend only 25 percent of an unstructured play period interacting with other children. In a study reported by

Briskin and Gardner (1968), Lisa, attending a preschool program, spent 54 percent of her time during structured activity periods in disruptive behavior. This percentage figure provided a baseline measure against which changes which coincided with the initiation of a behavior management program could be evaluated. Johnston and her associates (1966) used a percentage of total time spent on the playground during which a young child engaged in climbing on play equipment. The behavior management program was designed to increase the percentage of time spent in climbing activity.

Time Sampling of Events

In the examples presented above, continuous recording of the occurrence of a behavioral event was made. The total number of aggressive behaviors which occurred throughout the day was recorded. Such continuous recording may not be feasible or necessary in many instances. The frequency may be rather high and relatively stable over time. A sample of the frequency of occurrence may well be representative of a more time-consuming continuous recording of each occurrence. In this instance a *time-sampling* procedure would be followed. The initial five minutes of each 30-minute period during a four hour school day, for example, may be selected for recording. Every occurrence of the observed behavior during those designated time periods is recorded. The frequency data obtained during these small time samples are then used to represent the overall behavior strength.

INTERVAL RECORDING

The Briskin and Gardner study mentioned earlier is interesting as it illustrates other observational procedures. In this study, instead of a frequency recording of every occurrence of various behaviors during a designated time period, the teacher used an interval procedure. In *interval recording* the observation session is divided into a number of equal time periods. The observer records *only* whether the designated behavior did or did not occur during the interval, instead of recording the number of different times a specific behavior may have occurred. The observer may combine an interval with a *time sampling* procedure in which he may, for example, observe only during the last 30 seconds of a designated interval and spend the remaining time in recording or in other activities. The observer only samples the behavior at specific times during a defined time interval and then records its occurrence or nonoccurrence.

In the Briskin and Gardner study, the teacher recorded the child's behavior only during designated periods of time throughout the class periods of the day. In obtaining a measure of Lisa's disruptive behaviors, an observer recorded the occurrence of such behaviors during the initial five minutes of each of the seven activity periods throughout the day. Within each five-minute sample the observer would glance at Lisa for three seconds and then record for twelve seconds, look again for three seconds and record. If the behaviors were occurring during the three second glance period, a + was recorded; if not a 0 was recorded. In this manner, the observer was able to make 140 observations during a single school day. This procedure required only 35 minutes of observer time. The strength of Lisa's disruptive behavior was expressed as a percentage of the total time in which Lisa was observed to engage in disruptive behavior. Daily observation over six days provided an average rate of behavior strength during the pretreatment or baseline period.

Table 8.4 depicts another example of the use of interval recording. The observation represents the presence or absence during five-minute segments of stereotyped behavior—defined as rocking back and forth—of a five-year-old boy. The + designates the occurrence of the behavior during some part of the five-minute interval; the 0 indicates no such behavior occurred during the five-minute period.

Zeilberger and associates (1968) used this procedure of interval recording in obtaining a measure of the strength of aggressive behavior of a young child. The occurrence or nonoccurrence of aggressive behavior (defined as hitting, pushing, kicking, throwing, biting, scratching) was recorded in successive 20-second intervals during a one-hour play period. The behavior strength was expressed as a percentage of total intervals during which aggressive behavior was recorded. During baseline aggressive behavior occurred in 5 percent to 13 percent of the scored intervals. After initiation of a behavior management program the aggressive behavior occurred only rarely.

It may be helpful to emphasize again that a time sampling procedure can be used in combination with continuous-event recording as well as with an interval-recording procedure. The total occurrence of a behavior within designated time samples can be recorded. Or, in interval recording, only the presence or absence of the behavior during designated subunits of time will be recorded.

Table 8.4: Interval Recording Sheet

Child: Leif	Observer: Ms. Sham

Behavior: Stereotyped rocking

Physical/social situation: Classroom during a 60-minute play period.

Time interval: 5 minutes

Interval Number

1	2	3	4	5	6	7	8	9	10	11	12	%	DATE
+	+	0	+	+	+	+	0	0	+	+	0	66	11/14/73
+	+	0	0	+	+	+	+	+	+	0	0	66	11/15/73
0	+	+	+	0	0	+	0	0	+	+	0	50	11/16/73
+	+	0	+	+	0	+	+	+	+	+	0	75	11/17/73
+	+	+	0	0	0	0	+	+	0	+	0	50	11/18/73

LENGTH OF BASELINE PERIOD

Prior to a discussion of other measures of behavior strength, it will be useful to comment on the question "Over what period of time should baseline recording be taken?" The purpose of measurement during the pretreatment or baseline period is to provide an initial reference point for evaluating the effects of any subsequent behavior change which may result from initiation of a behavior management program. The goal is to obtain a reliable indication of behavior strength. The number of different observation periods needed to obtain a reliable measure of strength would depend upon the fluctuation and the frequency of occurrence of the focal behavior. Typically, daily recordings over a week or so would be sufficient. However, behavior which fluctuated considerably might require a longer period of baseline recording for obtaining a reliable index of typical behavior strength.

INTENSITY OF BEHAVIOR

In addition to being concerned about influencing the percentage of times defined behaviors occur or the rate of behavior within specified periods of time, the teacher may be concerned with the intensity or magnitude characteristics of a behavior pattern. Although more difficult to measure, especially in complex child behavior, the intensity or magnitude (i.e., "loudness," "vigor," or "enthusiasm") components of behavior are of importance at times. The rate of temper tantrum behavior may show little change initially after the teacher begins a specific program for controlling such behavior. However, there may be a steady decrease in the intensity of the temper outbursts. The child may not cry as loudly, thrash about as vigorously, or pound on his legs as rapidly as was characteristic prior to program initiation. A shy child may speak with such low volume that the teacher is unable to understand him when not standing close by. The behavior may be measured in terms of the approximate distance (number of feet) between the child and the teacher for her to understand the child. A program may be designed to shape increasingly louder speech. The effects of the program will be measured by an increase in distance between the child and teacher for understandable verbal communication. These and similar magnitude components of a complex behavior pattern should be defined and measured in one way or another in order to obtain adequate measures of behavior strength and change.

DURATION OF BEHAVIOR

Duration of behavior is another measure of strength which is useful in some instances. The length of time that a child engages in crying behavior once begun provides a measure of the strength of that behavior. This measure of behavior strength was used in an experience reported by Williams (1959) with a preschool child who would scream and fuss if his parents left his room at night before he went to sleep. After the parents decided to attempt to eliminate the crying behavior, the child was placed in bed and left. Recording of the duration of crying was initiated as the behavior management program was begun. Crying occurred for 45 minutes the first time. On subsequent nights the length of time the child spent in crying gradually decreased, that is, the strength declined. By the tenth occasion the crying behavior no longer occurred. Crying had not been eliminated completely; rather, the behavior showed no strength under this specific condition of being placed in bed and left alone. The child cried under other conditions at other times. This illustrates the concept presented in a previous chapter that behavior is never completely eliminated. It may just no longer occur in certain situations as new experiences are gained.

Duration recording may be useful for such concerns as the amount of time a child spends out of seat on each occasion of leaving the chair, time spent in isolated activities following each occasion of becoming upset, and amount of time sitting quietly after reprimand prior to another outburst. Such recording would produce rate data by adding the duration time of each observation period and dividing that sum by the number of observation periods. "During the observation period he got out of his chair on 15 different occasions. He remained out of his chair on an average of five minutes." "He remained in isolated activity following the 13 crying episodes for an average of 20 minutes." "He sat quietly for an average of 17 minutes after being reprimanded prior to becoming disruptive. This represents 20 observations of behavior following reprimand."

RESPONSE LATENCY

A final measure of behavior strength of importance in some instances is response latency. A behavior that occurs with promptness upon being requested may be described as representing a stronger pattern of compliance than that of a child who stalls and ignores the request for a time prior to complying. The objective of a behavior change program in this instance would be to reduce the time delay or latency between request and compliance. As another example, a distractible child has difficulty beginning work once it is presented to him. A measure of the amount of time which elapses between work assignment and the time the child initiates the work would serve as a valuable baseline measure for a program designed to decrease the time delay between assignment and work.

WHO SHOULD RECORD BEHAVIOR

Typically the teacher will do her own observations and recording. If this is not feasible, the assistance of a teacher aide or of independent observers such as parents, colleagues, or volunteers may be enlisted. In some instances the child may record his own behavior. In so doing, the child frequently is able to recognize the relationship between his own behavior and the effects it may have on others. In any event it is necessary that behavior recording be initiated and continued if program efforts are to be measured.

In teaching a child to record his own behavior, it is best to begin with easily defined actions such as the number of puzzles completed, pictures colored, or objects drawn. A hash mark will be made on a card after each task is completed. The teacher will next teach the child to transfer the total frequency to a bar or line graph. Young children are able to do this if they have basic number concepts. Use of a bar graph can demonstrate to the child whether the total number of his recorded responses is increasing or decreasing. The data kept by Kaye, a six-year-old child with severe visual-perceptual difficulties are presented in Figure 8.3. The child recorded the number of puzzles completed each day during the week. The teacher used the graph to challenge the child to "see if you can do more so that we can make the bar go even higher than yesterday." This apparently was reinforcing to the child as she did show improvement.

After the child has had experience with recording and graphing desired behavior, the teacher may then guide the child into recording designated inappropriate behaviors. The child may record every occasion he gets out of his seat during periods of time when he is to remain seated, or the number of times he blurts out while someone else is talking during language period. Initially the

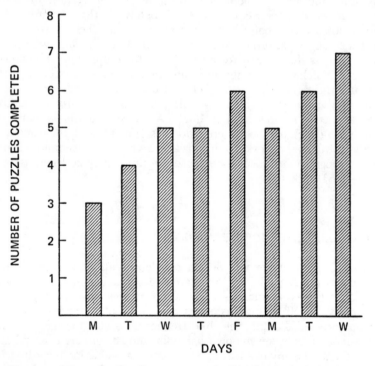

FIGURE 8.3:   *Daily Frequency of Number of Completed Puzzles*

teacher may find it necessary to assist him in such recording and to monitor it to insure that all occurrences are marked on the record card. After placing the initial frequency on a bar or line graph, the child may be challenged by the teacher to decrease the frequency in subsequent class periods.

Figure 8.4 shows the data recorded by a 6½-year-old boy who blurted out-of-turn frequently during language period. After recording of the first day frequency the child was challenged to "make the bars get smaller" by raising his hand before speaking out in language period. The child recorded his behavior for two weeks and was able to demonstrate a most impressive decrease in the disruptive verbal behavior.

SPONTANEOUS BEHAVIOR CHANGE

It is not unusual during baseline recording to observe an improvement in the observed behaviors. This has been reported by a number of different people (Ackerman, 1972; Patterson, 1971;

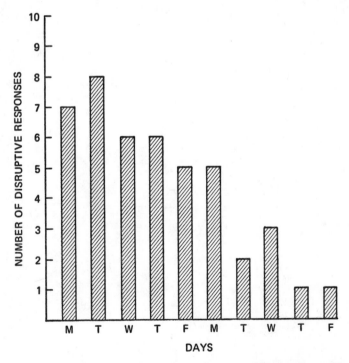

FIGURE 8.4:   *Daily Frequency of Disruptive Verbal Responses*

Tharp and Wetzel, 1969). Such improvement in problem behaviors during baseline recording appears to be related to the change in the manner in which the teacher or other observer interacts with the child being observed. The teacher may begin to focus more on what she is doing and the possible effect this has on the way the child is behaving. This self-analysis may result in changes in the manner in which the child is treated. The child's behavior may improve in this new relationship. It may also be true that the child on occasion may observe the teacher in her recording. Knowledge that the teacher is recording his behavior may create conditions (the child is embarrassed or fearful) which influence behavior change.

CHAPTER 9

Developing a Behavior
Management Program:
Guidelines

Learning new behavioral skills and continuing this knowledge under appropriate conditions pose a difficult task for the young child with learning and behavior problems. It becomes essential that the total learning experiences provided for the child be well-designed. A number of principles and related strategies and techniques for designing a positive learning environment have been presented in previous chapters. This chapter will elaborate upon some of these concepts and provide a number of other suggestions for developing and implementing programs of behavior management.

In arranging and presenting behavior management programs to children, the teacher will find direction from the previously discussed learning concepts. Once understood and practiced, the application of these principles should not interfere with the natural personal characteristics of the teacher. The teacher can be just as warm, enthusiastic, and spontaneous in a program of behavior management as she could be in following any other concepts of child development. She can be systematic and spontaneous at the same time. Only a skilled observer will be able to recognize that the teacher is making systematic application of behavior management procedures. Within a few minutes the teacher may be reinforcing four or five different behaviors by using various types and arrangements of consequences, may be extinguishing other behaviors, may be initiating the development of a needed discrimination, and may be discouraging other behaviors by skillful shaping of competing ones.

A group of visiting educators from several European countries were heard commenting on their impressions of a teacher whom they had just observed working with a class of young children. "She is a great teacher." "She seems so alive and enthusiastic." "Yes, she relates so well to the children—interacts freely. The children seem to enjoy her. I thought she was one of these behavior modification teachers, but apparently not. I did not see her giving out any rewards or punishing any children." These visitors were surprised to discover that they were in fact describing an excellent behavior management teacher. An example of what they observed and the manner in which the teacher made use of behavior management techniques in the normal flow of classroom activity will serve to illustrate the natural application of learning principles.

The teacher is standing in front of a semi-circular table around which six children are seated. The children are busily working individually on perceptual-motor problems which the teacher had provided a few moments before.

Susan sneezes loudly. Her peers look up. One boy giggles briefly.	Susan is a shy, overly anxious child who is highly embarrassed by any of her behavior that attracts attention from her peers.
The teacher moves toward her and softly says "Bless you," smiles warmly and touches her gently on the shoulder.	The teacher has established a good relationship with the child; she uses this opportunity to indicate to the child that her behavior is quite acceptable. By presenting an accepting social model she hopes to relax the child somewhat as such a relaxation response would compete with the anxiety and decrease its intensity.
Susan smiles in return and continues her work.	The child imitated the teacher's behavior. The anxiety reaction associated with attracting attention should be less intense in the future.

Jonathon, observing the interchange, fakes a sneeze and looks at the teacher, apparently expecting attention.

The teacher ignores the sneeze as she looks away.	The teacher knows that Jonathon finds teacher attention highly reinforcing. She does not wish to strengthen this disruptive attention-seeking behavior.
Jonathon fakes two additional sneezes.	
Teacher continues to ignore him. Jonathon returns to his task.	Teacher is careful not to attend to him, even to show her disapproval as it would probably be reinforcing. She recognizes that attention would reinforce both the disruptive behavior as well as his persistence. If she attends to him after the third sneeze she realizes that she would be teaching him to persist at the misbehavior and it eventually would pay off.
After a minute or so has passed with Jonathon busily at work, teacher moves behind him and comments on his work and praises him for staying with it.	Teacher is interested in strengthening Jonathon's task persistence and task completion behaviors. He receives the social attention which he was seeking, but only after appropriate behavior. He is now more likely to enjoy his table work and persist at it.
As the teacher is interacting with Jonathon, Kathy looks up and announces, "I can't do this."	
Teacher replies, "Wait just a minute and I'll look at it." After 15–20 seconds, teacher, noting that Kathy is becoming restless, smiles, winks at her and nods.	Kathy is an impatient child who requires immediate attention. Teacher is gradually reinforcing her for waiting for increasingly longer periods of time prior to fulfilling her requests. In responding to her as she begins to become restless, the teacher calms her with her smile and reassures her that she will be available in a short time.

As she begins to become restless again teacher moves to Kathy.

Teacher recognizes that Kathy may become too emotional if she further delays attending to her.

The teacher moves to Kathy, smiles, and states: "Thank you for waiting until I finished with Jonathon. Now let's see what you have done." She notes that Kathy had done her work incorrectly. She had not followed the directions provided earlier. Teacher suggests, "Let's do this one again. Now where do we start?"

Kathy touches the starting point on the page.

"Good."

Teacher reinforces Kathy for waiting. Note that she labeled the response pattern that she was pleased with. This helps Kathy to recognize the relationship between behavior and consequence.

Teacher, recognizing that Kathy does not remember the directions, begins to guide her step-by-step through the exercise.

Reinforcement is provided immediately for this correct response.

"Now tell me what you do next."

Kathy replies "Draw from green one to this red one."

"Great! You remembered well. I'm proud of you."

Teacher, instead of showing her what to do, is attempting to get Kathy to cue herself by verbally describing the activity.

The child was reinforced for solving the problem. Note that the teacher labeled the behavior of remembering as she reinforced the child. Kathy will associate remembering directions with pleasant consequences.

"Now show me how to do it and tell me what you are doing."

Kathy draws a line from the green circle down to the red one as she says: "Drawing a line from the green light to the red light."

Teacher wishes to associate verbal directions to motor behavior.

"Wow, you have it just right! What will you do with the others?"

Kathy is reinforced for the verbal and motor behavior patterns. The teacher now wishes to determine if Kathy can complete a new task without further prompting.

Kathy completes another sheet without assistance.

"Good. Now you finish all the others" as the teacher moves away.

Teacher now feels that Kathy can perform without further assistance. She enhances the child's independence and feelings of accomplishment as she does not leave until the child is being successful. The child continues on her own.

In this example, it becomes apparent that the teacher is influencing a range of behaviors. She is presenting a model of enthusiasm. She has the children smiling and pleased with their behavior as she finds some appropriate behavior to praise. Since she recognizes that her behavior can have a profound effect on the child's behaviors, she is quite sensitive to what she does and when she does it. As she recognizes that her attention can strengthen behavior patterns in a child, she seeks positive behaviors toward which to direct her attention. She finds herself being sensitive and accepting individual differences among children. She recognizes that children can learn if encouraged to do so in an adequately designed program. She views inappropriate behavior in its correct perspective: she looks at her program for ways of influencing this behavior and does not blame the child for it. The teacher's positive emotional tone is being associated with such child behaviors as attending, task involvement, and verbalizing directions. In this manner these behaviors are becoming more pleasant and satisfying to the children.

"DO'S AND DON'TS" OF PROGRAM DESIGN

Focus on Does Do Behavior

A behavior management program should focus on what the child does do under various conditions and on what you would wish him to do, not on what a child cannot or does not do. A learning environment must be created that will assist the child in developing and in engaging in desired behaviors. A child frequently does not comply with teacher request. The program emphasis should be to develop a plan for increasing compliance behavior. The following types of questions become pertinent: Is the behavioral requirement of compliance too difficult for the child at his present level of development? What are the consequences of compliance and of noncompliance? Has the child had sufficient experience with the consequences associated with compliance to insure that those behaviors have some strength? Is the consequence appropriate in kind and amount to the difficulty level of the behaviors requested? Are cues for competing behaviors of noncompliance too strong? These and similar questions focus on designing a program to improve the child's compliance behaviors.

Child Involvement Depends on Success

A child will participate in a learning program if he is being successful. The greater the number of positive experiences provided the child, the less the likelihood that he will engage in inappropriate behavior. If a child has a preponderance of failures, the program content and method should be evaluated as it is not appropriate at present for that particular child. The program should be redesigned to match the characteristics of the child. If, for example, a child's frequent emotional outbursts are disrupting Mrs. Johnson's class, the child is not a successful learner. In analyzing this problem as a basis for designing a strategy for handling it, the following steps are helpful:

(1)   The function which is served by the inappropriate behavior should be identified. Does it remove the child from an unpleasant situation? When or in what situations is the behavior most likely to occur? Is it more likely to occur during periods in which he is required to engage in especially difficult tasks? What are the cues which appear to control the behavior or render it more likely? For example, is it true that the child has more difficulty settling down on Monday mornings or after holidays or absences? If so, could additional support be provided during these "critical" periods in order to insure appropriate behavior?

Does the disruptive behavior produce peer and teacher attention which usually is not provided except following disruptive behavior? Does the child in fact have the skills to engage in the appropriate behaviors asked of class members? Does the problem follow other negative confrontations with teacher or peers? That is, is he in a "bad mood" and thus more likely to engage in disruptive or uncooperative and noncompliant behavior?

(2) The teacher should define and then label for the child the unacceptable behavior and indicate why it is unacceptable.

(3) On the basis of an analysis of the behavior and its relationship to various preceding and following consequences, a behavior management plan should be developed which will seek to decrease the likelihood of its reoccurrence and which will strengthen appropriate competing behavior to replace the disruptive outburst in the classroom.

A Plan for Each Child

As a general rule a specific behavior management plan should be developed with well-defined objectives along numerous behavioral dimensions for each child. The plan should include procedures for evaluating its usefulness and alternative strategies in the event the objectives are not attained.

Realistic Behavioral Objectives

The behavioral objectives set for each child must be realistic. Do the expectations for a child represent reasonable changes based on an appraisal of the child's present behavioral repertoire and his predicted rate of developing new behaviors? If there is reasonable doubt, the objectives must be redefined. The setting of realistic behavioral objectives requires an analysis of the prerequisite skills needed for successful attainment of more complex skills. If these prerequisite skills are not present, it will be necessary to teach them prior to exposing the child to the more complex learning task. Hamblin and his associates (1971) experienced considerable difficulty in an academic program designed for children with extreme expressive language problems. It was necessary to structure a special language program to teach the children to talk. Following development of talking skills, the children were again exposed to the academic program and were then able to make good progress. The talking skills apparently were an essential component of correct academic work.

Time for Adaptation to New Situations

The child must have time to adapt to a new environment before the development of specific programs to handle inappropriate behaviors. When a child is introduced to a new school, a new group, or to a new teacher he may engage in behaviors that are not characteristic of the way he will behave after a period of adaptation. He may be quite shy, inattentive, hyperactive, fearful, or relatively nonresponsive to your attempts to initiate interaction. In time the child may behave quite differently, especially if the new environment responds to him in a relaxed, nondemanding manner.

Focus on Influencing Appropriate Behaviors

The major focus of a behavior management approach should not be to eliminate undesired patterns of behavior. Rather, the major goal should be to strengthen prosocial patterns which successfully compete with or take the place of the undesired behaviors. If possible, disruptive and other undesired behavior patterns should be ignored, with attention or other forms of reinforcement provided appropriate competing behaviors. The child will acquire those behaviors which result in pleasant consequences. As emphasized, attending to an undesired behavior, even in the form of reprimand, criticism, or threat, may actually serve to strengthen rather than discourage the behavior. If the child engages in undesired behavior, the teacher should focus on acceptable behaviors and reinforce those which will replace the undesired one. If a child is being disruptive in class, it is best to encourage the child to engage in some acceptable alternative behavior. Such statements as "Stop that," "Let's don't do that," "John, would you like to stop that," or "I wish you would stop being noisy and do your work" are unlikely to produce more than momentary effect on the chronically disruptive child. The teacher must tell the child what *to do*, not merely remind him of what he should not do. If he pulls another child's hair, he must be taught other behaviors for interacting with peers. The teacher should guard against being "turned off" or becoming upset when a child misbehaves. A major source of the child's reinforcement resides in the teacher or other adults in the child's life. If the adult becomes too negative, she loses some of her reinforcement effectiveness.

The behavior which the teacher engages in will serve as a model for the children to imitate. Becker and his associates (1971) describe an experience of one of their teachers which illustrates the positive effects which modeling desired behavior can have on a class. The teacher writes:

As a result of training in behavior modification principles, I attempted to change my classroom environment completely. I previously scurried about, chattered constantly, and often found myself yelling at the children. It came to me while studying the nature of imitation that I was teaching the children, through modeling, the exact frenzied behavior I could not control. I began to walk about the room more slowly; I talked more softly, distinctly, and slowly. I carefully explained what I wanted and waited for questions. . . . I began deleting all useless words and unnecessary parts of lessons. . . . The results are astounding. My class now works quietly for long periods of time and is able to clean up much more quickly than before. The children are more relaxed and speak more quietly. They can change from one task to another easily. In general, a calm atmosphere prevails. This has reduced my fatigue and tension. This is extremely important because as my tension rises, so does the noise level in the room. (p. 169)

Structuring the Behavior Management Program

A relaxed but structured environment results in best overall behavior development and functioning for the young child with learning and behavior problems. An overly permissive orientation on the part of adults does not recognize the unique characteristics of young children with learning and behavior problems; nor does an excessive authoritarian approach. Whenever possible, the child should be exposed to a general school day routine. Within this routine there should be free time without scheduled activities as well as frequent opportunity to explore, to make decisions, and to engage in a variety of interpersonal experiences. The child should be provided a variety of behavioral alternatives. Children frequently engage in inappropriate behavior because they are bored. They become satiated with the same old routine. Although structure is needed, the child needs a variety of activities. He needs freedom to explore new activities, places, people, and objects. He needs direction; he also needs experiences in making decisions. He needs frequent opportunity for physical activity. He also needs time to rest. Problems are created when tasks requiring concentrated attention or persistence are presented and the child is fatigued or hungry. He needs to make his wishes known; he also needs to attend to the wishes and requirements of others. Teachers should be calm but confident, relaxed but organized, warm but consistent, flexible but with individual expectations for each child.

A structured environment reflects consistency, both in what is required of a child as well as in the consequences of various behaviors. Inconsistency creates confusion and confounds the already difficult problems of learning which characterize many young children.

Camp and Lathen (1967) described the classroom environ-

225

ment which they designed for children who were described as emotionally disturbed.

> Emphasis in the class is placed upon the structure necessary to help each pupil develop inner controls. Class routine provides well defined limits, but freedom is allowed within these limits. . . . Because these children have very little inner emotional control, however, structure must come, at least during the early months, from their external environment both at school and at home. Parents are encouraged to follow the example of the teacher, who places special emphasis on consistent behavior with the child at all times. Negative behavior on the part of the pupil, for example, is never reinforced by angry behavior by the teacher. The goal of the teacher is to behave in a calm but firm and consistent manner in response to *all* pupil behavior. (p. 34)

Child Involvement

Every child must be actively involved in the education program. A child may give the appearance of attending to verbal or visual cues, but may be doing something else. If the child is not actively involved, attention and productive participation may be enhanced by adding prompts, by presenting novel cues, by reducing response alternatives, and by providing more desirable reinforcing events.

Introducing Changes Slowly

The teacher should avoid rapid change in a child's environment at any given time or attempts to solve too many problems at once. Such changes require behaviors that the child may not have or that are of low strength. Such newness is upsetting for many children as previous experiences with new events have resulted in unpleasantness.

A focus on a limited number of new behavioral requirements at any one time will insure more consistent learning. New requirements, problems, and experiences should be presented slowly, in small sequential steps that permit the child to acquire new skills as he is making use of present skills. In this manner the child will learn to persist at a task as he is being successful. He learns that persistence results in pleasant consequences. If the new requirements are too difficult, he will experience little success: becoming involved and persistence at a task will be discouraged.

226

Displeasure with Difficult Tasks

A child will not be especially pleased with any program efforts which seek to strengthen behavior which is especially difficult for the child. The young child with learning and behavior difficulties will more likely attempt to avoid involvement and persistence at such tasks than is typical of other children. Enthusiasm over change, however, can be generated by a well designed program which is presented in a step-by-step fashion and which is based on immediate and frequent positive reinforcement.

Demonstrating New Behavior Requirements

The teacher should demonstrate to the child the behaviors that are desired in a given situation, and not assume that the child knows what to do. If the child refuses to participate in desired behavior (for example, will not return his play materials to the toy shelf after using them), the teacher should not blame such refusal on the child. It is easy to assume "Oh, he doesn't want to." If the desired behavior does not occur, the program is at fault. "How can the environment be arranged to get the child to engage in the desired behavior" becomes a legitimate concern.

Stating Requests Positively

When presenting requests for desired behavior, the teacher states them in a positive manner:

"John, join the group please."
"Sue, put your mat away."
"I cannot hear you, Tim. Please speak louder."
"You may play the new record as soon as we finish reading."

This type of statement tells the child precisely the behaviors which are expected. The positive approach is much preferred to one that threatens the child: "If you don't finish your reading, you cannot play the new record."

If the teacher wishes a child to make decisions in a choice situation, he must present alternative behaviors which would be acceptable. "John, you may remain and listen to the music or you may go outside." However, if John must go to the playground, stating this as if the child had a choice creates confusion. Suggesting, "John, do you not wish to go outside" when the intention is "John, go outside" is unfair to the child. The teacher should simply state, "Now, we shall go outside" and insure that such an activity will be enjoyable to him.

Process and End Product Reinforcement

The teacher should reinforce both the *end product* (for example, "Your picture is really pretty. I like your colors") as well as the *process* ("You really are coloring well. You stay in the lines nicely"). This is especially critical for tasks that require persistence, for example, "John, you can really stick to it." "Sue, I like the way you are trying different ways to put the puzzle together."

The child should know what the process behaviors are that result in a final product. He should rehearse and label these behaviors.

The child will learn to be pleased with task completion only to the extent that such behavior has produced pleasant consequences on *numerous* previous occasions. As both process behaviors and end products are labeled and reinforced these behaviors will acquire secondary reinforcement properties and will be self-maintaining through periods of failure (nonreinforcement from external sources). As new more difficult tasks are introduced, however, reinforcing events other than those associated with task completion or mastery may be required initially.

Individualized Reinforcing Events

Effective learning can occur with young children only if reinforcing consequences are individualized. Behavior patterns of enthusiasm, cooperation, and persistence are best encouraged by an environment which provides the novelty of a variety of events which are relevant to each child.

Using Natural Reinforcing Events

Maximum use of reinforcing events that are naturally available in the child's environment is important. Those activities and events which the child prefers should be identified and should occur after completion of low preference activities. "After we finish putting the toys on the shelf, we shall have a snack."

Emphasizing Social Reinforcement

Even if tangible or other consequences are provided, these events should be paired liberally with praise or other social reinforcers.

When providing reinforcers, the teacher should attempt to show in gesture, facial expression, verbal content, and verbal expression that he is pleased. Such behaviors would include smiling, winking, a pat on the shoulder, clapping—whatever is meaningful to the child being reinforced. In this manner, social events will become more influential as reinforcing events. Additionally, learning new behavior patterns and engaging in appropriate ones become meaningful social experiences.

Labeling Behavior

It is helpful to describe to the child the behavior that is being reinforced as it is occurring. "You picked up the toys and put them in the box. That's great. Now we shall have our snack." "You finished coloring the car. You did a good job coloring the car." "Look how well John wrote his name. John can now listen to his favorite record." In each instance, specific behavior was praised.

If reinforcement is delayed, it is especially valuable to describe the behavior being reinforced and have the child talk about what he did as he is being reinforced.

Attention to the Reinforcer

The teacher must be especially aware of the types of behaviors which may be reinforced by him and others in the child's environment. If the child receives attention ("Oh, that's all right") when he fails or becomes discouraged, non-involvement behavior may well be strengthened. If the task proves too difficult, it must be changed; the teacher should assist the child in making a successful response and then praise him. In this manner his "doing" behavior is strengthened instead of behavior patterns which interfere or compete with doing.

Realistic Encouragement

Comments like, "You *can* do the puzzle," "You are a big (strong, smart, fast) boy," should be provided as the child is demonstrating these or similar kinds of behavior. The child should label himself as he is engaging in competent behaviors. "I can really color." "Watch me cut this. I can follow the lines." Such experiences will insure that use of these behavior descriptions in the future will exert some prompting or reinforcing effect on the child as he is faced with various problems.

Clear Rules for New Behavior Requirements

In introducing new behavioral requirements, the teacher must specify precisely the behaviors which he wishes the child to acquire and the situations in which these behaviors are expected. He should state positively what the child *should do* instead of providing him with a long list of what he should not do. The teacher should provide clear rules for desired behavior so that the child knows when the behavior is expected. Children forget when too many rules are introduced, so they should be short, precise and few in number. The desired behavior and the resulting consequences should be demonstrated. Frequent reminders of desired behaviors and consequences are necessary, especially prior to occasions in which children are more likely to break the rules. A procedure of behavior rehearsal or of observing a model will insure that the child understands the contingency. The child should observe someone else obtaining reinforcement following the desired behavior pattern, or else he should "walk through" the behavior and sample the positive consequences. Rules which are not associated with reinforcement will not be followed: they will become important to the child only if behavior consistent with the rules is reinforced.

Behavioral requirements, consequences, and contingencies in nonspecific terms are open to misinterpretations or to varied interpretations. A statement such as, "If you are good today, we shall do something fun later," would be quite inappropriate. The young child can best learn if provided specific descriptions of behavior patterns which will result in specific consequences. "If we finish the work that I have given each of you and clean our tables, we shall play outside" becomes a more meaningful specification of the behavioral contingency.

Rules of Social Living

As suggested earlier, children must learn a variety of rules of social living. Prior to introducing a rule of how a child should behave in various social situations, these should be evaluated by the following questions:

1. Why is the rule needed?
2. Will the child understand it?
3. Can the child accomplish it?
4. What are the consequences of compliance? Of noncompliance?
5. Can the rule be enforced? If not, it is useless.
6. What time limit will be allowed for compliance?

Relevancy

A rule of social living should not be an arbitrarily imposed requirement. It should represent a desired behavior pattern that will contribute to the competency of the child as he interacts with a learning program and with others in a social situation. Rules become important to children if reinforcement is provided after following them.

Understanding the Rule

To insure that the child understands the rule initially, he should verbalize or demonstrate (rehearse) the rule behavior. Also, if the child experiences difficulty in following the rule, he should label the misbehavior and demonstrate the desired behavior. The teacher should remind the child of rules on non-reinforcing occasions and also review the rules prior to situations in which they are likely to be forgotten.

Accentuating the Positive

If much time is spent in objecting to the child's behavior with "Don't do that," "Stop that," "Come here and stop that noise," the program is wrong for that child. One educator (McClain, 1969), in emphasizing the need for a positive approach to children with learning and behavior problems, made the observation ". . . it is often remarked to a child that if he continues engaging in a certain behavior he will be punished. But has it ever been echoed that if he does so-and-so behavior he will be rewarded?" (p. 123)

Letting the Child Live a Little

A child can learn only through his own experience. If a child does not comply with a rule of social living, he should experience the unpleasant consequences. If it is a proper rule in the first place, the child can only learn about noncompliance by experiencing the consequences or through careful observation of others experiencing them. Until he is aware of the different consequences which distinguish compliance from noncompliance, he is in no position to make a choice between them.

If reasonable limits are set and if the unpleasant consequences are not drastic, the child will profit from experiencing the logical consequences of such behavior. He will be in a good position to make a choice and thus be responsible for his own behavior.

Pleasant and Precise Requests

In presenting a request (requirement, rule), the teacher should make it pleasant and specific, and not present a lengthy description of why the child should comply. "Clean up the play area" may be a rather simple activity for a teacher but quite difficult for a child. It may be helpful to develop a checklist in which various pictures or signs would depict aspects of a completed task. The child would check off each task segment as he completed it. "Clean up the toy area" may include:

—picking up toys
—picking up scrap paper and placing in waste basket
—arranging toy baskets in order on shelf
—arranging chairs around table
—putting colors, paste, and scissors in appropriate drawers.

With this type of behavioral specification, the child and teacher can tell at a glance the condition or quantity of task completion.

To increase the child's interest in the sequence of tasks, and to facilitate his memory of the steps in completing it, colored Polaroid pictures of the child engaging in each segment of the task may be prepared. These may be arranged in a booklet which the child can use to cue him through the task. The reinforcing consequences associated with task completion may also be represented. Naptime routine may be depicted by the following pictures:

—teacher pointing to shelf on which mats are stored
—child spreading mat on floor
—child lying on mat in resting position
—child folding his mat after naptime
—child placing folded mat on storage shelf
—child walking from rest area to work table
—child sitting at work table looking at teacher as she hands him his table work
—teacher smiling at child (or any other reinforcing consequence which can be depicted by picture).

Maintaining Present Behavior

When the teacher is introducing new behavioral requirements that are intended to replace well-established but inappropriate behaviors, the child will probably object. The teacher must be prepared to ignore these objections. These will disappear as the child is reinforced for following the new rule. The child will test the rule with emotional outburst and noncompliance. These are natural and predictable reactions to frustration, but they should be viewed as irrelevant behaviors that serve no useful purpose. If the teacher responds to these objections in an angry manner or if he becomes otherwise punitive, he runs the risk of prolonging the very behavior he wishes to eliminate. Scolding, lecturing, reprimanding, and taking the child's objections personally will not be beneficial to the child. The teacher must remain calm and persistent in representing the new behavior requirements and be prepared to reinforce compliance.

Providing Lead Time

A child should learn of a new behavior requirement in advance of requiring the behavior, especially if it represents distinct change. For example:

"Tomorrow we shall . . ."
"On Monday I want you to . . ."
"After the weekend . . ."

It is also useful to rehearse the new requirement to insure that the child understands what is expected. "Now let's practice this so that tomorrow we can . . ."

Consistency Is In

Consistency is essential in representing behavioral requirements and in providing consequences. The child should know what to expect. The child should be informed of the behavioral objectives set for him and should experience the contingency and consequences associated with alternative behaviors.

Inconsistency produces unpredictable contingencies which may result either in the child's withdrawal or hesitancy over becoming involved in other learning experiences.

Empty Threats Are Out!

A teacher should never represent a consequence to a child that is unrealistic or that will not or cannot be provided. "If you don't stop that, I'll send you home" may be completely unrealistic in terms of what will be done if the threatened behavior continues to occur. Such unfulfilled threats soon lose any behavior-influence functions which may be present. It is just as important that statements of positive reinforcers which are to follow appropriate behavior be realistic and fulfilled.

Describing Consequences

It may be useful to describe the consequences associated with requested behaviors. "Remember, after we finish cleaning the table, we shall get our finger paints out."

Dealing with Problems as They Arise

Whenever possible, the teacher should deal with problematic behaviors as they occur in the natural environments of the child. If the child behaves inappropriately in the classroom, on the playground, on the bus, or during lunchtime, the teacher should deal with the behaviors at the time they occur in that setting.

Removing the child from the natural settings for "special" therapy or treatment frequently creates more problems than are solved.

Presenting Unpleasant Consequences Logically

The teacher should present behavioral requirements in a positive manner and not threaten the child. "This behavior results in a positive consequence" is preferable to "Do this or I'll punish you."

The teacher may state realistic negative consequences for specific behaviors, but should do so in a factual manner. "If you continue with that noise, Sue, you must go to the quiet chair. You may remain with us if you choose to sit quietly." This represents a realistic choice contingency and is preferable to the threat, "Stop that noise or I'll send you to the quiet chair."

Threatening a child limits the manner in which he can be handled if he does not comply. In this instance, the teacher must follow through with the threat or teach the child that threats are empty.

Additionally, threats frequently elicit negativism or negative emotional reactions in children. Such reactions may be strengthened if these result in the removal of the threat.

Nagging Is Out!

Cajoling, debating, arguing, or attempting to convince a child to engage in certain behaviors is useless: nagging is out! As emphasized earlier, warning a child repeatedly merely teaches him that his misbehavior will only produce warnings. The teacher should explain to him why required behaviors are desirable. Most of the convincing, however, should be left to the effects of the positive consequences which follow the occurrence of the desired behavior.

Remaining Calm

The child's negativism or other irrelevant behaviors should not upset the teacher, who might reinforce these behaviors by exploding. Becoming emotionally upset after the child yells, "I don't want to do that stupid thing," will only serve to provoke him more. The expected behavior will serve as a model for the child when represented in a firm, deliberate manner. He is more likely to acquire "calmness" behavior under such provoking situations.

Admitting Mistakes

An effective child management program requires the honest and enthusiastic involvement of the teacher. If the teacher has been wrong or unreasonable, he should *admit it* to himself and the child. How can a child learn to do this himself unless he sees a human model?

Self-Knowledge

An effective behavior management teacher is aware of the events in the classroom environment which influence her own behavior. She recognizes that various characteristics of children and their behaviors have an effect on her behavior. She is open, flexible, and nondefensive about viewing herself as a possible factor in problem behaviors which children present.

A child who frequently engages in disruptive behavior will come to influence the teacher's emotional reactions to him. The teacher may begin to avoid the child as he is unpleasant to her, or to overrespond to minor behavioral deviations in an effort to avoid the child's more obviously disruptive or undesirable behaviors. These teacher behaviors may be strengthened by the immediate control over the child's behavior which these tactics produce. An objective appraisal of such teacher behaviors, however, may reveal that they serve the teacher but contribute little to the child's appropriate behavior development.

It should be recognized that the teacher may be unaware of

what she is doing and of the factors which are influencing this behavior. In other instances the teacher may well recognize and be dissatisfied with the manner in which she responds to some children. She may become upset too frequently and find herself yelling at the child or otherwise attempting through aversive means to control the child's behavior. Because such behaviors are unpleasant to her, she recognizes that the mere presence of the child, or his presence in situations in which disruptive behavior is highly likely to occur, produces excessive emotionality in her. She then begins to avoid the child whenever possible by keeping him occupied in activities which do little to contribute to his behavior development.

These illustrations serve to emphasize the need for constant teacher evaluation of her own behavior in relation to children. Such evaluation and modification of one's own behavior serve both the teacher and the child.

Criticism Is Out!

Criticism must be used sparingly, if at all. It is easy to criticize a child who does not behave as desired. However, such behavior on the part of adults serves no useful function in a behavior management program. The adult may feel better, but it does not assist the child. Scolding, shaming, making derogatory statements, (e.g., "that is really stupid"), punishing physically, or coaxing— these are demeaning actions and can only result in negative emotional reactions and related disruptive behaviors on the part of the child and teacher. Under such derogatory conditions, the child is likely to *label himself* as stupid, inadequate, or weak, and use these same labels in describing others.

If a child does not attain a behavioral objective, it is best to analyze the situation to identify the inadequate components of the program. If it is necessary to point out various unacceptable components of a child's behavior, the teacher should attempt first to identify some desired behavior and praise it prior to identifying the inappropriate ones. A child in a positive emotional state is more likely to accept and profit from correction or mild reprimand. "John, you put the toys away and you put your coat on. That was great. Now as soon as you straighten the chairs and put the colors away, we shall go on the playground." This is much preferred over one which declares, "John, you never remember to do everything. Now straighten the chairs and put the colors away. When will you ever learn!"

The statement, "Accentuate the positive, eliminate the negative, don't mess with Mister in-between," represents good advice.   Criticism and other forms of punishment are easy to deliver.   It is more valuable, however, to find some behavior to reinforce positively if the objective is to influence prosocial behavior.

Encouraging Self-Direction

A child with developmental difficulties will learn to make appropriate choices and to develop adequate self-direction skills if he is exposed to systematic experiences designed to foster these habits. Although structure and routine is needed, the child must be permitted to do things on his own.   Exploration and curiosity should be encouraged by introducing new events and problems in an enthusiastic manner and by reinforcing the child richly for approximations of these behavior patterns.

Whenever possible children should participate in selecting activities or in setting behavior goals.   "Which would you like to do—color the pictures or put the puzzles together?"   "We can listen to the music or we can look at color slides of animals. Which would you like to do?"   "How many pictures should we color today?   Two or three?"   "Do you think you can do three without stopping?"   "Johnnie, how many puzzles do you think you can do today?   You did two yesterday."

Mixing Easy with Hard

In arranging the learning programs, relatively easy experiences can alternate with more difficult ones.   Presenting a series of difficult tasks runs the risk of producing a dislike for learning tasks and thus strengthens inappropriate avoidance patterns which remove the child from the learning experience.   Having success with easy tasks initially provides more impetus to task involvement and persistence when the problems become difficult.

Shortening Difficult Tasks

Keeping difficult tasks short initially and providing an enriched schedule of high-preference reinforcing consequences are supportive to the child.   The more difficult the task, the more important it becomes to reinforce immediately and frequently.

The difficulty level of requirements should not be increased too quickly.   If the class becomes less manageable as tasks become difficult, the program is at fault, not the children.   The requirements may be too great, the reinforcers provided may be inadequate, or too much unpleasantness may be associated with the program.

Providing Distinct Cues

Prompting events for desired behaviors ought to be distinct and appropriate for the child. If behaviors occur which interfere with desired behavior, those events which prompt the competing behavior should be eliminated. For example, a child who is sitting next to a shelf containing toys or other attractive items may look at and reach for these during storytime. Moving the child closer to the teacher or covering the shelf will reduce the likelihood of this competing behavior.

Stimulating Multiple Senses

Use of materials and methods of presentation which utilize multiple sense modalities facilitates learning and memory. The child should touch an object as he looks. He should smell and touch as he looks at and listens to an animal.

Reinforced Repetition

Although repetition of a newly learned behavior in itself does not strengthen the behavior or insure effective retention, repetition that results in reinforcement does. Repetition to the point of overlearning should not be restricted to the initial teaching experience. Once a behavior is learned, use should be made of this new behavior in a variety of experiences and settings. This improves both retention and transfer to situations other than the teaching one.

Reviewing Frequently

Frequent review of newly acquired behaviors under varying environmental settings facilitates long-term retention. This should be conducted in a pleasant fashion which emphasizes the natural use of the newly acquired behavior pattern.

Learning Can Be Slow

New behavior patterns may be strengthened quite slowly. Reinforcement may be provided time and time again before obvious gains become apparent. In the early stages of learning a new behavior, consistency in providing reinforcers upon every occurrence of the behavior is essential.

Reinforcing Initial Effort

As the child initially enters into a new or a difficult task, his *effort* requires reinforcement initially. "Trying" refers to a set of behaviors which require reinforcement. Gradually, the performance criterion shifts and the teacher requires, through appropriate guidance, increasingly higher levels of performance prior to reinforcement.

Insuring Correct Responding

In the early stages of learning a new behavior pattern, it is essential that the child engage in the desired behavior or some acceptable approximation of it (i.e., that he makes the right response instead of an incorrect one). This requires that the child receive frequent feedback about the correctness of his behavior. Inappropriate behaviors should be provided immediate feedback and guidance to insure that the correct behavior can be engaged in and reinforced. If the child engages in inappropriate behavior, he must be informed immediately as to how he should behave. Considerable prompting may be needed initially, but will be removed gradually as the child is able to engage in the desired behavior on his own. It is easier to fade redundant cues than it is to remove a wrong response that has been reinforced on past occasions. If approximations of the desired behavior do not occur from the beginning of the program, the behavior unit expected is too complex, the cues are inappropriate, or the reinforcing events used are of insufficient value. These should be modified to the extent required for successful learning.

CHAPTER 10

Developing a Behavior
Management Program:
Design and Implementation

SETTING BEHAVIORAL OBJECTIVES

The concept of *should do* behaviors was introduced previously to refer to the behaviors which teachers and parents would like children to learn. These expectations may represent the desired behaviors in relation to both excessive and deficit behavior patterns and become the goals or objectives of a program of behavior management. It is perhaps true that many early education programs for children with learning difficulties have been somewhat unsuccessful or inefficient because no clear delineation has been made of the specific behavioral objectives of such programs. The behavior management approach, in contrast, identifies in precise descriptive and measurable terms the behavioral objectives which the program seeks to attain. This orientation will permit the teacher or parent to know what is being attempted and when the goal has been reached. This chapter will focus on the specific components of a program and the manner in which these factors are integrated into a meaningful educational experience.

It is essential, then, that the behavioral objectives designed for a specific child or for groups of children be realistic—not only are they possible for the children to attain but the behaviors will be acquired within a reasonable period of time. Setting realistic behavioral objectives can only result from a detailed knowledge of each child's learning characteristics and his present behavioral repertoires.

Target and Terminal Behavioral Objectives

In setting program goals, it is useful for the teacher to distinguish between *target* and *terminal* objectives. *Terminal* objectives refer to those behaviors within a developmental or curriculum dimension or subdimension which represent reasonable *progress or change* from the present behavioral patterns. The terminal objective may also represent the *should do* behaviors in relation to an excessive behavior pattern such as noncompliance, stereotyped behaviors, or crying. These terminal goals at any one time are arbitrarily defined and will differ from child to child. They may represent components of a child development curriculum or may be behavioral objectives which have been devised uniquely for an individual child.

Within a group of preschool children the curriculum or terminal goals could be defined in terms of what would be expected by the end of the semester or the end of the school year. They should represent *reasonable* goals that most children would attain. The definition of reasonable is rather arbitrary, however, when used with children with developmental difficulties since such children frequently do not acquire new behavior patterns in any normal progression and rate. It has been found quite valuable to establish goals for individual children which can reasonably be expected to be attained within two or three months. As these behaviors are approached, other higher level or more complex terminal goals are set.

Once the terminal behaviors are set, the *target,* transitional, or short-term behavioral objectives are described as a series of steps which represent closer and closer progression toward attainment of the terminal behaviors. The targets which represent immediate sequential steps along the various terminal behavior dimensions become the focus of the program at any moment in time. Some targets become more critical than others and may receive the major focus at any given time in a child's program. In fact, after the child is placed in a program, an initially set target may turn out to represent a rather difficult goal. This would necessitate the development of a series of smaller behavior goals.

The following terminal and target behavior objectives represent components of an early education curriculum. One of the expectations which Ms. Kahn has for the children enrolled in her early education class is that each will be able to become independent in fulfilling nap-time requirements. She developed the following terminal and target behavioral objectives:

Terminal Behavior:

Following lunch and when requested to do so by teacher, the child will follow in an independent manner nap-time routine from start to finish.

The components of nap-time routine and the definition of "independent manner" are included in the related target behaviors.

Target Behaviors:

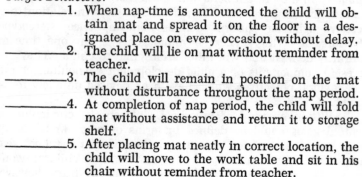

1. When nap-time is announced the child will obtain mat and spread it on the floor in a designated place on every occasion without delay.

2. The child will lie on mat without reminder from teacher.

3. The child will remain in position on the mat without disturbance throughout the nap period.

4. At completion of nap period, the child will fold mat without assistance and return it to storage shelf.

5. After placing mat neatly in correct location, the child will move to the work table and sit in his chair without reminder from teacher.

A child may meet some of the target behavioral objectives and not others. By observing the child in the classroom situation during nap-time the teacher can determine which of the specific target behavior objectives the child has met and which ones the child does not demonstrate satisfactorily. The unmet ones then become the focus of a behavior management program.

Tim satisfactorily met Target Behaviors 1, 2, 3, and 5. Due to physical and perceptual problems, he experienced difficulty with Target Behavior Number 4. The program would focus on teaching the motor skills required for satisfactory performance of this target behavior. This may require the development of three or four additional subunits or targets in this single area. It should be emphasized that in setting target objectives, each successive step must be relatively easy for the child to accomplish. If the initial set of target behavioral objectives is too difficult, they must be further subdivided into simpler steps to insure successful participation by the child. This emphasizes that the initial target behaviors set for a specific child as representing step progression toward reaching a terminal behavior objective must be viewed as tentative and subject to possible further elaboration as the child is exposed to the program.

It is important to recognize that at any single time the developmental education program for each specific child is based on numerous terminal and related target behaviors. The teacher is constantly providing the child with some experience. Ideally, this experience should be based on a plan to influence designated excessive and deficit behavior patterns.

Characteristics of Behavioral Objectives

Behavioral objectives, both terminal and target, should be stated in a form that will permit the teacher to know if the objectives have been attained or not. Goals such as "increase his understanding," "improve his social skills," "teach him more independence," or "encourage more initiative" are all much too general to be acceptable as behavioral objectives. How much is implied by "increase"? "How would "understanding" be defined and measured? What is "independence" and "initiative" in terms of what the child will do in specific situations and how will these be measured?

Even statements of *should do* behavior in the form "I want him to mind me" are too general. What is implied by "mind me"? What would the child do in certain situations or under what conditions that would lead the teacher to conclude "Now he minds me." How frequently should the child comply with teacher requests or directions in order to satisfy her that he does mind her? Would an independent observer agree with the teacher that the child's behavior has changed from a level of "poor compliance" to a level of "acceptable compliance"?

A statement of *should do* behaviors in the following form represents a distinct improvement: "When I make a request to Jim, he will comply with the request without excessive delay or negativism." However, even this statement requires further elaboration. What does "excessive" imply? What is "negativism"? Until these behavioral characteristics are objectively defined, it would not be possible in any satisfactory manner to determine if the behavioral goal had been reached or not.

Previous discussion focused on the necessity of behavior measurement. If behavioral objectives are not defined in terms that will be measurable in some manner or another, the strength or nature of the initial behaviors cannot be measured; nor can changes be evaluated.

In developing both terminal and target behavioral objectives, four conditions, as recommended by Mager (1962), should be met:

243

1. *The objective must be stated in performance terms.* What will the child do in order to demonstrate that he has reached the behavioral objective?   The following statements illustrate this requirement:

The child:		
names	goes	hangs up
identifies	does	folds
selects	says	draws
points to	places in	colors
repeats	picks up	writes
imitates	goes under	traces
puts on	ties	completes

Descriptive terms like knows, understands, feels, believes, or perceives are inadequate because they are too general.   Different teachers are likely to define them in a different manner.

2. *The objective will designate the important conditions under which the behavior is to occur:*   In the classroom, during lunch period while sitting with his peers, after nap-time is announced by the teacher, when given three puzzles from the Zee Series of Motor Skill Development.

3. *The objective will include a statement of the criterion of acceptable performance.*   This aim will designate how well the behavior is to be performed.   "The child, during lunch time in the school kitchen and eating with his peers and teacher, will eat his meal with the proper utensils without spilling.   This objective will be demonstrated on five consecutive days."   "The child, when shown pictures of a dog, cat, boy, ball, car, house, table, and chair, will label these with the correct name.   He will do this daily for four days."

4. *The method of measuring the desired behavior must be described.*   "The teacher will record the frequency of the *should do* behavioral objective during five-minute observation periods.   A wrist counter will be used."

An example of a worksheet used for preparation of behavioral objectives is included in Table 10.1.

Many behavior patterns which the teacher may wish the child to develop are difficult to define and measure in an objective manner.   Such characteristics as "to be happy," "to relate freely with others," "to be curious," or "to be socially sensitive" are examples of these abstract goals.   But if the teacher is to influence the attainment of these behavioral characteristics, she must attempt to define them in terms of observable behavioral units.   She may have the impression that Hieta does not "relate to other children."   She would describe a series of behaviors which, if

Table 10.1: Worksheet for Preparation of Behavioral Objectives

Child's Name: Eudora Jones	Teacher: Ms. Kahn
Date: Dec. 3, 1973	Setting: Child Development Classroom

1. *Behavior objective* (Target/terminal). Specify what the child must do or perform when he is demonstrating that he has acquired the objective.
   Eudora will select all red and blue items from among a group of items which are red, blue, green, yellow, black, brown, and purple.

2. *Conditions.* Under what conditions is the behavior to occur? The items will be presented to Eudora during class time at her desk with the request: "Put the red ones in this red box and the blue ones in this blue box. Tell me when you have finished." The teacher will be working with other children while Eudora is completing the task.

3. *Criterion of performance.* How well should the child perform? Eudora will select the items with 100 percent correctness without assistance from others within ten minutes of presentation. She will meet the criterion on three consecutive days.

4. *Measurement procedure.* How will the performance be measured and by whom?
   Ms. Kahn will observe Eudora on occasion to insure that the child is working without assistance. Ms. Kahn will evaluate the correctness of the task at the time Eudora informs her that she has finished.

present, would result in her concluding "Ah, now Hieta is relating to her peers." These might include such behaviors as:

—Hieta will look at others when they call her name.
—Hieta will look at other children when they are the center of class attention.
—Hieta will interact with other children when they initiate interaction with her.
—Without prompting from teacher, Hieta will move close to other children.
—Hieta will approach other children and initiate interaction with them.
—Hieta will initiate and maintain cooperative play with her peers.
—Hieta will smile and laugh appropriately when playing with other children.
—Hieta will engage in affectionate behavior in response to affection provided by a peer.

With these more observable behavioral goals, the teacher is now in a position to assess Hieta's present behavior in each segment as a beginning point for the development of behavior management programs. As progress is made, the child would be described as having more desirable behaviors of "relating to others."

COMPONENTS OF A BEHAVIOR MANAGEMENT PROGRAM

The next step is to decide what will be done to attain the behavior objectives developed for a child or for groups of children. What program experiences will be provided the child? To effectively reduce the learning and adjustment difficulties of the young child, these program experiences must be systematic and individualized. These experiences should be provided in an environmental setting that is most conducive to the occurrence of the desired behaviors. The environment should be arranged to minimize the likelihood of occurrence of inappropriate behavior. The teacher must have reasonable control over the discriminative events as well as influential consequences in order to insure a predictable learning experience for the children.

If a teacher has little control over the noise level of a class, she may have extreme difficulty in influencing auditory attending of a distractible child. If she has insufficient control over the events in the classroom setting which influence the child's distractible and hyperactive behaviors, the teacher may find it necessary to remove him from the class and into a "special environment" in which she can present the discriminative and reinforcing events in a programmatic manner. After the desired behaviors are strengthened in this controlled environment, the child may be moved through a series of steps back into the original classroom environment. The noise level in the classroom may be unchanged, but may no longer serve as a distracting event. The attending behavior may now be under the influence of those events which the teacher does control.

The present section provides a description of the components of a program experience and places these into the context of target and terminal behavioral objectives and their measurement. The behavior management program focuses on the gaps which exist between the present behaviors of a child and those behavioral patterns which we would like the child to develop. The program experiences provided the child are designed to eliminate this gap and include both (1) *exposure components* and (2) *consequence components*. The exposure components refer to that stimulation which will be presented in an effort either to overcome the deficits and to get the desired behavior to occur or to decrease the likelihood of excessive inappropriate behavior. The consequence component refers to those events which will be provided after behavior occurs. Each of these will be described in more detail shortly, along with a procedure for evaluating the effectiveness of the behavior management program. The following review presents a step-by-step description of this program development and evaluation process:

> **Decision made that child has problem.**

1. The child's behavior in a situation does not meet the expectations of the teacher. At this initial stage, impressions about the child's *does do* behavior as well as the *should do* behavior are usually subjective and nonspecific. "He doesn't pay attention," "He seems to be uninterested," "He has trouble with auditory perception," "He doesn't relate well to other children."

> ***Does do* behaviors defined and measured.**

2. These general impressions are translated into defined *does do* behaviors as observed under specific conditions. The behaviors are described in clear terms and measurements of these behaviors are obtained. These become the behaviors with which a child enters (his *entering behaviors*) into a specific behavior management program.

> ***Should do* behavioral objectives described.**

3. The impressions of what the child *should do* are translated into specific and objectively defined *terminal* and related *target* behavioral objectives.

```
┌─────────────────────────────────┐
│ ┌─────────────────────────────┐ │
│ │ Exposure components are     │ │
│ │ specified.                  │ │
│ └─────────────────────────────┘ │
└─────────────────────────────────┘
```

4. A program of exposure is designed. The program will describe what will be done to get the desired behaviors to occur under the desired conditions and to decrease the likelihood of occurrence of excessive undesired behaviors.

```
┌─────────────────────────────────┐
│ ┌─────────────────────────────┐ │
│ │ Contingency and conse-      │ │
│ │ quence components speci-     │ │
│ │ fied.                       │ │
│ └─────────────────────────────┘ │
└─────────────────────────────────┘
```

5. The program environment is arranged so that specific consequences will follow the occurrence of the desired and undesired behaviors. The goal of these consequences, of course, is to influence the strength of the preceding behaviors.

```
┌─────────────────────────────────┐
│ ┌─────────────────────────────┐ │
│ │ Procedures for measuring    │ │
│ │ program effects specified.  │ │
│ └─────────────────────────────┘ │
└─────────────────────────────────┘
```

6. As the program is implemented, procedures are specified for measuring the effects of the behavior management program.

This initial program sequence continues until the designated target behavior objective is reached. This new behavior becomes the entering behavior for the next target behavior objective. After the terminal behavior objective is satisfied, the teacher uses this behavior pattern as an entering behavior for a more complex behavioral objective. The total developmental education experiences thus represent a never-ending cycle of specific behavior management programs, each with a set of objectives and related program strategies for meeting these objectives.

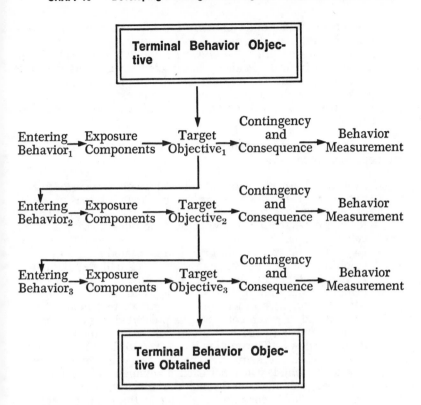

Exposure Components

The exposure components of the behavior management program define those events that will be provided the child in specific situations in an attempt (1) to get the target behavior, or some acceptable approximation, to occur under desired cue conditions and (2) to reduce the likelihood of occurrence of inappropriate behavior. The prompting procedures used to enhance the occurrence of the behavior as well as the discriminative cues which eventually will come to signal the time and place of the desired behavior should be designated. The manner in which the redundant prompts will be faded and eventually removed will be included. Additionally, components which will be used to enhance generalization of the desired behavior should be described. The exposure components will include a specification of:

1. *the physical setting:* the classroom, the speech therapy room, on the school bus, in the hall, on the playground;
2. *what the teacher will do:* the teacher will model the word and ask the child to repeat; the aide will sit by Tim and gently

249

touch his shoulder and comment "finish it" whenever Tim stops prior to completing the task;

3. *the materials or other stimulus events which will be provided:* the puppet from the Peabody Language Kit will be used by the teacher to get the child's attention; the child will be provided a work sheet with 15 circles and 15 squares drawn on it; the child will be provided puzzles one through five of the Zimmer Series, Level II.

The following programs illustrate this aspect of the behavior management program:

1. *Problem:* Kathryn received only 40 percent correct in a two-choice task which required her to match pieces of red or green paper when presented a color sample. The teacher expected her, under these conditions, to match the colors with perfect accuracy.

   Exposure Component: Kathryn will be seated in front of a teaching machine placed on a table in a small well lighted room. No other furniture is in the room. The face of the teaching machine includes a one inch square sample window, with two other similar windows two inches below. A red or green color will be presented in the sample window and both red and green will be presented in the lower windows. The child will be asked to choose the color that matches the sample. The teacher will demonstrate this to the child, will label each component of the tasks, and then guide Kathryn through the choice exercise.

2. *Problem:* Tim is constantly looking at the other children and at other objects and activities in the room when given a coloring task. He never finishes his task even though he does have adequate coloring skills.

   Exposure Component: Competing stimuli are reduced by placing a two foot cardboard screen around Tim's desk.

3. *Problem:* Melinda pulls her hair and begins to cry when confronted with a difficult task.

   Exposure Component: Melinda is presented with tasks she can complete successfully within short periods of time. Appropriate reactions to frustration will be described and modeled by the teacher. The difficulty level of tasks will be increased gradually as Melinda's frustration tolerance improves.

Consequence Component

This component of the behavior management program refers to (1) the specific consequences which the behavior will produce, (2) the manner in which these consequences will be provided and (3) the specific contingency in effect, including the frequency or schedule of providing the consequences. Brief examples will illustrate these components:

—Upon completion of the puzzle within the time period provided, the teacher will smile at Susan on every occasion and indicate "You can do those well," "I like the way you did that," "That was great work" or some similar praise.

—Upon putting the toys on the shelf, the teacher announces, "Now we shall go outside and play. You put the toys away nicely."

—Whenever Tom makes a spontaneous comment during unstructured play period, the teacher will approach him, smile warmly, and give careful attention to him.

—On an average of once for every three problems completed, the teacher will place a "Smiling Face" on Helen's card.

—Whenever Sue bites a child, she will be placed in time-out chair for three minutes.

—When Tom engages in "crazy" talk, he will be told "when you stop that nonsense I shall talk with you." He will be ignored until he initiates appropriate conversation.

—When Johnnie leaves the table prior to completing his meal, his plate will be removed. He will receive no more food until snack time.

—Social praise will be provided less and less frequently following spontaneous verbalization and eventually terminated.

INDIVIDUALIZING PROGRAM COMPONENTS

The specific exposure and consequence components of the behavior management program devised must be based on detailed information about the individual child. Description has been provided of procedures to use in obtaining measures of specific behavior patterns which are of interest. As noted earlier, direct observation of behavior in the natural situations in which it occurs is valuable in providing a preprogram (baseline) index of the strength of that behavior. The present discussion focuses on additional types of assessment data which are useful in developing the specific *exposure* and *consequence* components of a behavior management program.

Assessing Behavior in Specific Situations

It has been emphasized that behavior patterns should be described and assessed in relation to specific situations. Deficit behavior patterns should be evaluated in relation to specific stimulating conditions which attempt to get the behaviors to occur.

An example of a general procedure to follow in analyzing specific behavior deficits is presented in Table 10.2. The example emphasizes the relationship of a specific behavior being analyzed to broader behavioral dimensions which comprise a developmental education curriculum.

In observing excessive behaviors which vary in strength across situations, an attempt is made to identify possible relation-

Table 10.2: Specific Deficit Behavior Analysis Report

Name of Client: John D. Dear   Name(s) Of Evaluator: S. Gardner

Date(s) Of Evaluation: Jan. 26–28, 1973   Date: Feb. 14, 1973

MAJOR BEHAVIORAL DIMENSION: Language
SUBDIMENSION: Expressive language

SPECIFIC SKILL AREA: Using single words to label objects

TERMINAL BEHAVIOR OBJECTIVE: To name correctly commonly present objects* when requested by teacher to do so.

SPECIFIC TARGET BEHAVIOR OBJECTIVE: To name correctly toy object of ball, cat, boy when requested by teacher to do so.

PRESENT BEHAVIOR: Child does not label any objects when requested by teacher to do so.

RELATED BEHAVIORS: Child does point to objects correctly when requested to do so. Child can say words "cat, ball, boy" in imitation of verbal model of teacher.

EVALUATION PROCEDURES: Child presented with objects one at a time and questioned by teacher "what is this" or "what do you call it?" Procedures presented three times on each of two occasions separated by 2 days.

* man, woman, boy, girl, baby, ball, car, dog, cat, and similar objects

ships between differences in behavior strength and differences in the environmental conditions in which these occur. Knowing that a child bites other children on an average of eight times daily is valuable in deciding that a problem exists, but it does not provide the specific information needed in devising a behavior management program to deal with the biting behavior. Specific questions become more pertinent: When does Sue bite? Is she more likely to bite at one time than at another or under certain conditions than others? In the example of Sue described in Chapter 8 (p. 205), it was discovered that the child was much more likely to engage in biting and other aggressive behaviors during unstructured class periods than in structured periods. Further observation indicated that Sue was more likely to engage in aggressive behaviors during times when neither teacher nor peer was interacting with or otherwise attending to her. These observations suggested that the behavior management program developed to deal with the aggressive behaviors should begin with these specific conditions.

In another example, Lisa was more likely to become disruptive in structured class periods than in unstructured class periods. The major program effort for this child, as described in Chapter 6 (p. 155), focused on the structured periods. Tim was observed to engage in lengthy crying episodes on an average of six times daily. But most of these occurred during play periods when his peers would take toys away from him. Cal is much more likely to be excessively hyperactive after being brought to school by his mother than on those days when he rides the bus. These types of observations provide information about more specific factors involved in a designated behavior pattern. Hunches can be developed by the teacher concerning those events which precipitate or which render more likely various behavior patterns.

Identifying Potential Reinforcing Events

In addition to developing hunches about the consequences which may be maintaining specific problem behaviors, it is necessary to identify a series of additional events which may be reinforcing to each child for use in the behavior management program designed to strengthen more appropriate behaviors. These events should be arranged in terms of their relative importance to each child. In this manner, as illustrated earlier, a reinforcement hierarchy will be developed. It must be remembered that the success of a behavior management program depends upon both the *accessibility* and *use* of those reinforcing consequences which are of high value to each child. Relatively weak reinforcing consequences may be maintaining highly bothersome behavior patterns due to the unavailability of more influential positive events for appropriate behavior. Or the child may be unsuccessful in acquiring new behavior patterns due to the use of low value reinforcing events in program efforts.

In identifying a group of reinforcing events for use with specific children, the teacher should be highly specific. It is not sufficient to indicate that Timothy is influenced by social reinforcement. It would be necessary to identify the types of social reinforcement (attention, praise, approval, affection, control of others) and the classes of influential social agents (peers, older males, boys, young teachers). A child, for example, may be influenced by social approval from an adult male, but not so by a young female teacher.

Observing the Child in Natural Settings

The naturalistic observations of the child as he functions in the school setting will be used to complement information about the child that may be obtained from other sources. Information obtained by such means as standardized tests, checklists, and developmental inventories may provide information about learning rate, strengths and weaknesses in certain skill areas, and the types of materials to which the child responds most readily. This information will provide assistance both in setting realistic behavioral objectives and in deciding upon the specific materials and procedures to use in a behavior management program.

Identifying the Consequences of Excessive Behavior

In observing an excessive behavior pattern, attention should focus on the consequences of such behavior. What happens to the child as he engages in the focal behavior? These observations can provide hunches about the events which are reinforcing the behavior. In observing both Sue and Lisa it was noted that aggressive and disruptive behaviors produced immediate teacher attention. At other times, the teacher would stay away from the child as much as possible as she feared that any attention would upset the child. Both Sue and Lisa appeared to enjoy both adult and peer attention as these children stayed close to others even during free play periods when they could have isolated themselves. These observations suggested that the inappropriate behaviors were being maintained by the social attention that they produced.

In observing Tim's crying behavior, it was noted that in

many instances the crying resulted in the return of the lost toy by the peer or teacher. This observation led to the hunch that the crying behavior was being maintained because it provided the consequence of a regained toy. On occasion the teacher would soothe him with extra attention. Both positive and negative reinforcement were speculated as possible factors in the high-rate crying behavior. These hunches would be incorporated into a behavior management program designed to encourage more appropriate social behavior.

Programming for Excessive Behavior Patterns

A behavior management program devised to deal with excessive behavior patterns will consist of two sets of closely interrelated procedures: (1) those concerned with decreasing the strength of the excessive behavior, and (2) those directed toward increasing the strength of behavior which will replace the excessive behavior pattern. The behavior objectives for an isolated child who unexpectedly bites other children may include reducing the biting behavior to a zero level, and increasing the number of appropriate social responses by 30 percent. In evaluating the excessive behavior pattern as it occurs in various situations, the teacher should carefully observe the possible function which this behavior may serve for the child. The following example emphasizes the importance of this type of concern. Becky has a difficult time getting along with other children. She is isolated by other children and spends most of her time in solitary activity unless guided specifically by the teacher to become involved in structured interaction with peers. During these times she appears to enjoy this peer contact, but will quickly withdraw whenever the teacher is not present. Gradually, over the course of the first six weeks of the school term, Becky developed a variety of aggressive and other disruptive behaviors that involved her peers. The teacher attempted to ignore the behavior initially but finally decided that she had to do something to "get rid of that bothersome behavior. She is upsetting her peers too frequently. They really isolate her now. I have difficulty getting them to interact with her at all."

During the baseline observation period, the teacher wondered about the consequences which were maintaining the behavior. She hypothesized that the peer attention, although of a seemingly negative nature, was the reinforcing event. It then occurred to her that this child, who had been quite shy, isolated, and without peer interaction skills, had at least developed some, although inappropriate, social behavior. If a behavior management program were designed to eliminate these behaviors, the child would once again be without any means of interacting with her peers. A program was developed to teach more acceptable social interaction skills through modeling and guided participation. Peer and teacher attention paired with tangible events were used as reinforcers. The disruptive behavior was ignored whenever possible. As the child acquired skills interacting with her peers, first in highly structured situations and gradually under increasingly unstructured conditions, the disruptive behaviors disappeared.

This example emphasizes that no behavior pattern should be evaluated or dealt with in isolation. Any specific behavior must be viewed as one aspect of highly complex repertoires of behavior which characterize a child. The events which are maintaining a behavior pattern, the interrelationships of various behavior patterns, and the behavior patterns which may be viewed as acceptable alternatives of present behaviors must all be viewed from a point of view of "what is best for the child."

The checklist presented in Table 10.3 provides a guide to developing a program for eliminating inappropriate behavior patterns.

Table 10.3: Steps in Analysis of Excessive Behavior Pattern

————— 1. What behavior (or behaviors) are creating difficulty?

————— 2. In what setting does the behavior occur (place, time, conditions)?

————— 3. What is the strength of the behavior (frequency, rate, duration, magnitude)?

————— 4. What consequences does the behavior produce which may be maintaining the behavior? (Remember that reinforcement may occur only infrequently and still maintain the behavior—getting attention, avoiding unpleasant duties or situations, etc.)

————— 5. Is the presumed reinforcement positive or negative?

————— 6. Can the presumed reinforcing consequences be eliminated?

————— 7. Can the presumed reinforcing events be used to strengthen acceptable competing behaviors?

————— 8. Does the child have acceptable alternative behaviors in his repertoire which would be suitable in the situation?

————— 9. Does the environment provide sufficient opportunity to obtain positive consequences for acceptable behavior?

—————10. What behaviors should be taught which will replace the excessive behaviors?

What Specific Procedures Should be Used

In deciding on the specific exposure and consequence strategies to use with any child, numerous decisions are made. If a child engages consistently in some excessive behaviors that disrupt the class, what specifically should be done? A number of different procedures are available to the teacher. The teacher may decide:

—to arrange for aversive consequences to follow the behavior,
—to ignore the behavior or to otherwise remove any reinforcing consequences which may be maintaining the behavior, thus following an extinction procedure,
—to reinforce a specific incompatible behavior pattern to replace the undesired excessive ones,
—to use a time-out procedure,
—to use a response-cost procedure,
—to identify and remove or modify the external discriminative stimulus events which cue the behavior,
—to identify and remove or modify situations which provoke disruptive emotional behavior which in turn may increase the likelihood of the excessive behavior patterns, or
—to differentially reinforce all other behaviors that will serve to replace the excessive pattern.

In planning for the development of new behaviors and the strengthening of existing ones, a similar large number of decisions must be made. As examples:

—What will be done to insure that the desired behavior does occur? Will physical guidance, modeling by a peer, verbal prompting, or removal of distracting stimuli be used?
—What types of reinforcing events will be used—primary, social, token?
—How will the reinforcing events be managed? If tokens are used, for example, how will they be presented to the child? How will the tokens be exchanged?

The specific procedures or combination of procedures will depend upon numerous factors. These include characteristics of the child, of the behaviors being changed, of the physical and social settings, and of the teacher and other persons who will administer the program. A program designed for a child may be ideal from a theoretical viewpoint, but may be difficult if not impossible to implement due to the characteristics of the physical and social environment in which the child resides. The room may be too noisy. The seating arrangement may not permit suitable reduction of visual distraction. The room may not permit a time-out location. There may be no area of the room which could be used for a reinforcement area. There may be too many children in the class for highly individualized programs.

It is true also that the teacher may be unable to use various procedures. She may feel highly uncomfortable, for example, in using any type of punishment procedure. Or she may be unable to use an extinction procedure with disruptive behavior as she will not tolerate the temporary added disruption that is likely to occur. Another teacher may be quite able to use secondary reinforcers but refuses to use primary ones due to her philosophic concepts.

There are no "pre-packaged" or "cookbook" programs that can be used effectively by everyone. Each teacher will develop those programs that are most feasible in view of the particular combination of child-environment-teacher characteristics.

IMPLEMENTING THE PROGRAM

Now the stage is set for implementing the program. The behavior has been described and measured, the program objectives have been set, the exposure and consequence components have been decided upon, and a procedure for continuing evaluation of the program effects has been selected. The checklist presented in Table 10.4 may prove useful in evaluating the thoroughness of the

Table 10.4: Checklist for Program Evaluation

YES		No
_____	1. Have you identified the behaviors which you wish to influence today?	
_____	2. Are these target behaviors related to broader terminal behavior goals?	_____
_____	3. Have you specified the environmental setting in which you will present the procedures?	
_____	4. Are the exposure procedures appropriate for the behaviors which you wish to influence?	_____
_____	5. Are consequences available for the desired behavior and are those appropriate?	
_____	6. Have you specified the schedule of providing the consequences?	_____
_____	7. Have you specified the procedure of providing the consequences?	_____
_____	8. Have you specified the procedure to determine if the target behavior is being influenced?	
_____	9. Do you have alternative strategies if the program fails?	_____

program. If the checklist uncovers some program deficiencies, the program should be delayed until these have been clarified.

RECORDING AND EVALUATING BEHAVIOR CHANGE

The measurement of behavior which was initiated during the baseline period should be continued throughout the behavior management program in order to determine the effectiveness of the program components. These recordings can be transferred to a graph (as illustrated on p. 260) to provide a visual display of the changes in behavior that may coincide with the initiation of a specific behavior management program.

If suitable progress is not being made in the behavior management program once it has been initiated, the teacher should examine each component of her program and make changes in those components which she feels are contributing to the program difficulty. A checklist is presented in Table 10.5 to provide guidance to the teacher in this evaluation.

Table 10.5: Trouble–Shooting Checklist for Evaluating Program Difficulties

YES		No
_____	1. Are the target behavioral objectives too difficult for the child?	_____
_____	2. Are the exposure procedures (including prompting) appropriate?	_____
_____	3. Are cues for inappropriate competing behaviors present? (What are they? How can they be eliminated?)	_____
_____	4. Are the reinforcing or punishing consequences appropriate for the behavior being influenced?	_____
_____	5. Is the child aware of the contingency?	_____
_____	6. Is the promptness of the consequence appropriate?	_____
_____	7. Is the consequence presented frequently enough?	_____
_____	8. Does the classroom environment have aversive components which may produce avoidance behavior?	_____
_____	9. Are competing behaviors present which may be under negative reinforcement control?	_____

In evaluating the effects of specific behavior management procedures, it may be valuable on occasion to use a *reversal procedure*. Figure 10.1 illustrates the four components of this technique in a program in which teacher and aide provided immediate social reinforcement following a compliance response of a seven-year-old negativistic child.

Baseline recording indicated a compliance rate of 28 percent. Following this baseline period and continuing for five days, immediate social reinforcement was provided upon compliance. This procedure produced an average percentage of compliance of 47 percent. In order to determine if the social reinforcement procedure was in fact the critical factor that produced the increase in compliance behavior, the teacher and teacher assistant again made an effort to respond to the child as they had during the baseline period. The rate of compliance behavior showed a steady decline during the following four days. The social reinforcement procedure was then re-introduced, with the result of a steady and rapid increase in compliance behavior during the following five days. The reversal or return-to-baseline procedure demonstrated the

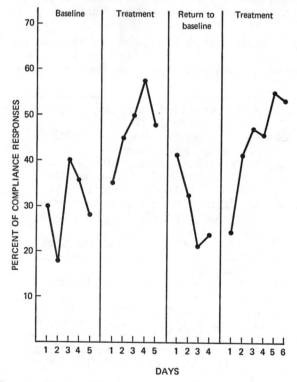

FIGURE 10.1:   *Illustration of a Reversal Procedure*

effectiveness of the immediate social reinforcement in increasing the rate of compliance behavior.

A similar procedure is used to determine if the behavior management procedure used to change the behavior needs to be continued. Compliance behavior, after being reinforced continuously for a period of time, may continue at high strength without the necessity of continuous immediate social reinforcement from the teacher. Such behavior may be reinforced (and thus maintained) by peers, or by other aspects of the environment. This can be determined by removing teacher reinforcement, that is, by a return to the procedures used by the teacher during baseline. If the child continues to comply with teacher request, the behavioral objective will be met and the program changed to focus on other target behaviors.

PART IV

Application to Learning and Behavior Problems

CHAPTER 11

Applications: Promoting
Desired Behavior Patterns

This section on application will focus on the use of behavior management principles and related procedures in influencing various deficit and excessive behaviors. This chapter describes behavior management strategies to use in facilitating the development of some general behavioral patterns which are viewed rather universally as desirable objectives of an early education program. Consideration will be given to the topics of curiosity, self-concept, frustration tolerance, and self-confidence. Next, suggestions for facilitating the development of incidental learning skills and memory skills are provided. The latter part of the chapter will describe programs for the development and improvement of imitation skills and skills of social interaction. Finally, selected references are provided for the teacher who wishes to design behavior management programs for the development of various self-help skills and basic language skills in young children who exhibit severe deficits in these behavioral areas. Chapter 12 will provide program suggestions for influencing a number of other prevalent problem behavior patterns.

GENERAL BEHAVIOR PATTERNS

As described in the opening chapter, the behavior management approach finds it useful to view general and complex behaviors as representing various repertoires or classes of behavior. Behavioral descriptions reflected in adjectives (he is a *patient* child), adverbs (he behaves *patiently*), and nouns (his *patience* is) are viewed as having reference to classes or types of behaviors which the child demonstrates with some consistency. Instead of speaking of a child's self-concept, reference is made to his self-concept behaviors. Likewise such child characteristics as being independent, affectionate, and persistent all refer to patterns of identifiable behaviors. These and similar terms are labels for general classes of behavior. They are not viewed as internal personality traits which cause a child to behave in a specific manner in various settings. These are behavior patterns which can be influenced by the teacher in the classroom setting.

GENERAL PATTERNS DEVELOP FROM SPECIFIC RESPONSES

A child does not suddenly demonstrate general behavior patterns, nor do they develop in some mysterious fashion. These inclinations begin with very specific behaviors acquired in quite specific situations. A child learns, for example, sharing behavior or self-confidence behaviors in terms of the previously described social learning principles which also underlie learning to dress himself, to distinguish red from green, to feel positive emotionality in a situation, or to write his name. Specific behaviors of sharing or specific behaviors which may be defined as self-confidence behaviors become more generalized patterns as they result in varying reinforcing consequences in numerous situations. Again, these behaviors are acquired initially by a child as a response to a specific situation. Then he learns to generalize that behavior to another situation. Gradually, consistency appears in the child's behavior as a result of frequent reinforcement in numerous situations. A child's sharing behavior pattern may reflect 100 or perhaps even 5000 previous learning experiences in which sharing behavior has been reinforced. The more the behavior is reinforced in various settings the greater the likelihood that it will reoccur, even in new settings.

The discussion to follow is only suggestive of the types of experiences which may contribute to the behavior patterns described. These descriptions, albeit brief, are intended to provide the teacher with some general direction to designing and implementing a variety of additional experiences for facilitating the various behavior patterns. These experiences cannot be presented haphazardly or left to chance when working with young children with learning and behavior difficulties. The likelihood is small that the child will acquire the behaviors which make up patterns of self-confidence, frustration tolerance, curiosity, or positive self-concept unless systematic and long-term attention is provided in these behavioral areas.   The effects of the child's excessive experiences of failure are too influential to expect otherwise.

CURIOSITY

As suggested in Chapter 2, young children with severe learning and behavior difficulties frequently are rather restricted in their curiosity behaviors. As a result the child is less likely to attend to and interact with various unfamiliar aspects of his environment, and possible learning experiences are restricted.

Curiosity behaviors may be developed and strengthened in the young child by:

1. Exposing the child on a daily basis to new events—toys, foods, textures, shapes, auditory stimuli, people—when the child is relatively relaxed and in a good mood; presenting events in a positive enthusiastic manner which doesn't force new events on the child; reinforcing the child initially for any approach behavior.
2. Encouraging exploration which makes use of multiple sense modalities. As the child begins to interact with new events he should describe what he is experiencing. He should be encouraged to rub, squeeze, smell, look at, hear, and taste events.
3. Having a peer model exploring the new event and encouraging the child to imitate the model if the child is hesitant.
4. Encouraging the child to label new events and to ask questions about aspects of them.
5. Presenting exploration as a fun activity: a child explores new events as his peers observe, and the teacher encourages group participation in describing aspects of the events.
6. Remembering that an adult who is warm, sociable, and outgoing and who encourages divergent behavior is likely to get children to demonstrate curiosity behaviors.
7. Presenting problems that have numerous acceptable solutions. Although major emphasis in an educational program for young children with learning and behavior difficulties is on a structured environment in which acceptable behaviors are distinct, the teacher must move beyond this structure as she encourages exploration.
8. Encouraging the child to explore various aspects of himself— his feelings, his physical characteristics, his behavior; offering him new labels for aspects of himself which he is unable to identify or describe.
9. Encouraging free, uninhibited, and even exaggerated ex-

pression as the child explores new events. This can be encouraged initially by modeling the behaviors and having the child imitate these.

SELF-CONCEPT

Self-concept behaviors refer to the verbal labels that a child uses to describe aspects of himself and his behaviors and to the positive and negative emotionality that is influenced by these labels. The self-concept behaviors of the young child with severe learning and behavior difficulties is frequently of a predominately negative nature. The child is described as "not liking himself," "doesn't believe that he could do if he would try," "not thinking much of his capabilities." These verbal-emotional behavior patterns do serve as conditioned and discriminative events which influence what the child does do in numerous instances. If a child labels himself in relation to a task or social situation as "I am ugly," "I am dumb," "I can't do that because I'm not strong," he is most likely to avoid appropriate interaction with the situation. This correspondence between a child's verbal-emotional behaviors and other non-verbal behaviors has been demonstrated by studies with young children (Lovaas, 1961; Lovaas, 1964; Risley and Hart, 1968). Thus, a promising behavior management strategy is one which seeks to teach the child a range of verbal behaviors denoting various appropriate non-verbal behaviors. These would include such labels as "I can do that," "I like to play," "It is fun to work," "I am strong," "I am fast," "I like you," "I am good at that," "I can hit the ball hard," "I can really do those puzzles," "I am pretty."

These verbal behaviors are best taught as the child is successfully engaging in various activities. The labels not only acquire influence over the future occurrence of the behavior but also become associated with the positive emotionality that results from the positive reinforcer. When confronted with the situation in the future the child will suggest, "I like that. I want to do that." These verbal behaviors will arouse positive emotional behaviors which in turn will increase the likelihood that the child will approach and interact with the activity.

More specifically, positive self-concept behaviors may be strengthened as illustrated in the cue sequence:

CUE	BEHAVIOR	CONSEQUENCES
"Color this" as the teacher places a picture and crayons on the child's table.	Child colors the picture.	Teacher exclaims, "You can really color well. What a nice picture. You selected such pretty colors."

The social reinforcement is a conditioned event for positive emotionality. This becomes associated with the activity of coloring. While the child is feeling good in the presence of the picture, the teacher labels the child's behavior again with such comments as "You colored well," "You are skillful." The labels become associated with the positive feelings and, after a few pairings, become conditioned events for positive emotionality. In the future, whenever these labels are used, they will result in positive emotionality. Such positive emotionality increases the likelihood of approach behavior in similar situations in the future. After this and numerous other experiences of this nature are repeated on ten, 100, 1000, 3000 occasions, the child gradually develops appropriate positive self-concept behaviors. It should be emphasized that the child, on numerous occasions, should be prompted to label aspects of his behavior with positive and realistic labels.

FRUSTRATION TOLERANCE

The young child with learning and behavior difficulties is likely to behave in a variety of disruptive ways when confronted with frustrating events. Behavior patterns of patience and persistence in the face of difficulty are minimal. He may be described as being unable to delay gratification sufficiently to maintain appropriate behavior in the absence of immediate and frequent reinforcing events. More appropriate frustration tolerance behaviors may be encouraged by the following types of strategies:

1. Remember that a child who is in a good mood is less likely to engage in disruptive emotional outburst when frustrated. Providing the child with frequent and varied reinforcing events for engaging in a range of appropriate behaviors creates the positive emotionality which makes up the good mood.

2. Teach increased persistence in the following manner:

    (a) Place child in a minimally distracting situation and present him with a task which he enjoys. Reinforce him initially for any persistence which he exhibits. Label this persistence. When the child presents signs of leaving the task, prompt him to continue for a short additional time. Reinforce this additional persistence immediately and label it with such comments as "I'm glad you worked a little longer," or "Timmy, you stayed at that for a long time. I'm proud of you."

    (b) In selecting a task, insure that the child will be successful with it. Be sure that persistence will pay off in problem solution or in the increased number of units of a task which are completed. If the child is able to sit and work at a given activity for five minutes, for example, provide additional prompts for him to remain at the task for six or seven minutes. Provide definite physical cues for "time at task." This may consist of an hour-glass sand timer, a clock timer, music, a special light, a metronome, or teacher cueing. These should be apparent but nondistracting. These should be presented in a direct positive manner: "Susan, color the picture until the music stops" or "Put the puzzles together until this light goes off." Initially stop the music or turn off the light within the child's present persistence level. Gradually increase the time interval in an irregular fashion—five minutes, then four minutes, then six minutes, then three minutes, then seven minutes, then 5½ minutes, then 7½ minutes, then eight minutes, then five minutes, until a desired level is reached.

(c) Gradually introduce more difficult tasks after stable control has been established over persistence behavior in the easier tasks. Intersperse easy and more difficult tasks as the child learns to persist. Require longer periods of persistence for the easier tasks to insure that the child is being successful.

(d) Reinforce the child consistently with high-preference reinforcers.

(e) Gradually fade out the physical prompts and set specific behavioral goals for the child to attain prior to termination of a specific task or activity.

3. If a child experiences difficulty in maintaining persistence as the types of tasks or activities become difficult, the following procedure may be helpful:

(a) Identify a series of tasks that change slowly from easy to difficult for the specific child.

(b) Identify a range of high preference reinforcers which can be used.

(c) As the child is presented with tasks that are difficult for him, permit the child to select a high preference reinforcer and display it on the work table. Immediately upon completion of the difficult task, provide the reinforcer. It may be necessary to sit with the child and to assist him whenever he encounters too much difficulty. Remember, the child must be successful if he is to acquire persistence behavior in the face of difficulty. Use whatever prompts and provide whatever assistance is needed. These may be faded gradually as the child's persistence behaviors become more stable.

4. The child who is unable to maintain his appropriate behavior in the absence of immediate and frequent reinforcement will require systematic experiences in which reinforcing events are moved from immediate food items, to tokens which are exchanged for food immediately, to tokens which are provided frequently to be exchanged for events at the end of a specific activity, and finally to tokens which are provided after task completion and exchanged later in the day or week for high-preference reinforcing events.

SELF-CONFIDENCE

A description of a child as having "self-confidence" refers to a range of specific behaviors which the child demonstrates in various settings. Generally such behavioral descriptions would include: enters into problem situations without unnecessary caution, reacts with curiosity to new or puzzling events, is open to experiencing new situations or events, will enter into difficult situations, is not unduly upset by failure, has verbal behaviors of the positive self-concept kind, "I can do," "I am strong," or "I am a good worker," is free to use his skills in an uninhibited manner, and relates easily to others.

The teacher can facilitate the development of such self-confidence behaviors in children with learning and behavior difficulties by:

1. *Providing the child with numerous experiences of being successful.* This requires that the school environment is structured to complement the present behavioral repertoire of each child.

2. *Recognizing that each new skill a child develops and uses in a variety of situations adds to his self-confidence behaviors.* That is, the greater the number of appropriate behaviors a child has in his repertoire, the more likely he is to enter into difficult situations. He will use these behaviors consistently and spontaneously at appropriate times if they have a consistent history of positive reinforcement.

3. *Labeling skill attainment and appropriate use of these behaviors; with such positive labels as "You are fast," "You can do that well," "I am pleased with the way you did that one."*

4. *Exposing the child to a variety of new tasks and social situations and reinforcing both his initial approach to the situations as well as his continued involvement and successful solution of problems.*

5. *Keeping failure and punishment to an absolute minimum.* The child can best learn to use his skills if he has an abundance of success. He also will learn 'positive emotional behaviors and related positive labels depicting competency under conditions of frequent success and infrequent punishment.

6. *Reinforcing a realistic approach to problems.* This will require careful and systematic presentation of situations which require that the child make realistic discriminations between what he can accomplish presently and what he cannot do.

INCIDENTAL LEARNING SKILLS

As noted in Chapter 2, young children with severe learning and behavior difficulties often reflect deficits in incidental learning skills. They experience unusual difficulty in acquiring new behavior patterns incidental to well-structured learning tasks. These difficulties in incidental learning reflect attentional deficits, deficits in curiosity behavior, and motivational deficits. In some instances, the limitations in incidental learning are a reflection of widespread avoidance behavior. The child is fearful of many aspects of his environment and thus views these as aversive situations to be avoided.

Incidental learning may be enhanced by the following types of procedures:

1. *Decreasing the fear-provoking qualities of the school environment in the shy and fearful child.* This may be accomplished by carefully guiding the child into participation with those aspects of the environment which produce negative emotionality and by providing liberal and frequent positive reinforcement for such participation. As the conditioned stimuli for negative emotionality are extinguished and replaced by events which control positive emotional responses, the child is more likely to attend to and interact with more aspects of his environment. As a result he will be reinforced for behaviors other than those strengthened in the structured teaching program provided by the teacher.

2. *Increasing the reinforcement value of exploration.* The child is guided into interacting with aspects of his environment and reinforced for this interaction. He is observed at times when he has not been instructed to behave in a designated manner and reinforced for any exploration behaviors which may occur.

3. *Increasing the cue components of the school environ-ment.* The child is reinforced for recall of various cues even though he was not instructed to attend to and remember these cues. For example, a green lantern is placed over the coat rack, a loud record plays during lunch period, or someone wears different colored shoes in a story. The children who recall any of these events are reinforced. If this is repeated at various unscheduled times, the children are more likely to attend to and otherwise inter-act with various components of their environment. Such inter-action increases the likelihood of learning new behaviors.

4. *Encouraging the child to describe his behaviors as he moves through an activity;* also encouraging him to describe the events which he views as influencing this behavior. This activity will increase his awareness of cue-behavior-reinforcement se-quences.

5. *Stopping an activity at unscheduled times and having a child describe an immediately preceding experience.* The child is reinforced initially for any recall, and the quality and complete-ness of the recall is increased for reinforcer attainment. This should increase the child's attention to various behaviors in rela-tion to cues and reinforcers.

6. *Providing experiences to improve the child's imitation skills.* The child role-plays, imitating various models. Initially, the teacher will model some behavior and have everyone imitate her as she engages in some exaggerated behavior. Gradually, he decreases the exaggeration to encourage the child to be more atten-tive to more subtle aspects of the model's behavior. After the child has been reinforced for increasingly complex imitative be-haviors, have a peer serve as a model. The child is reinforced for imitating a wide range of peer behaviors in a variety of settings. Such increased imitation skills should enhance the child's inci-dental learning skills.

MEMORY SKILLS

In view of the difficulties which children have in learning new behaviors, it becomes essential that the environment be designed to enhance retention of behaviors once they have been acquired. In addition to the previously discussed factors of immediate and appropriate reinforcing events, reinforced repetition, and frequent review in various settings, the following strategies may be helpful in improving retention of desired behavior patterns:

1. The teacher is careful to avoid excessive emotionality. Anxiety over behaving correctly can interfere with the recall of

previously practiced behavior. In a relaxed and pleasant environment, the child is less likely to engage in excessive emotionality which interferes with memory of previously learned behaviors.

2. During the learning experience, the teacher arranges for the simultaneous presentation of cues which stimulate multiple sensory modalities. As an example, a child may look at and touch an object as he labels it.

3. The teacher provides distinct and exaggerated (redundant) cues when possible during the learning experience. The exaggeration can be faded as the child engages repeatedly in the correct behavior.

4. Memory is facilitated when new concepts and skills are developed through a gradual and systematic progression from well-established behaviors presently in the child's repertoire. Concrete materials and related experiences involving the child doing something should be used whenever possible to increase the retention of concepts.

5. The teacher distributes practice to facilitate retention. If the teaching sessions are too long and require too much attention and effort, the child soon forgets what he has learned.

6. Better memory occurs if only a few new behaviors are taught in a given period of time. This is especially true if the new behaviors are highly similar. The child becomes confused if he is taught too many new labels at one time. Memory would be facilitated if each lesson contained material which is highly dissimilar to that which precedes or follows it in the daily class schedule. Rest periods should be provided between structured learning experiences. The most important materials should be presented at the beginning or at the end of a class period, as these are the behaviors that are most likely to be retained.

7. Retention of motor behaviors may be facilitated by having the child label the motor behaviors.

8. Memory is facilitated when the materials involved are familiar and meaningful, for example, when new associations are formed between familiar events.

GENERALIZED IMITATIVE SKILLS

Generalized imitation skills are essential for the effective acquisition of many types of learning in young children. As described in Chapter 2, many children with severe learning and behavior difficulties have poorly developed skills of imitation. There is evidence (Baer, Peterson, and Sherman, 1967; Martin, 1971; Metz, 1965) that even the more severely disabled child not only will imitate the behavior of others when this imitated behavior is reinforced but also he will acquire generalized imitation skills. In an appropriate training program, the child will gradually begin to imitate even new behaviors that have never resulted in previous reinforcement. In the absence of a generalized imitative repertoire, the teacher is left with a slow process of arduous shaping of new behaviors. The teacher of young children with developmental difficulties must evaluate the generalized imitative skills of each child and provide a remediation training program when the child demonstrates limited imitative behaviors.

In teaching imitation skills, the teacher should:

1. *Select a group of behaviors to be imitated.* These should begin with relatively simple movements early in the training program and move progressively to more complex behaviors. Behaviors which the children will use in social situations and which may be used in shaping speech should be selected.

Bricker and Bricker (1970) used the following movements in a program designed to train a motor imitation repertoire. These are ordered according to increasing difficulty:

1.	Step on board	11.	Swing feet
2.	Token in box	12.	Walk in place
3.	Sit on box	13.	Hands on mouth
4.	Cups in cups	14.	Bow up and down
5.	Pat box with hand	15.	Raise foot
6.	Blow cotton	16.	Finger on feet
7.	Pat knees	17.	Turn around
8.	Open mouth	18.	Move head up and down
9.	Hands on head	19.	Arms waving
10.	Touch ear	20.	Wave arms extended

Baer, Peterson, and Sherman (1967) used 130 motor responses in training generalized imitation skills in severely retarded children who initially showed no imitation whatsoever. These behaviors ranged from simple ones such as "Raise left arm," "Nod yes," and "Tap chair seat" to more complex ones such as "Walk and hold book on head," "Put heads on door knob," and "Place box inside ring of beads." Examples of the motor behaviors used by Metz (1965) in his successful program of teaching generalized imitation to young children with severe autistic behavior patterns include:

Throw softball	Slide block across floor
Clap hands	Run across room
Squat	Throw bean bag
Squeeze horn	Arrange configuration of blocks
Mark with chalk on slate	Place cloth over blocks

2. *Identify reinforcers.* Food may be necessary initially. It is desirable, however, to establish tokens and social events such

as praise as effective reinforcers as quickly as possible as they provide more efficient and flexible training possibilities.

3. *Initiate training.* After the behaviors to be imitated have been selected and the reinforcing events and procedure of delivery have been established, training begins. Training should occur in an environmental setting with minimal sources of distraction. At the start, it is desirable to use both a trainer and an assistant. The trainer calls the child by name and says "Do this." He then demonstrates the desired behavior. If the child imitates the behavior within a specified period (ten to 20 seconds), he is promptly reinforced with "Good" and a token or food reinforcer. If the child does not imitate the behavior, the trainer again repeats the sequence. The assistant then physically guides the child through the behavior and promptly provides a reinforcer. As this sequence is repeated, the external guidance is gradually faded until the child spontaneously imitates the demonstrated behavior following the trainer's discriminative cue "Do this."

As the child imitates the initial behavior with high consistency, a second behavior is presented. As the child imitates this one spontaneously, he is provided practice in imitating both responses. This procedure is continued until he is able to imitate a number of demonstrated behaviors. The frequency of reinforcement is reduced to whatever level is possible to maintain a high level of correct response. The behaviors to be imitated should be demonstrated in a random fashion to avoid the development of specific chains of behavior.

4. *Intersperse new behaviors which have not been presented previously and which have never been reinforced among ones previously reinforced.* These are not provided reinforcement. If the child imitates them with consistency, a generalized imitative pattern is demonstrated. The training should be continued until the child is able to imitate both previously reinforced and new behaviors without hesitation or error.

5. *Use different trainers at this stage to enhance generalization of this imitative repertoire.* Additionally, the training should occur in various settings which become increasingly similar to the child's natural environments.

The trainer will find that as the child becomes skillful in imitating the demonstrated behaviors, inappropriate motor and emotional behaviors will decline. The experience becomes a fun activity for many children. It will be found that as the child begins to imitate some responses, it becomes progressively easier to obtain new imitative behaviors.

After the generalized imitative repertoire of motor behaviors has been established, the teacher will be able to use the specific behaviors and the generalized repertoire to teach other behaviors. The use of these skills as a foundation for teaching speech behavior is described in the next chapter. The following section describes its use in the development of social interaction skills.

Paloutzian and his associates (1971), after initially training non-imitative children to imitate 24 motor responses, used these newly acquired imitation skills to teach social interaction with peers. The children were taught to imitate the following social interaction behaviors: passing a bean bag, walking to a peer and gently stroking his face, pulling a peer in a wagon, pushing another child in a swing, and rocking another child in a rocking chair or hobby horse. The children required fewer training sessions to learn to imitate these more complex behaviors than required initially to learn the relatively simple motor responses. The trainers also reported that the children began to demonstrate positive emotional reactions of delight during training sessions.

Prior to and following the training, the social interaction behaviors of these children were rated during daily scheduled free-play periods. The children demonstrate considerably more and a higher level of social interaction behaviors in free-play settings following the imitation training experiences than was evident prior to training. Thus, the social interaction skills acquired in the training sessions generalized to other settings.

BASIC LANGUAGE AND SELF-HELP SKILLS

The following references are provided for the teacher who may wish to develop behavior management programs for development of basic language skills and various self-help skills such as dressing, toileting, feeding, and grooming.

Basic Language Skills

Bricker and Bricker in *A Program of Language Training for the Severely Language Handicapped* (1970) describe a sequence of language training procedures. The procedures are based on the authors' research as well as the recent investigations of other speech and language specialists. Language components specifically dealt with are receptive vocabulary, imitation, naming, and sentence production.

The Sloane and MacAulay book, *Operant Procedures in Remedial Speech and Language Training* (1968), contains a number of chapters which provide detailed description of procedures found useful in instituting speech in severely impaired children.

Watson's *How to Use Behavior Modification with Mentally Retarded and Autistic Children* (1972) describes a ten-phase language training program which he has used successfully in teaching receptive and expressive language skills to nonverbal children.

Self-Help Skills

Watson (*How to Use Behavior Modification with Mentally Retarded and Autistic Children,* 1972) also provides a step-by-step description of behavior management procedures for use in the development of the following self-help skills: toileting; eating with utensils; taking off pants, shirt, socks, and shoes; putting on pants, shirt, socks, and shoes; bathing; and tooth-brushing.

CHAPTER 12

Applications: Management of
Some Recurring Problem
Behavior Patterns

This chapter will consider some of the more prevalent problem behavior patterns presented by young children. These patterns do not suddenly appear at the time the child enters an educational program outside the home. Such patterns develop out of the social learning experiences gained in the home and in related settings. Regardless of the specific experiences involved in the learning of such patterns, or of the present social learning experiences which may serve to perpetuate and to maintain them, the school setting represents a significant new social environment. If this school setting is designed to promote a wide range of behaviors of social and personal competency, the problem behaviors can be dealt with in a calm, matter-of-fact manner.

The patterns of dependency, excessive fearfulness, excessive shyness, excessive temper tantrum behavior, negativistic behavior, excessive aggressive behavior, and hyperactivity and distractability will be described. The chapter will conclude with a brief description of autistic behavior patterns. In discussing each, attention will be devoted to (1) possible factors involved in the development of the behavior pattern and (2) suggestions for managing and modifying the behavior pattern. Cautions which should be exercised in implementing a management program will be enumerated. Examples from home and school settings will be provided to emphasize the need for cooperative behavior management endeavors between home and school.

Any child may exhibit the above-mentioned and related problems either in isolation or in various combinations. Problem behavior patterns may be highly interrelated in some children. For example, a child who is generally negativistic may be likely to engage in violent temper tantrum behaviors on occasion. In other children, the factors involved in one behavior pattern may be quite distinctly different, with specific problem behaviors occurring in isolation. Additionally, the following points should be remembered in consideration of these behavior patterns:

1. *Although the problem behavior patterns which different children exhibit may appear to be highly similar, both the historical factors involved in the development of these behaviors and the present factors which exert influence over them may be quite different.* One child's aggressive behavior may be a result of a rich history of positive social reinforcement from parents, siblings, or peers for such behavior while a similar pattern of behavior in another child may have been strengthened as it removed a source of unpleasantness, for example, a younger sibling stopped aggravating him when he yelled and hit the sibling.

2. *The factors involved in the initial development of a pattern of behavior may or may not be those factors which presently influence the behavior.* This emphasizes the necessity of analyzing the present social environment in which the behavior is occurring in order to understand it. It may be valuable to identify the historical conditions which resulted in the strengthening of present behavior; nevertheless, major consideration must be given to present conditions as they are the ones with which the behavior management program must deal.

3. *Describing a child as being aggressive, shy, or negativistic does not imply that the child has behavior traits or personality types which reflect some basic internal or central causes.* These are not all-or-nothing characteristics of a child. The basic concern is not one whether the child is shy or not shy, for example. Shyness, as is true of other behavior patterns mentioned, is merely a class name for behaviors which create certain reactions from those in the social environment of a child. These terms are used merely in a descriptive sense to refer to the behavior patterns which characterize the child.

Describing John as aggressive does not tell us much about what John actually does. To become meaningful as a basis for an intervention program, it would be necessary to describe the specifics of what John does, the strength of these behaviors, and the conditions under which they occur.

It is important to recognize, for instance, that aggressiveness or shyness reside in the view of the observer and are not absolute characteristics of the behavior observed or of the child.

The same child may be labeled aggressive by one observer and delightfully assertive by another. The behavior thus must be viewed in the context of the social environment in which it occurs.

It is also true that a behavior pattern may be highly specific to a particular social context or it may occur across numerous settings. The child may be quarrelsome, fight with other children, and be hard to get along with at home, but exhibit few of these behaviors when in school. Other children may exhibit a consistent pattern of acting in an aggressive manner across a wide range of social and environmental conditions.

4. *This position which views the acceptability or nonacceptability of specific behaviors in a relative manner avoids the diagnostic problem of deciding if a child is really aggressive or shy, or negative, or not.* It avoids such unnecessary problems as deciding, for example, just how shy a child must be before he can be labeled a shy child.

5. *The following discussion of probable conditions which result in a given set of problematic behaviors should be viewed as suggestive only.* These suggestions are supported by various writers (e.g., Patterson, 1971; Becker, 1971; Krumboltz and Krumboltz, 1972) and are consistent with the concepts and principles of social learning and with a plethora of treatment studies (see Bandura, 1969; Mischel, 1971; Staats, 1971).

A word about prevention seems in order prior to consideration of the problem behavior patterns. If the adults in a child's life provide him social reinforcement on a frequent basis as he engages in a wide range of appropriate behavior, if a free and pleasant interaction exists, if the adults are able to "get on the child's level" in playing, talking and in being serious, if the adults stay calm, are pleasant in their manner, nondemanding, and above all only seldom if ever become angry or harsh, the likelihood is greatly reduced that serious behavior problems of the nature described in the following section will develop. Under these "positive interpersonal relationship" conditions, adult requests will more likely be fulfilled as a result of the social reinforcement of a pleased or happy teacher or parent. Children learn a great deal by observing the behavior of others. If adults and children have a poor relationship, if they are grouchy, loud, defensive, unhappy, and harsh, children are likely to exhibit these same inappropriate behaviors.

TEMPER-TANTRUM BEHAVIORS

All young children engage on occasion in temper-tantrum behavior whenever they do not have their way, do not receive expected positive consequences, when placed in conflict situations, or when something interferes with their ongoing, goal-directed behavior. The temper tantrums include a combination of anger and aggressive behaviors such as crying, screaming, thrashing about, attacking others verbally or physically and self-directed aggression. Children with developmental difficulties are even more likely to engage in such frustration behaviors as their disabilities frequently increase the difficulty of task accomplishment. As a result, they are faced with more barriers to goal attainment and generally exhibit low tolerance to frustration.

How the Behavior Develops

Parents, teachers, and others are more prone to "feel sorry" for the young child with learning and behavior problems whenever he is experiencing difficulty and to provide him with extra attention or assistance during a temper outburst. It is not unusual under these circumstances for the adult to reduce the requirements or to give in to the child. In this manner the child learns that a successful way to stop the adult from requiring him to do something is to engage in temper tantrum behavior. Stated more technically, the child's temper-tantrum behavior has been strengthened under these conditions through a combination of negative and positive reinforcement. The behavior not only removes an aversive condition (negative reinforcement) but also may result in increased attention in the form of soothing comments and sympathy (positive reinforcement).

As it will be illustrated, such behavior patterns under certain learning conditions can become quite frequent and, under the slightest provocation, rather intense. It is also true that the temper outburst can become discriminative, occurring only in the presence of certain people or only under highly specific conditions.

John, a four-year-old physically handicapped boy, has been given candy on numerous occasions recently as his mother was under emotional stress and used the candy as a means of keeping John happy and quiet. John learned to come to mother and ask for candy at an increasingly frequent rate. These requests had been reinforced since they produced the candy which the child promptly ate.

Mother, becoming concerned when John began to be fussy about his food at mealtimes and when he began to leave too much food on his plate at dinnertime, decided to cut out the candy between meals and to provide it only immediately after meals.

When John asked her for candy between meals, she refused him, explaining her new plan. Although logical, it did nevertheless represent a removal of a reinforcing event which previously had been provided following John's request for it. This change in mother's procedure, an extinction one, produced a frustration reaction. He began fretting and, failing to obtain the candy, sat down on the floor and began crying. Mother, feeling sympathy for him and feeling guilty that she had upset him, gave in after a few minutes of his sobbing and provided him with the candy, with the declaration, "This is the only piece that you will get until dinner."

This episode is repeated many times over the next few weeks. Mother is able to stick to her resolution on occasion to cut the candy out between meals. At other times, she gives in immediately saying, "Oh, okay. Just one piece, though." On still other occasions she makes unsuccessful attempts to withstand the temper outburst. The longer she waits, the louder the crying and the more vigorous the thrashing about becomes. The child kicks the floor and pounds on mother with his hands. Mother becomes afraid that he will hurt himself and gives him the candy to quiet him down. In this manner John is reinforced for increasingly vigorous temper-tantrum behaviors. The less intense temper-tantrum behavior which appeared initially following withholding of the candy had failed to produce the reinforcer. More intense forms were shaped gradually in the child as these more vigorous temper tantrums, and only these, resulted in the mother giving in and providing the candy.

Behavior Management Program

When setting up a program to alter temper-tantrum behavior, the parent or teacher should follow these guidelines:

1. Define precisely the behaviors which make up the temper tantrum. Define the time, place and social setting in which these behaviors occur. What produces or precipitates the temper tantrums?

2. Obtain some measure of the strength of the behavior. How many temper tantrums occur per morning, day, or during other designated time periods? How long does the outburst last once it begins? How intense is it? It is necessary to obtain some objective measure of the strength of the temper tantrums prior to initiation of a behavior management program in order to determine if the program is being effective.

3. Describe what occurs in the child's environment as the tantrum behavior occurs. What happens whenever the child engages in such behaviors? These consequences most likely are serving to maintain the tantrums and thus must be evaluated carefully.

4. If the program involves a change in reinforcement schedule or in the contingency, inform the child that the reinforcing event or activity will no longer be provided except at designated times or following designated behavior. Do this prior to the occasion in which the reinforcer is usually available to the child, that is, prior to frustration, so that the child knows what to expect under the new arrangements.

5. If the temper tantrums are more likely to occur at certain periods of time or in certain situations, attempt to get the child involved in behaviors which will reduce the possibility of frustration and the resulting temper tantrum.

6. If the child does not understand language, demonstrate to him (in those instances where this is possible) what he must do to obtain the desired consequence or some appropriate substitute.

7. Do not provide reinforcement following the initiation of temper-tantrum behavior. Let the temper tantrum run its course. After a few occurrences the length and intensity of the tantrum will typically decline. The child may be placed in a room by himself. If the teacher remains in the room to insure that the child does not harm himself or damage property, care must be exercised to keep attention at a minimum. Even looking at the child or responding to him in any manner may only intensify and prolong the tantrum.

8. Provide both the withdrawn reinforcer or one of comparable value and positive social attention (approval, praise, playful interaction, affection) at other times during the day when the child is involved in appropriate behavior.

9. Reinforce the child richly in those instances in which he demonstrates appropriate behavior in the face of frustrating conditions. As he begins to decrease the frequency of temper-tantrum behavior, provide him with frequent praise and approval for being a "big boy" or "big girl."

10. Be prepared for long and loud temper tantrums on the first few occasions of this behavior being placed on extinction. Remember that giving in, even occasionally, will greatly prolong the episodes.

11. If the child is left alone during temper tantrums, be sure that there is minimal possibility that the child's behavior will require that you provide him with attention. If the child inflicts minor injury which you attend to, the possibility exists that such behavior will be strengthened.

12. Inform the child of the consequences of the tantrum (e.g., "John, you can cry if you wish. I shall leave you until you finish.") Be consistent in fulfilling stipulations (e.g., "You cannot come out of your room until you have stopped your crying." "You may join the class again after you choose to stop your tantrum.")

13. Do not let the child's temper tantrum arouse your sympathy or guilt. He will survive. If you provide him with sufficient acceptance and affection at other times in a natural manner, any emotional trauma that he may experience or any feelings of being rejected or mistreated will be short-lived. In fact, by being consistent in your treatment of temper-tantrum behavior you will assist the child to develop a concept of responsibility for his own behavior. As his temper tantrums begin to occur less frequently, his concept of himself as a person who has self-control will be enhanced.

14. It is also crucial that the social environment recognizes the manner in which chronic temper-tantrum behaviors can be strengthened and avoids the trap in the future.

As noted initially, all children engage in temper-tantrum behaviors on occasion as things do not go right for them. These tantrums become excessively intense and chronic, however, only under conditions where they are too frequently reinforced by the social environment and other competing behaviors are not provided sufficient reinforcement.

NEGATIVISTIC BEHAVIOR

Some children are actively negativistic to many requests made by parents and teachers. *Stubborn, oppositional, noncompliant,* and *passive-aggressive* are other terms used to describe a behavior pattern which is accentuated by "No," "I don't want to," or "I'm not going to do that." Usually these verbal negatives are accompanied by whining and other similar obnoxious behaviors which accompany the failure to comply with or to fulfill the requests made by others—peers, older siblings or adults.

Some children are more passive in their noncompliance. They do not verbally refuse to comply or engage in whining or other disruptive emotional behavior—they just do not perform. They drag through the requested behavior for an inordinate period of time, or may postpone action until the request is finally presented in a harsh and threatening manner.

The child with various types of developmental difficulties frequently comes to control the household and to attempt to control the school environment. Parents and teacher may spoil the child by permitting him to set the pace. If the child objects to adult requests, these requests too frequently are removed and the child is permitted to do as he pleases. On those occasions when adults do attempt to obtain compliance, the child responds with increased negativism, much to the surprise of the adults because "we require very little of him. I don't know why he objects so much to our few requests."

It is not unusual to observe that parents, teachers, and others do not respond or relate to the negativistic child too frequently. Most of the interaction occurs when the adult is presenting requests or is attempting to enforce compliance. This becomes such an unpleasant experience that both adult and child tend to ignore each other due to the limited positive reinforcement associated with interaction. It is also true that many noncompliant children do not seem to pay attention. Whenever a request is made, the child sits as if he did not hear the request. He has found it more comfortable to turn the social environment off as it frequently is unpleasant to him.

How the Behavior Develops

It should be recognized initially that no child will comply with adult requests on every occasion. However, it is evident that the social environment, regardless of intentions to the contrary, can teach a child to be excessively noncompliant by gradually shaping this behavior pattern over a period of time.

The child's negativistic or noncompliant behavior has been strengthened as it has resulted in the termination of the adult request, has postponed compliance, or has resulted in excessive attention from parent or teacher as she attempts to nag him, reason with him, or argue with him.

The following situation illustrates such noncompliant behavior. Mother calls from the kitchen, "It's time to take your nap. Put your toys away." Johnnie quickly replies, "I don't want to," and begins to fuss. Mother, not feeling well and not up to a battle with Johnnie, makes no reply and lets him continue his play activity. After thirty minutes or so she makes another attempt and suggests in a calm voice as she walks into the playroom, "Johnnie, don't you think it is time for your nap now?" Johnnie screams, "No, no, I won't," and begins to cry as he scoots across the room. Mother becomes upset, storms out of the room and yells, "Just do what you want to then." Mother's actions are teaching Johnnie that he should refuse and put up a fuss when requests are made of him because these behaviors will result in the termination of the unpleasant requests.

Another child may be taught to resist passively or to ignore requests if such behaviors avoid or postpone termination of pleasant activity or initiation of requested unpleasant activity. The child at school may be playing in the sand box and be requested to join the group for music period. The child ignores the request and makes no move, or if he acts as if he did not hear what the teacher requested, he can prolong his pleasant activity.

On other occasions, the teacher will nag the child. The request will be repeated, "Sue, get your mat and prepare for naptime." "Sue, I told you to get ready for your nap." Finally, in aggravation, the teacher yells in a harsh manner, "Get your mat this second or I'll send you out of the room." The child may prepare for naptime after this demand; however, the teacher's approach may also have two other effects. It may teach the child that compliance with teacher request is unnecessary unless the teacher becomes angry. Additionally, the teacher is reinforced for yelling at the child since the behavior did provide a solution to the problem. As a result the teacher is more likely to yell under similar conditions of the child's noncompliance.

When a teacher repeats a request a number of times prior to requiring the child to initiate, persist at, or complete an activity, two learning processes are possibly in operation which strengthen negativistic or noncompliance behavior. First, refusal results in continued attention from adults as they repeat the requests or otherwise reason with, argue with, or scold the child. Second, if the requested activity is unpleasant (complete a difficult visual-motor task, pick up your toys, stop playing and prepare for work), refusal serves to postpone the initiation of the unpleasant activity. This has an immediate effect of strengthening the refusal behavior.

As noted earlier (and as is true in many problem situations) the major behavior which results in social attention for the child is that of being negativistic. As the child becomes more negativistic, he is left alone more and more at other times because "he is such a brat," or "he's such an unpleasant child."

Some children have also been taught that after refusal, parents will occasionally bribe them into compliance. Under these conditions the children are reinforced for refusal as a result of the subsequent bribe. As the reward is not provided on every occasion, the behavior becomes even more difficult to eliminate due to the intermittent nature of the reinforcement.

Behavior Management Program

The adult attempting to alter the behavior of a noncompliant child should consider these suggestions:

1. Define precisely the behaviors which are viewed as negativistic. When do they occur, where, and under what conditions? What are the major types of requests which produce negativistic behavior? Is the child negativistic most of the time or

mostly under certain time or situation conditions?   Identify occurrences of compliance and attempt to identify those factors which distinguish compliance from negativistic behavior.

2. What is the strength of the negativistic behaviors?   In obtaining a record of the number of times negativistic behaviors occur during designated periods of time, also note the types of requests and the manner in which they are presented to the child. A child may have developed highly discriminating negativistic behaviors; that is, he may be negativistic with mother or the teacher aide but not with father or the teacher.

3. What happens after negativistic behavior?   Attention should be given to the cueing as well as the possible reinforcing events.   Does the social environment repeat a request a number of times prior to becoming firm and requiring the behavior?   If so, the initial requests are redundant and have no appropriate behavior control function.   What are the consequences of the negativistic behavior?

4. Make no request of a child that he is not fully expected to fulfill.   Do not change requests after the child balks.   Insure that the child follows requests even if it becomes necessary to actively assist him; if the child refuses, take it in a matter-of-fact manner.   Perhaps the teacher may take him by his hand and gently guide him through the activity to demonstrate to him that he should comply with the request the first time it is made.   This may be a novel experience for the child since, as suggested earlier, the child has been trained to respond only after persistent requests from adults.

Stay *calm* in this activity.   It is highly likely that the child will put up a fuss.   If the teacher becomes too emotional, the child's emotionality will be intensified.   If the child complains or cries, he should be ignored.   Sufficient physical guidance or verbal prompts should insure that the initial request is fulfilled.

If, under this new approach, the child becomes too disruptive (highly emotional and physical), it may be necessary to postpone his compliance until a later time.   However, he should not be permitted to continue the activity which the request interrupted.

5. Be prepared to reinforce compliance with natural social consequences ("Thank you for putting your mat up." "You are a big help.")

6. If a child is being requested to terminate or disrupt some activity which he enjoys, *provide a lead time*.   "John, after you finish the next picture, put your toys away." "Sue, we'll go wash our hands after the sand stops falling," as the teacher places a five-minute sand timer on the finger-painting table.   Again, do not become upset if a child shows displeasure.   This is a natural

reaction; do not reinforce it with an excessive reaction. Act as if it did not occur and provide a model of more positive emotional reaction. Assist the child by providing initial support, "Come on, I'll get you started." Take the child's hand or put an arm around him.

7. Be pleasant. Sudden, curt, demanding, or harsh requests will most likely provoke increased negativism.

8. Be positive and definitive. Instead of "John, how would you like to take the trash out, please," or "Would you get the paper for me," state, "John, take the trash out," or "Hand me the papers on my desk. I would appreciate it."

9. If the child is engaging in an undesired behavior such as talking too loudly, provoking a younger peer or the like, suggest some alternative activity which he also enjoys. "Jack, get the puzzle out and play a game with me. That yelling hurts my ears."

If the behavior is one that the child understands is taboo, suggest a natural negative consequence of continuing the behavior. "John, if that does not stop immediately, you will be sent to the quiet room." Also, suggest some alternative acceptable behavior. Again, *be prepared to fulfill the stated consequence.* If the child continues, send him to the quiet room. Without a follow-through, the child will merely learn that the threat is an empty one and he will not be influenced by it; he will learn to ignore it.

10. It becomes important, as implied earlier, that the child is in fact able to comply with the request made. Demanding in an unrealistic manner that the child behave in a given manner only intensifies his difficulties.

11. Be prepared to reinforce cooperative compliance behavior in many situations. Identify those instances in which the child is most likely to comply and reinforce the child richly for his cooperative behavior. Label his compliance in a positive manner. "Thank you for doing that. You are a big help." Provide him with a concept that fulfilling adult requests is a pleasant activity. "I appreciate your helping me." "Thank you for picking up your toys. That's a big help."

12. Again, reinforce the child consistently for compliance. Do not assume that the child should comply merely out of gratitude, love, appreciation, respect, or the like. Don't be afraid to express pleasure. Only under such conditions can a child learn to express his happiness.

13. It may prove helpful in cases of high rates of noncompliance to use a time-out procedure in combination with one of reinforcing compliance and other desired behaviors. Wahler (1972) has found in his work with children with oppositional behavior patterns that differential social reinforcement of cooperative behavior may not result in reduction in noncompliance. This

perhaps is a result of the relatively ineffectual nature of adult social attention. The child has found little in his interaction with teachers and parents that has been pleasant. Wahler (1969b) and Patterson and his associates (1970) have reported successful reduction of inappropriate behaviors in highly oppositional children with a skillful use of a time-out procedure combined with the differential reinforcement of cooperative behaviors.

A reduction in the oppositional behavior following use of a time-out procedure provides the adults and child with opportunities to relate to each other in a more positive manner. The parents and teachers will attend to and enjoy the child more as he is no longer so obnoxious. The child will like his teachers and parents more because they no longer are yelling at him or are angry at him.

14. It may be valuable to initiate a token system in which the child would be reinforced immediately for compliance behavior. This may be needed with children who do not appear to care much for adult attention. If a token system is used, start it in a setting in which the child is likely to comply. Gradually extend the token system into problem behavior areas as the child is assured that compliance will result in reinforcing events. Extend it into more difficult areas as the token system becomes more influential.

DEPENDENCY

Children with developmental difficulties are quite prone to develop behavior patterns of dependency. Some dependent children are unable to do much without the presence or assistance of adults, require an excessive amount of adult attention and suport, and are apt to become fearful or excessively docile or inactive when adults are not prodding or assisting them. As the child grows older, he clings to mother or teacher, prefers to stay with an adult instead of being with other children, and may even insist on sitting next to teacher or even sleeping with parents. Under these conditions, adults are constantly available for assistance of one kind or another and generally to "do for the child" whenever a problem arises.

How the Behavior Develops

Children with developmental difficulties are likely to learn patterns of dependency as a result of (1) the difficulty which such children have doing things they see others doing or which the social environment requires of them and (2) the tendency which adults and older siblings have to provide too much assistance to the child when he is confronted with difficulty. Stated differently, children are taught by others to be excessively dependent. Children with physical, cognitive, and sensory handicaps of one kind or degree often do require the assistance of others. However, if the adult continues to do for the child, or encourages the child to seek his assistance, even with those things that the child could do or learn to do himself, the child becomes excessively dependent. Whenever the adult does for the child that which he could do himself, the child is being reinforced for not doing, for being passive and dependent.

Many parents of handicapped children overprotect their children. They do not expose them to the range of experiences required for adequate development. Whenever the parent is not present, the child is helpless. Being helpless earns the solicitous attention of mother, teacher, and others. This is quite satisfying to some adults since they feel important and needed when asked for help by a dependent child.

The following example illustrates the development of dependency behavior. Jane, a retarded child with physical handicaps, experiences difficulty in dressing, self-feeding, and in walking. Mother did everything for her, providing her with excessive attention and assistance. Whenever Jane faced a problem, she would call for mother. She seldom let mother out of her sight. However, when a new baby, Sue, was born, mother was no longer available for the constant solicitous attention. The child's dependency behavior no longer produced mother's immediate attention. Jane was placed under a change in schedule of reinforcement, a process which produces emotional or frustration behavior if imposed too suddenly. As a consequence Jane engaged in long crying episodes and exhibited extreme jealousy and aggressive outbursts toward her young sister. The mother's close attention on occasion following the crying episodes only served to strengthen this behavioral reaction.

Dependency, once developed, can be maintained at high strength merely by infrequent reinforcement. Consider the following interaction between child and adult. "Help me." "No, do it yourself." The child whines, stalls, pleads, grumbles. On occasion the adult feels sorry for the child, is in a hurry, gets aggravated at the child's demands, and does provide the requested assistance. Such assistance serves to strengthen the whining, stalling, pleading and grumbling, and thus prolongs these behavior patterns.

Some children have a difficult time leaving mother.

291

Whenever mother is out of sight, leaves home, or leaves the child at school, the child cries excessively. This type of pattern is highly likely when mother is the child's sole or major source of positive reinforcement. Such children have a history of obtaining little reinforcement without mother being present. Mother has hovered over the child, attended to her, encouraged the child's dependent behavior. As a result other persons or situations become relatively unimportant. In some cases, it also may be true that the child has experienced several unpleasant experiences (has been punished or frightened) when away from mother.

Under these conditions, the child becomes highly upset when mother is not present as her absence represents a withdrawal of reinforcement. As noted earlier, a child is quite likely to display disruptive emotional behavior whenever a familiar reinforcing event (in this case, mother) is no longer available. The child may sob, scream for mother to return, and display other fearful behavior. If the crying results in mother's return, the behavior can become a predominant one whenever mother attempts to leave or is absent. Parents frequently go to extremes to meet the child's requirement of no separation as they "feel so badly when I leave him crying like that." It is not unusual under such conditions for children to learn to cry intensely or for prolonged periods of time since these actions have resulted in the reappearance of the parents. Some parents attempt to leave their crying child but return after varying periods of time during which the child is crying. The child thus learns to persist at his crying and mother will return.

Montenegro (1968) provides a description of a six-year-old boy who would begin to "cry and shout desperately" when mother left him in kindergarten. The boy, Romeo, had seldom been away from his mother. He had never been left with a baby-sitter. He always got his way with mother. If she did not comply with his wishes, he would engage in tantrum behavior until he got his way. The mother bathed the boy, helped him dress, and sometimes gave him his food. He had no sources of social reinforcement independent of parents.

Behavior Management Program

The following program provides suggestions for dealing with the dependent child:

1. Define the child's dependency in specific observable behavioral terms. Identify both what the child does in various specific situations as well as what he should be doing. Distinguish between those things that the child can do but does not do with

sufficient independence and those behaviors that should occur but which the child has never exhibited.

2. Obtain objective measures of the dependency behavior. For example, what percentage of the time does the child remain undressed after being requested to dress without assistance? How many times does the child cry when left alone? How long does he cry after he is left alone?

3. What happens when the child requests "Help me," or "Show me how," or "I can't do that," or some similar indication of dependency? Does the social environment do for the child too frequently? Some social learning experiences have encouraged and strengthened the dependency. Develop some hunches about what has created and reinforced these behaviors.

4. As has been emphasized in previous chapters, a child with learning and behavior problems can learn to be independent in many behavioral areas if the learning experiences permit this. It is essential that the parents and teacher be aware of what the child is able to do or could learn to do and to provide a systematic series of experiences designed to strengthen these behaviors. Why should a child dress or feed himself if the adult world does this for him? Why should he assume responsibility for cleaning up his mess if the adult does it for him?

It often happens, as suggested earlier, that the adult has been too busy, too impatient or too overprotective to permit the child to develop independence in those areas that are within his realm of possibility. In some cases the adults may have expected the child to engage in behaviors which were beyond his level of development at the time or which required considerable vigilance on his part. The child, failing these tasks, may have engaged in dependency behavior which the adults reinforced. New tasks may come to be viewed as aversive. The child may avoid them by displaying dependency behavior.

It may be difficult for a child to do certain things. It may require considerable effort for a child to finish a task. But the child can learn "I can do" only if he is permitted to do and is reinforced for his efforts. Thus, the initial step in decreasing the dependency of a child is to adopt the position that the child can in fact be more independent and self-sufficient if *realistic* expectations are set and *appropriate* learning experiences provided.

5. Refrain from reinforcing the child for dependent behavior. However, do not suddenly withdraw all assistance: this could be too upsetting to the child. Identify a limited number of behaviors initially and reinforce him for increased independence in these areas.

6. As the child acquires new behaviors of independence (dresses himself, picks up his toys, remains in the room while

mother runs an errand, plays with a small group of peers while teacher is engaged with another group), have the child engage in these activities frequently in order to give the child experience in obtaining positive consequences associated with doing for himself. Label the child's independence as being "big boy," "strong," "able," and with other competency terms.   Have other persons in the family and school environments recognize the independence and attend to these.   As new skills develop, adopt a policy of ignoring dependency behavior and reinforcing competing independent behavior.   If a child cries excessively when he has a minor accident, does not have his way, or the like, such behavior should be ignored.   Whenever the child is not crying, he should be attended to for being a "big boy" or "big girl."   It is not being suggested that a child should not be provided comfort on occasions when he is frightened or is really hurt.   Be certain that there is a distinction between these occasions, however, and those in which the child uses this means of getting attention for dependent behavior.   Again, do not suddenly withdraw directions or support. Gradually move from a position of directing his dependency behavior toward one of providing less and less assistance as the child becomes able to do for himself.

7. In handling separation crying, either when left in bed at night or at various places and times during the day, the following procedures should be initiated:

(a) Insure that the child will not have frightening or otherwise unpleasant experiences when left by the adult.

(b) Increase the range of social reinforcers provided the child.   Have other people, especially peers, interact with the child and provide pleasant activities and events.

(c) As the child begins to respond to other reinforcing events, separate adults more and more.

The specific procedures used will depend upon the strength of the crying and related behaviors and upon the presence and number of other dependency and fearful behavior patterns.   If separation crying is one of numerous dependency reactions, a program emphasizing gradual separation should be followed as new independent behaviors are acquired.   If the behavior is an isolated pattern, separation at specific times in familiar and comforting settings may be initiated early in the program.

8. It may be necessary initially to reinforce the child for trying.   Following this, reinforce progressively more complex approximations of the desired independent behavior.   Consistency becomes important.   It is important to recognize that many children may be able to accomplish certain tasks (has the skills of dressing, self-feeding, playing without adult present) but will not

do these things independently of the adult. The task is to reinforce independence in these areas. In other cases, the child may be unable to accomplish certain tasks as he has not acquired the necessary basic skills. In both instances, specific behavior objectives denoting increasing independence must be identified and provided frequent and consistent reinforcement.

9. Provide the child with experiences in making simple decisions. Give him two foods and permit him to select one. Offer two puzzles and have him select one. Let him select one of two shirts or her select one of two dresses provided. Be prepared to accept and reinforce the child's choices. In this manner the child's independence is being enhanced.

EXCESSIVE AGGRESSIVE BEHAVIOR

Some children are described as aggressive, hostile, and having associated patterns of negativism and general noncompliance. These behavior patterns not only interfere with the child's learning of more appropriate ways of behavior but also disrupt others in the social environment. Children are often unpredictable, embarrass parents, create turmoil because they tease and fight siblings and peers, will not comply with parental or teacher requests, and engage in temper tantrums when aggravated. These behavior patterns may occur in isolation or in various combinations. Unfortunately for child, family, and those in the school setting, some children are characterized by all.

When this combination occurs, parents and teachers frequently are puzzled, discouraged and overwhelmed. They frequently feel that something is wrong with the child which causes him to behave in this manner. It is not unusual for parents and others who attempt to manage the child to be drawn into a battle with the child. Similar patterns of shouting, striking out, and temper-tantrum-like behavior result.

The major difference between the behavior of the aggressive child and other children is that the behavior rate or intensity of the aggressive child is greater and he engages more frequently in such behaviors in inappropriate situations. Most children are noncompliant at times, display temper tantrums, and attack others either verbally or physically in the normal course of development. When these events become too frequent or when an aggressive episode becomes highly intense and prolonged, the home and school environments usually become concerned and begin to look for factors which may account for these behavior patterns.

How the Behavior Develops

Teasing, yelling, and attacking others (hitting, shoving, verbally abusing) are behaviors acquired by children because they produce consequences which are either positively or negatively reinforcing. In most instances, yelling "Stop that or I'll poke you" increases in strength as the threat removes an unpleasant source of teasing from siblings or peers. Hitting, kicking, and biting become major reactions to situations which interfere with the child's plans or activities as these behaviors remove the interruption. The child may learn to be aggressive as these behaviors terminate a range of unpleasant situations (teasing and reprimanding from others).

The child pushes another child and gets a toy. He is reinforced for pushing. A child yells when his big brother attempts to recover his book which Frank is reading. Frank's yell brings a demand from father, "Let Frank keep the book." In this way the child is trained to yell whenever his brother interferes with him.

It has been observed that the crying which hitting another child may produce serves as a powerful reinforcer to the child who does the hitting. It frequently does become a secondary positive reinforcer to the aggressive child as crying so frequently becomes associated with getting his way. If a child "gets away with" hitting, pushing, demanding, grabbing—the aggressive child causes another child to cry and he gets the toy, book, tricycle, privilege, following such behaviors—these ways of behaving will become more frequent and may become the more dominant form of peer control.

It is understandable that parents and teachers are sometimes puzzled by the persistence of aggressive behavior in some chidren. "Why, I'm always scolding or spanking Jim for hitting his younger brothers, but he keeps doing it in spite of the punishment. He's good for a while but I can't spank him all the time."

In a recent study of an overly aggressive child, it was observed that Jim attacked his younger siblings four or five times in a morning. Almost invariably the younger boys would begin crying. Most frequently, Jim would win the argument before mother would appear and would get the toy, TV choice, food or reinforcing event from the other boys. Mother fluctuated considerably in her handling of the problem. Frequently she would ignore the fracas. At other times, she would yell at Jim and threaten to punish him if he did not stop being naughty. Even less frequently, usually after the fighting became too intense, she would lose her patience, scold Jim and send him to his room. But for every punishment, Jim was reinforced many times by the crying of his younger brothers and by the positive events which his hitting produced. The inconsistent manner in which mother was handling the problem merely compounded the problem. She was becoming a grouch, was losing her temper, and was yelling in a manner similar to that which she was attempting to eliminate in Jim.

Aggressive behavior also may be strengthened by the social attention which it creates. Parents and teachers come running when a child attacks another child. Also, whenever the child is aggressive toward adults he is sure to obtain considerable attention. The fact that the adult attention may be a reprimand is not a factor in many cases. As emphasized earlier, it is not unusual for such attention to have a strengthening effect on the behavior that produces it. Also it is probably true that both positive and negative reinforcement underlie the development of high-rate aggressive behavior, with negative reinforcement being the major process involved.

An additional factor involved in development of aggressive behavior is imitation. Children are more likely to engage in aggressive behavior if parents, siblings, peers, or teachers display aggressive behavior. It is not invariably true that aggressive children have aggressive parents or teachers. It is true, however, that aggressive children frequently have parents or teachers who have behaved quite inconsistently in their handling of the child's aggressive behavior. On occasion, adults will punish such behaviors, sometimes rather harshly. But on too many other occasions such behaviors are ignored, overlooked, tolerated, or permitted to occur and be reinforced.

Behavior Management Program

Control of aggressive behavior might be achieved by following this management program:

1. As behaviors which may be viewed as aggressive vary considerably, the initial step in a behavior management program is to define the behaviors and describe the time, place, and social settings in which these events occur. The program is designed to deal with the behaviors—hitting, pushing, yelling, smart talk—and not with aggression. It is necessary to specify the behaviors which are creating difficulty.

2. The second step is to obtain some measure of the frequency with which the behavior occurs. Children will not suddenly stop being aggressive. However, if aggressive outbursts are well-defined and measured prior to and during the behavior management program, the adults can readily determine if the rate of aggressive behavior is being reduced. The objective is to lower the rate of aggressive behaviors to a tolerable level.

3. Third, prior to initiating a program, observation should be made of precisely what the behavior produces. Does the child get his way? Does he get attention which he otherwise would not obtain? Do the adults in the environment become upset with the child and engage in disruptive emotional behavior? Any of these and similar events may be maintaining the behavior.

4. How frequently does the child receive positive social reinforcement for behaving appropriately? It is likely that the excessively aggressive child gets little positive social attention. Adults and peers have learned to turn him off because he is so obnoxious so often. They avoid interaction with him when he is behaving satisfactorily in fear of creating a situation in which he will behave aggressively. He is likely to be attended to only when he behaves aggressively, and then only inconsistently.

5. The child should not get his way following aggressive behavior; he does not get a toy which was snatched from another child, or does not get his choice of records after screaming at another child. That kind of behavior must not result in positive consequences. When this extinction procedure is initiated, be prepared for emotional outbursts from the child. Recall that whenever certain behavior no longer produces reinforcing consequences, a frustration reaction is highly likely for a period of time. These periods will decrease in frequency and intensity, however, as the child experiences no positive consequences following aggressive behavior.

6. In initiating a behavior management program, inform the child of the new rules which will be in effect. Ignore complaints. Do not argue with the child or attempt to defend the rules. Whenever possible, involve the child in a discussion of his aggressive behaviors and in the desirable consequences associated with more socially appropriate behavior. Encourage him to set new behavioral goals and to select positive consequences to be obtained by non-aggressive behaviors.

7. It frequently becomes valuable to impose some negative consequences following inappropriate aggressive behavior. This is especially needed at times in which it is impossible to remove all positive consequences for aggressive behavior and in those instances of high strength and frequently practiced behaviors. Under the condition of consistency, such contingent and predictable consequences also provide the child with a realistic relationship between inappropriate social behavior and unpleasant consequences. A five to ten-minute time-out procedure has been used successfully with many aggressive children.

8. As emphasized earlier, it is essential that the punishment procedure be accompanied by a plan for reinforcing the child frequently for appropriate behavior. Be sure to identify specific

behaviors to reinforce which may serve to take the place of the aggressive behavior. These may include such activities as playing with children, sitting quietly, complying with requests, cooperating with peers, watching without disruption, taking his turn, sharing his materials. Upon initiation of the punishment procedure, it is critical that additional effort be made to recognize and positively reinforce appropriate behaviors. Otherwise the relationship with adults will be one predominantly associated with punishment. As the reinforcement value of social praise or approval provided by parents and teachers is relatively weak, it would be desirable to utilize reinforcers of a concrete nature such as trinkets, toys, or candy. A token system might be initiated to make available a wider range of reinforcing events. In addition, after some success has been realized and the child's aggressive behavior shows a noticeable decrease, the token system would permit the easy use of a response-cost procedure.

Frequent pairing of social praise and approval with the presentation of the token and other tangible reinforcers is essential as a means of increasing the reinforcement value of these social events.

9. Make a point of reinforcing desired behaviors in other children while the child with excessive aggressive behaviors is observing. This demonstration of appropriate behaviors which produce valuable positive consequences may well increase the likelihood of these behaviors on the part of the observer.

10. Be as consistent as possible in managing the new contingencies. Whenever deviations of the rules occur, regardless of the time and place of infraction, provide the negative consequence. Children learn to be aggressive in highly selective situations—public places such as church, grocery store, bus; when visitors are present—because this behavior has resulted in immediate reinforcing consequences. These immediate consequences become highly influential in strengthening aggressive behavior and serve to offset the suppressing effects of punishment which is inconsistently provided but at a much delayed time. At the same time, be sure to immediately and frequently reinforce desired reactions.

11. It is best to initiate the behavior management program at home and at school. There is no basis for expecting behavior which changes in one setting to change spontaneously in another. It may occur to some degree but unless both environments change the manner in which aggressive behavior is handled, there is no basis for expecting a generalized change.

12. Demonstrate to the child and have him rehearse those socially acceptable behaviors which will produce reinforcing consequences comparable to those produced by the aggressive be-

havior. Some children have had little practice in engaging in nonaggressive behaviors in some conditions. Tell him, show him, have him observe other children engaging in the desired behaviors, physically guide or prompt him through desired behaviors, have him role-play or otherwise rehearse the behaviors—and be sure to provide positive reinforcement for these.

13. Remain calm as the behavior management program is implemented. If the teacher becomes angry, loud, explosive, loses his temper, or otherwise loses his control, he is merely providing an aggressive model. Firmness and consistency produce much better results.

THE SHY-PASSIVE CHILD

Some children generally isolate themselves from others. When in the presence of others, they are relatively inactive. In response to direct comments or approaches, the child may turn away, provide only limited reply, seldom look directly at others, and may display positive affect only in highly familiar situations. Other children and adults soon begin to avoid the shy child as he provides them with too little social interaction. These children find solitary activity such as playing with toys or looking at pictures more enjoyable than being actively involved with others.

How the Behavior Develops

A child who interacts little with others may be exhibiting either one or both of two processes. The child may find people nonreinforcing if parents and siblings have used an excessive amount of punishment in their interaction with him. Those who provide the punishment become generally unpleasant, and the child feels uncomfortable around them. Punishment may be physical or it may take the form of verbal abuse. Parents, siblings, and teachers make numerous derogatory remarks—criticizing, complaining, reminding the child through gesture, facial expression, or verbal content that he is undesirable and inadequate. As a result of this experience a child learns that the less he interacts with or is even in the physical presence of others the more he can avoid unpleasant consequences.

In other instances, a child may have been isolated from contact with others. He may not find others aversive through any direct painful experience. He just has been reinforced only infrequently for such interaction. Social interaction skills are relatively weak or poorly developed. It is not unusual for the parents of such children to be quiet and somewhat isolated themselves.

Behavior Management Program

Positive reinforcement for the shy and passive child could be supplied by the interactions suggested in this behavior management program:

1. The shy and passive behaviors must be defined in terms of situations and people. What does the child do in relation to *should do* behavior goals involving social interaction that may be set for him? Since shyness and passivity are such general behavior characteristics it becomes essential to define them in objective and measurable behavioral units.

2. After adequately defining the observable behaviors, they should be measured in specific situations. Reliable measures of behavior strength are critical as change is frequently slow.

3. Children and adults must acquire positive reinforcement characteristics for the shy child. This is accomplished (1) by reducing to an absolute minimum the use of punishment (preferably eliminating it completely) in the child's presence and (2) by having adults and peers provide the child, or be associated with, positive reinforcers. In this manner, these persons will acquire reinforcing properties.

In the cases of children with high anxiety reactions which underlie much of the avoidance shy behavior, it is valuable to identify a situation that is least likely to create anxiety. This may involve a play situation with favorite toys and an older sibling or a particular peer. As the child relaxes in this setting, a new child or the teacher assistant is gradually introduced into the activity. Easing in the unknown will serve to reduce the anxiety associated with interacting with some unfamiliar person.

4. It may be necessary to reinforce approximations of desired social interaction or other patterns which compete with the shyness. Be careful that attempts at interaction are devoid of punishment. For example, do not place this child in a class in which there is another child who is overly aggressive. Antagonism would not only serve to inhibit the shy child's interaction, it may also lead to direct punishment if the shy child becomes the target of the aggressiveness of the other child.

Many shy children actually do not know how to interact with others in a manner that will result in positive feedback. Such interaction behaviors must be taught in a step-by-step manner. In shaping social behaviors, the teacher should begin with a simple one that is within the child's comfort level, gradually increasing the complexity of the social behaviors and the social situation. Patience is necessary: such a shaping program may require numerous approximation steps prior to obtaining the desired behaviors. If the child is pushed or forced too quickly to interact, the child's anxieties may only be intensified. More severe withdrawal may result.

5. Reinforce the child for a wide range of behaviors which involve interaction with others. Attempt to make him feel worthwhile and important by listening to him and by attending to him as he attempts new behaviors. Be prepared to reinforce successful as well as approximations of successful behaviors. Also reinforce other children for outgoing behavior as the shy child observes. Use a "follow-the-leader" game and be prepared to reinforce the child for interaction behavior.

A shy child frequently is avoided or ignored by other children because he has so little to offer them. He does not reinforce their approach behavior. Steps may be taken to increase his value to other children and thus to insure more interaction. As mentioned earlier, Kirby and Toler (1970) induced a five-year-old child with a low rate of interaction with his classmates to pass out choices of candy to his peers. He was reinforced with social praise and tangible events by the teacher when he finished the daily task. Following initiation of this procedure, there was a dramatic increase in social interaction. He was approached by other children, included in their activities, and talked to more by his peers. Patterson and Brodsky (1966) first reinforced peers with tangible events for initiating social contact with a shy boy and in turn reinforced the boy for initiating contacts on his own. The behavior management program of Ross and associates (1971) described earlier in Chapter 7 represents another approach to increasing the social skills of a shy child. Various modeling and guided participation procedures were most effective in eliminating the intense shy behaviors of a six-year-old boy and in replacing them with a variety of social interaction skills.

THE FEARFUL CHILD

It is quite natural for children to learn to fear various objects, events and situations in the course of development. In fact, children are taught frequently to fear such things as fire, dangerous objects such as sharp knives, large dogs, guns and the like. In addition to developing the normal fears of childhood some children demonstrate rather intense fears of a number of specific situations. In some instances a fearful child may also demonstrate the general shyness described earlier. He is insecure and hesitant over becoming involved in any new activity or interacting with new adults or children.

How the Behavior Develops

Young children learn to fear things that adults and peers in their environment fear. If a big sister is fearful of the dark, for example, the young child may imitate this fear. Hearing others talk about their fears of certain events or objects or observing a fearful reaction in relation to specific situations may create fearfulness in a child.

Children also acquire fear as a consequence of fear-provoking experiences. A child may be afraid of dogs because of a bad experience with a dog, or cars as a result of an accident. Strangers may be feared due to previous aversive experiences with strangers. However, although children have specific fears due to painful traumatic experiences, it is unusual for a child to develop a generalized disposition as a result.

As noted in the discussion of the dependent child, some children express fear when left alone or separated from mother. When mother leaves, the child may become frightened. Closely related is the pattern of fearful behavior which some children exhibit when left alone at bedtime. Crying often insures that mother will stay in the room until the child is asleep.

Behavior Management Program

A successful program to alleviate the worries of the fearful child would:

1. Define precisely the fear reaction, including a description of the conditions (event, situation, person) in which the fear reaction occurs.

2. Obtain some measure of the strength of the fear reaction. If the child fears furry animals how close will he get to an animal? What will he do if the animal is brought closer? Does he cry, scream, run? How long does he cry? These and other frequency, duration, and intensity measures should be obtained.

3. Use a counterconditioning procedure for reinforcing responses which brings the person closer to the feared object. The child is provided a series of graded exposures to the feared events at a time when he is engaging in a positive emotional reaction. These graded exposures involve events which are increasingly similar to the feared one. Initially the situation presented to the

child when he is in a relaxed state is only minimally similar to the feared object. The goal is to avoid any fear reaction as these events are presented. As the child adapts to these occurrences, he is exposed to others which are more and more similar to the actual feared event. The positive emotional response will render a fear response less likely. This procedure is also known as *systematic desensitization*. As an example of the procedure, a child who fears furry animals may be exposed to:

a) pictures of animals
b) plastic animals
c) a furry pillow
d) a small stuffed rabbit
e) a color slide of a friend with a big smile on his face holding a rabbit
f) observation of peers playing with a rabbit. The peers are having great fun
g) a rabbit in a cage
h) touching a rabbit held by someone else, and finally,
i) touching and holding a rabbit.

In each stage of the experience, the child is provided positive reinforcement for any progress that is noted. Whenever possible, maximum use should be made of the procedure of having the child observe others in positive interaction with the feared object. If this can be managed, it may reduce the amount of time required for extinction of the fear.

4. Employ strategies described for the shy child for children with more generalized fears.

THE HYPERACTIVE CHILD

Many developmentally-handicapped children exhibit patterns of excessive activity and of distractibility and limitations of persistence at specific activities. While it may be true that physical factors account for some of the excessive motor activity, it is also true that a child may learn some of these behaviors through inadvertent reinforcement by others. Even if the basis for the overactivity is primarily a physical one, it is possible that the child can learn to slow down.

How the Behavior Develops

The possible learning factors involved in the development of the hyperactive behavior pattern include both positive and negative reinforcement. First a child may learn to move from one activity to another as he avoids situations that are unpleasant. He may not stick to a task or activity if that involvement has frequently resulted in aversive consequences. Mother, for example, may constantly be attempting to show him what he is doing wrong, how he can do something better. Such experiences may produce a generalized anxiety reaction which increases as he becomes involved in or persists at any particular activity. Terminating or avoiding this activity reduces unpleasant emotionality and thus reinforces the preceding behavior. His hyperactivity thus may represent perpetual avoidance behavior. As he moves from one activity to another, his anxiety is temporarily reduced. Moving away from a task becomes strengthened through negative reinforcement. Remaining in a task is a conditioned cue for an increased anxiety reaction as his history has demonstrated that the longer in a task the greater the likelihood of failure and punishment.

Hyperactive behavior may also be strengthened by the social attention which it produces from others. Parents, siblings, peers, and teachers will respond socially to the child in one way or another in an attempt to slow the child down and to focus him on some specific activities. The social reinforcement value of this interaction is not infrequently enhanced by the fact that the child may be relatively isolated by others unless he is behaving in a hyperactive manner. The emotional relationship between the child and others in his environment is likely to be a negative one due to the high frequency of his bothersome behavior. The child is "shut off" unless he is engaging in hyperactive and aggravating behavior. Due to the social reinforcement which these behaviors produce, they may become a consistent means of obtaining attention.

The level and type of activity which the child may engage in may also be shaped gradually by the social reaction of others. As parents and others learn to tolerate and "shut off" a given level of noise and activity, children are trained to become louder and more active in order to obtain social attention.

It is interesting to note that the hyperactive child may train parents and teachers to develop highly inappropriate ways of responding to the hyperactive behavior. The adult may discover that shouting, yelling, or threatening the child to remain still or to stick to a task may have some immediate effect. The child may slow down for a short time. Such removal, albeit temporary, of the disturbing behavior, reinforces the adult behavior which removed the unpleasantness. The adult may develop a strong pattern of scolding and nagging behavior.

Behavior Management Program

The following suggestions should assist a program aimed to reduce the excessive motion of the hyperactive child.

1. Describe the specific behaviors involved, and relate these to types of situations. Under what conditions is the child most likely to display the hyperactive behavior?

2. Identify the situations in which the behavior is less likely to occur. Some children, for example, can sit for extended periods of time watching TV, listening to music, or playing certain games. What are the differences between these two types of situations?

3. Obtain some measurement of the hyperactive behavior in relation to specific situations.

4. Avoid punishing, yelling, scolding, threatening or otherwise attending to the child for his hyperactive pattern. This will only serve to perpetuate the behavior.

5. Follow a major procedure of reinforcing competing behaviors. Strengthen behaviors through positive reinforcement that will take the place of the hyperactive behavior.

6. In following this strategy, begin with a high-preference activity in a highly-structured situation. Reinforce persistence at this activity for gradually increasing periods of time. Provide sufficient cues and prompts to insure that the child will be successful. Reduce distracting cues to an absolute minimum. Be sure that the child is aware of the behavior which is expected and the consequences which will follow performance of the desired behavior. Reinforce him for attending to and persisting at a task for increasingly longer periods of time.

7. Use a successive approximation procedure and gradually increase the behavioral requirements and the situations in which the behavior is to occur. Attempt to ignore any hyperactivity which may occur, avoiding reinforement by attention if at all possible.

8. Provide immediate and high-preference reinforcers for improvements. Remember the hyperactive behavior has been practiced hundreds of times and will require strong competing behaviors to replace it.

9. As the child shows improvements, praise him before other adults and peers. Specify the behavior that is pleasing to you. "Jill did her table work today very quietly and had fun. I'm proud of her."

10. Provide many pleasant interpersonal experiences. These will reduce the anxiety reactions which the child has developed in relation to numerous aspects of his social environment.

11. Insure that the child has a high preponderance of

successful experiences.   This can be accomplished only by careful selection of tasks and the programming under optimal conditions in small progressive increments.

AUTISTIC BEHAVIOR PATTERNS

Many young children with severe learning and behavior difficulties become rather detached on occasion from their social environment and exhibit limited responsiveness to social stimulation.   However, the detachment is not a general characteristic nor is it long lasting; the social environment does become important to the child as interactions with people result in numerous positive emotional experiences.   A few children, however, exhibit profound, generalized, and long-lasting autistic behavior patterns.   Various labels have been used to describe the behavioral syndrome.   The most common labels are autism, childhood schizophrenia, early infantile autism, and schizophrenic syndrome in childhood.   As the teacher of young children with learning and behavior problems will have contact with children with autistic behavior patterns, brief description will be provided (1) of the outstanding characteristics of such patterns and (2) of behavior management procedures which have been used with some success in dealing with some of these characteristics.   Since there is considerable controversy over the factors which underlie such extreme patterns of autistic behavior, the format previously followed to describe possible social learning factors will not be followed.   The interested reader should consult Ferster (1961) and Rimland (1964) for discussion of various physiological and psychological factors which have been suggested by various writers as being involved in the development of such behavioral characteristics.

Behavioral Characteristics

The following characteristics frequently are present in children with autistic patterns:
 1. *Limited responsiveness to external stimulation.*   The child attends to or is influenced only infrequently by the things that go on around him.   Changes in the physical environment usually have no effect on the child.   He is especially nonresponsive to social stimulation.   He actively avoids eye contact with others and seldom acknowledges that he is even aware that others are around unless they physically attempt to force him to attend to them.

2. *Self-destructive behaviors.*   He is likely to engage in such behaviors as head-banging, face-slapping, hair-pulling, and face-scratching.

3. *Tantrum behavior.*   When frustrated, the child is quite likely to shout, whine, cry, kick, and engage in similar disruptive tantrum behaviors.

4. *Self-stimulatory behavior.*   The following behaviors may be present in many children with extreme forms of autistic behavior patterns: finger-flicking, rocking in sitting or standing position, gazing at lights or at hand or fingers, spinning objects, wrist-flapping.

5. *Failure to imitate.*   The child exhibits an obvious deficit in imitation skills.   This limitation in imitation skills increases his learning difficulties, especially in the language area.

6. *Isolated behaviors.*   Such behaviors as "staring off at something," "blank stare," "expressionless," and "sitting very still for long periods" frequently are present.

7. *Echolalic speech or absence of speech.*   Many children with severe autistic behavior patterns do not speak.   They give an impression of a severe hearing loss as they do not respond to verbal stimulation.   The nonspeaking child also tends to be quite disruptive and destructive.

Other children have speech, but it frequently is of an echolalic nature.   Those who do mimic the verbal productions of others are generally able to learn more normal speech than children who are nonverbal at the initiation of a behavior management program.

8. *Short attention span.*   The child displays a short attention span when he becomes involved in any learning task.   This involvement is frequently momentary.

Behavior Management Program

The following discussion provides brief summaries of behavior management procedures which have been used with some success with children characterized by extreme forms of autistic behavior. The reader is encouraged to refer to the suggested readings provided throughout the section for more detailed and comprehensive accounts of these procedures.   Hamblin and associates (1971) provide the following suggestions:

1. The first step is to find effective reinforcers.   Food items are most typically required initially.   This is difficult in some cases as the children have highly individual and variable food preferences.   In selecting food for use in a behavior shaping program, preference should be given to items which can be presented in

small bites, which the child cannot play with, and which the child can eat rapidly. Ice cream, sherbet, and soft puddings have been found most effective as have such items as small bits of sugar-coated cereals. It may be necessary to enhance the usefulness of food as a reinforcer by using the child's meals. Once the child begins to respond with some consistency to food items, a token procedure should be introduced. As the child responds appropriately to tokens, the training sessions can be increased in length as the satiation effect which results with the use of food items will not be present.

2. Negativistic behaviors are quite likely to occur with high frequency early in training. Hamblin and associates report such behaviors as refusals, reversals (smiling or laughing at incorrect behaviors), tantrums and pouting.

3. Keep trial and error learning to an absolute minimum in early stages of working with the child. This indicates that a well-sequenced task should be used with very careful shaping of each component to insure errorless learning. Negativism becomes more frequent and intense if the child experiences frustration in trial and error learning.

4. If the child does make an error it is best initially to ignore it. Informing the child that he has made an error tends to increase his negativism.

5. Make single requests in the beginning. Multiple requests increase the negativistic behaviors.

6. To avoid negativistic behaviors, move slowly from a continuous reinforcement schedule to an intermittent one.

7. Ignore bizarre behavior initially. Avoid making demands on the child until considerable success has been attained in influencing his behaviors. Demands early in the behavior management program are quite likely to result in excessive negativistic behavior.

Teaching Speech

One of the most central deficits of children with autistic behavior patterns relates to functional speech. Studies have suggested a significant relationship between the early development of speech (by the age of five) and later social adjustment (see Eisenberg, 1956). It is essential that the initial focus of the behavior management program is to teach functional speech. One of the first steps is to insure that imitative behaviors are present. The following steps described by Hartung (1970), Lovaas (1968) and Risley and Wolf (1967; 1968) have been found to produce favorable results:

1. Attention and eye contact must be shaped initially. The child cannot learn to imitate the motor and verbal behaviors of the teacher until he is able to attend to her. Attention and eye contact may be maintained initially by holding the food reinforcer directly in front of the teacher's face. Later, attention may be attracted by the use of loud noises such as shouting the child's name ("John, look!") or a sharp slap on the table top. Additionally, the child's head may be held or turned so that he faces the teacher.

2. After some attention has been shaped, the next step is to teach the child to imitate motor behaviors demonstrated by the teacher. It is valuable to teach the child a pattern of consistent motor-imitative behaviors prior to the beginning of speech training.

3. The motor behavior is used as a basis for shaping verbal behaviors. The child is requested to initiate a series of motor responses and then is presented a verbal model to imitate. The progression may start with gross motor imitation, then fine motor imitation, then motor imitation involving facial movements and finally may involve verbalizations.

4. The child is reinforced initially for all vocal sounds and for visually fixating on the teacher's mouth and eyes.

5. In teaching specific vocal sounds to nonverbal children, those sounds that can be prompted by manually assisting the child should be selected, e.g., the sound "b." The teacher makes the sound "b" and prompts the child to make the sound by holding the child's lips closed with her fingers and quickly removing them when the child exhales (see Lovaas *et al.*, 1966, for a more detailed description).

6. Those sounds are selected that have concomitant visual components which can be exaggerated when the teacher pronounces them, e.g., the labial "m" and the front or open-mouthed vowel "a." The exaggeration emphasizes the lip and mouth placements.

7. For the child who does have some verbal skills, the teacher selects words or sounds which the child uses and builds on them.

8. The teacher initially avoids sounds that have only auditory components such as the "k," "g," "s," and "l."

9. After the child is making vocal sounds, the teacher begins to reinforce the child for making the sounds within a designated period of time (5 to 10 sec.) following the teacher's sounds.

10. Next, sounds are reinforced that resemble those of the teacher's modeled sound. It is helpful to prompt the child by holding and guiding the child's lips. This assistance is gradually faded as the child begins to imitate correctly.

11. New sounds and words are added as the child correctly and consistently imitates a single word. New and old themes are alternated to insure frequent success.

12. After the child has successfully imitated a few words, it is not unusual to find the emergence of echolalia. The child begins to imitate numerous words and even short phrases.

13. After imitative responses occur with consistency, the child is taught to name objects. This is accomplished by presenting an object, labeling it, and having the child imitate the name. The labeling prompt is gradually removed as the child is able to spontaneously name the object. Following naming, the child is taught to answer questions, use phrases, and finally to use functional speech.

As noted at the outset, this discussion is only suggestive of some of the procedures which have been used with children with autistic behavior patterns. It should be emphasized that the behavior management program is quite time consuming and prolonged. The results, however, are quite dramatic in some instances. The teacher who wishes to obtain more information about the strategies used is encouraged to study the references mentioned. Stuecher's (1972) detailed report of his successful experience with a young child and the description of a kindergarten program for a group of children by Martin and associates (1968) are especially recommended for the teacher as they provide description of numerous components of comprehensive behavior management programs. Finally, the teacher will find the recent description by Kozloff (1973) of a parent training program valuable for working with autistic behavior patterns of children.

PART V

Facilitating Behavior Change
in the Home

CHAPTER 13

Behavior Management Programs
in the Home

The rules of social learning described throughout the book emphasize that what a child learns and how the child behaves are potentially influenced by any social experiences that he may have.
Although the school environment can exert a most significant
influence on the young child, the home environment continues to
provide the child with numerous inappropriate as well as appropriate learning experiences. The young child spends many more
hours each week in the social environment of the home than he
spends at school. This time in the home represents a potentially
valuable asset to the school program, so it becomes highly desirable for the educational program to include a well-defined and
ongoing home-school component. The school program, isolated
from the family, obviously will contribute to the child's behavior
development. However, the severe learning and behavior problems of young children can be dealt with much more effectively in
a joint school-home endeavor.

Parents and other members of the family frequently are
quite eager and capable of providing more appropriate learning
experiences in the home for the young child with problems. But
too often parents do not know what to do when confronted with
difficulties in parent-child interactions, or how best to deal with the
problems. They have lived with the child's problems for some
length of time and are often quite frustrated and overwhelmed by
these difficulties. They may not understand why their child does
not learn or behave like other children. They have ill-defined
concepts of some internal causes of their child's difficulties. But

the professionals with whom they have consulted have not provided specific guidance in ways of dealing with the child's problems.

It is true that many of the learning and behavior difficulties have been created, or at least intensified, by inadequate behavior management procedures in the home. Some parents require little of their children; they pander to them excessively. Other parents are dominated by their children, and they fulfill all requests made by them. Still other parents respond in an overly demanding and negative manner toward their child simply because they are at their wits' end. They have tried everything they know to do but the problem remains. This was illustrated by a recent experience with a father of a child who would not speak in nursery school although she was quite verbal at home. As one step in decreasing the selective mutism of his young daughter, the father was requested to encourage the child to record her voice on a tape recorder. The father became quite enthusiastic over the behavior management program that was devised and was highly motivated to fulfill every suggestion made by the teacher. But the child balked at recording her voice. After encouraging her in every way, the father suddenly lost his temper and started shouting at and threatening the child. After this failed to get the child to comply with his request, the father finally spanked her rather severely. The father's behavior merely served to intensify the child's shyness.

Many parents do need assistance in recognizing that what they are doing may create additional problems for the child. Many could benefit from guidance in modifying the manner in which they interact with or respond to their children. They do not need the teacher to place blame on them or to lecture them on what they have done wrong or how they have created the child's problems. They do require information, guidance, and support. They need information about how specific and general problems can be approached and how their day to day interactions with their child can contribute to the child's development. They do not need generalities about being a good parent. They do need specific, concrete, and practical suggestions about how they can best promote optimal adjustment for their child.

Many things can be done by family members in the home to contribute to and complement the behavior management endeavors of the school program. Family members can reinforce and enhance new behaviors that have been acquired in the school setting. They can contribute tremendously to the positive emotional experiences which are required by the child with learning and behavior difficulties. They can provide their child with meaningful expectations and the extra support necessary for the child to fulfill these behavioral objectives. Parents can learn, in short, to become more skillful at utilizing effective behavior management procedures if provided appropriate information, training, and followup assistance.

OBJECTIVES OF A HOME-SCHOOL PROGRAM

The ideal arrangement from the child's viewpoint is one which reflects a high degree of consistency between the school and home in the behavioral objectives set for the child and in the general behavior management procedures used. Although this ideal consistency is seldom realized, there will be numerous unplanned opportunities for cooperative concern and programming between home and school. Parents occasionally will seek the guidance of school personnel in dealing with specific problems which the child presents in the home; the teacher will seek the cooperation of parents in understanding behavior difficulties which the child may be presenting or to enlist the parents' assistance in extending the school program into the home. Although these types of unplanned and unsystematic interactions between home and school have many positive features, the child's total learning experiences will be enhanced substantially by more formal and consistent types of cooperative endeavors.

The teacher and other school personnel may provide assistance and enlist the cooperation of parents and other family members in three ways. First, the school may work cooperatively with parents in setting joint school-home behavioral objectives for the child. The parents also could be provided direction in reinforcing or in otherwise dealing with certain behaviors which the child has acquired in school. Consistent home support will serve to strengthen the behavior and also to facilitate its generalization to the home and other settings. Second, the school may provide specific consultation to the parents in developing behavior management programs for general and specific problems which occur in the home or in both home and school settings. Third, the school may provide a systematic program to the parents designed to promote development of general behavior management skills. Each of these approaches will be discussed.

JOINT HOME-SCHOOL PROGRAMS

It is essential that the home and school agree on a common set of goals for children with learning and behavior problems. Thus, at a very minimum the teacher can plan cooperatively on a scheduled basis with parents in setting behavioral objectives for the young child. As a starting point in this planning, the teacher can provide initial impressions about what she feels the child can accomplish along various behavioral dimensions. These initial impressions may be based on psychological and educational evaluation data, on the experiences with the child reported by other teachers, or on her own previous contacts with the child. The parents can expand on these impressions, add new ones, or delete or modify others. Also, parents should be encouraged to express their opinions about how realistic these objectives appear to them.

In setting behavioral objectives, the child's present level of performance in relation to each behavior objective should be discussed. This should prove valuable since it emphasizes the nature of the gap between what the child presently can and does do and what he is being expected to learn to do. The parents will recognize that the child does function and learn in many areas. Also, the parents will be in a position to assume a more optimistic view of their child's behavior development. As program objectives are set along numerous behavioral dimensions, the parents are more likely to recognize that the child is learning something instead of being overwhelmed and discouraged by the fact that he has so many learning and behavior difficulties. The behavioral objectives set will emphasize what the child can learn instead of focusing on what is wrong about him.

In planning cooperatively with parents, the teacher is in an ideal position to enlist the parents' assistance in supporting the behaviors which the school program will attempt to strengthen. If the school and home can agree on some common behavioral objectives, the child will be the beneficiary since he will not be expected to behave one way at home and a different way at school. The teacher may recognize that the child is overly dependent on adult assistance or is too prone to be physically aggressive toward peers. She may wish to teach more independence and more acceptable means of social interaction in conflict situations or of handling frustration. Open discussion of these behavioral goals with the parents and means by which both home and school can encourage the development of these patterns of behavior will identify and clarify differences of opinion and approach.

Joint teacher-parent planning will provide the teacher with some insight into the types of learning experiences provided for the child in the home. She will understand what the parents expect of the child and of some of the child-rearing practices of the parents. With this information the teacher will be in a better position to understand and successfully deal with many of the behavior patterns which the child brings into the school program.

The parents and teacher can work out some procedure so that the family can be informed routinely how the child is progressing in relation to the behavioral objectives set for his school program. Also, specific ways should be devised by which the parents can support the new behaviors acquired in school. For example, a child may learn to recognize and label red, blue, green, and yellow colors. The teacher may wish the parents to use these color names in describing objects and to encourage and reinforce the child for using these names within the home environment. The particular types of involvement of the parents and the specific communication system devised obviously would vary from family to family. Some parents may routinely demand too much from a child; others would be highly inconsistent in providing any follow-through. Still others may be highly reliable and effective in any role agreed upon.

Procedures may be developed for the child to take finished products home regularly (e.g., paintings, drawings, colorings, visual-motor practice sheets, printing worksheets). Caution must be exercised, however, in setting up this program. The teacher should not send anything home that will result in negative consequences for the child. If the child is reprimanded or otherwise criticized for materials brought from school, he will like school less. The teacher should not send anything home that implies inadequate performance. Some teachers have used the procedure of sending a "smiling face" home to denote that the child had a good day at school and a "frowning face" if the child did not perform satisfactorily. This procedure is not to be recommended for the child will be punished twice—at school and at home—for behaviors which did not meet the teacher's expectation. School experiences become less pleasant to the child when this type of procedure is used. Also, the punishment provided by the parents upon receipt of a "frowning face" (disappointment, reprimand, response cost, or however the parent responds to the child) is so noncontingent and nonspecific. It comes some hours after the inappropriate behavior has occurred. The parents and perhaps even the child have little notion of what specific behaviors were inadequate.

A more acceptable procedure would be one in which the teacher routinely finds something that the child did that was appropriate and communicates this to the home. Remember, the school program is designed to teach appropriate skills—including emotional ones. The child must be provided experiences that result in good feelings about something that he has accomplished. If not, the school experiences, especially negative ones that could be extended into the home, will result in the child feeling even more inadequate than he already does.

If the teacher is dissatisfied with the child's behavior in relation to the goals set, she should communicate this to the parents in a face-to-face conference.   In this manner, parents and teachers can discuss means of facilitating more appropriate behavior.

CONSULTATION WITH PARENTS

In addition to encouraging follow-through in the home of behaviors acquired in the school, the teacher or other school personnel may provide assistance to the parents in developing behavior management programs for specific and general behavior problems which the child exhibits in the home setting.   In developing these programs it generally is best to present highly detailed and specific suggestions.   As the parents are successful in implementing the highly structured programs, the consultation can gradually become of a less frequent and of a more general nature.

An illustration of the specificity and detail of recommended programs is provided by Zeilberger and associates (1968).   These consultants provided program recommendations for parents to follow in dealing with noncompliance and aggressive behavior in their four-year, eight-month-old son, Rorey.   Examples of the twelve instructions outlined for the parents included:

1. Immediately after Rorey acts aggressively or disobediently, take him to the time-out (TO) room.   One of the family bedrooms was modified for this use by having toys and other items of interest to a child removed.

2. As Rorey is taken to the TO room for aggressive behavior, say "You cannot stay here if you fight."   As Rorey is taken to the TO room for disobedient behavior, say "You cannot stay here if you do not do what you are told."   Make no other comments.

3. Place Rorey in the TO room swiftly and without conversation other than the above.   Place him inside and shut and hook the door.

4. Leave Rorey in the TO room for 2 minutes.   If he tantrums or cries, time the 2 minutes from the end of the last tantrum or cry.

. . .

7. Ignore undesirable behavior which does not merit going to the TO room.   "Ignore" means you should not comment upon

such behavior, nor attend to it by suddenly looking around when it occurs.

. . .

9. Reinforce desirable cooperative play frequently (at least once every 5 minutes) without interrupting it. Comments, such as "My, you're all having a good time" are sufficient, although direct praise which does not interrupt the play is acceptable.

10. Always reward Rorey when he obeys.

. . .

12. Follow the program 24 hours a day. (p. 49)

In providing consultation to parents, the teacher is in a position to encourage the parents (1) to develop consistency in their interaction with their child, (2) to facilitate as much independence as possible and (3) to provide the child with as much success and subsequent positive emotional learning as possible. These will be discussed briefly.

Facilitating Consistency

As emphasized and illustrated throughout the book, consistency in presenting behavioral requirements to children and in the manner in which parents respond to the way the child behaves are extremely important in facilitating stable and desirable behavior patterns in the child. Inconsistency produces considerable problems. The following points should be emphasized to parents:

1. The parents should clearly identify for themselves just what they expect of their child. The behavioral requirements should be examined in terms of their purpose and reasonableness for the child. If the parents are unable to define for themselves why certain behaviors are desired, they are likely to be inconsistent in requiring and supporting such behaviors.

2. The behavior expectations of the parents (many of which can be stated as rules of behavior) should be explained or demonstrated to the child. The conditions under which the behavior is expected to occur should be clearly delineated.

3. The parents should plan the manner in which the child will be requested or otherwise cued to behave in a specified manner as well as the way in which the child will be reinforced for engaging in the behavior.

4. The parents should decide what they will do if the child fails to engage in the expected behavior. Parents should be

encouraged to ignore a child's objections when he is being required to fulfill a rule. The parent should understand that children will test the rules set for them. If the child is able to disregard rules on occasion following objection on his part (crying, whining, stalling, ignoring), the parents should recognize that they will be teaching the child inappropriate behavior patterns. The child will learn to follow rules only if parents are consistent in requiring compliance and in reinforcing it with meaningful reinforcing events.

5. Parents should understand that consistency on their part will produce stable behavior patterns in their child. Children soon learn not to waste their time "testing rules." If parents are inconsistent, children spend an excessive amount of time engaging in irrelevant behavior.

6. It must be emphasized that a child is more likely to engage in behavior that is not particularly enjoyable to him if he has a good relationship with his parents. If the child enjoys being with his parents, if parents engage in play and other fun activities with their child frequently, if parents "catch their child being good" and reinforce him frequently, and if parents are generally available to him when he needs assistance, support, or reassurance, the child is more likely to behave appropriately.

Facilitating Independence in Home Setting

One important behavioral goal for exceptional children is gaining independence in as many behavioral areas and as high a level as possible. The family can contribute significantly to the child's independence by setting *realistic* behavioral goals in such self-care and related areas as dressing, feeding, grooming, keeping room clean, and basic household chores. It is important to provide the child with opportunities to contribute to the family. Chores should be presented in a pleasant matter-of-fact manner. The child should be provided with frequent praise and presented with such concepts as "being helpful," "smart," "strong," "big," "fast." When these labels are associated frequently with task involvement and completion they add to the child's concept of competency.

In assigning chores or responsibilities the parent should:

(1) Provide specific tasks to be completed within specific time periods. This can be facilitated by using a timer which rings at the end of the period.

(2) Arrange the contingency so that high-preference activities follow low-preference ones (e.g., after toys picked up, TV may be turned on; after room picked up, bedtime story read).

(3) Emphasize the strategy of providing positive consequences for appropriate behavior instead of depending upon behavior control through threat or negative consequences. If a child learns to complete tasks in order to avoid negative consequences, he does not learn to enjoy these activities. In contrast, if the behavior is under the influence of subsequent positive reinforcers the child learns to enjoy task completion. He gains satisfaction from pleasing others as well as being proud of himself.

Providing Successful Experiences

It is highly critical that the child be successful in the vast majority of his endeavors. Parents should be assisted in recognizing that young children with learning and behavior difficulties who have failed excessively have developed too much negative emotionality. The experiences in the home, just as those in the school, must become positive ones. The learning environments must be structured to insure success and contingent positive consequences.

PROGRAM IN BEHAVIOR MANAGEMENT PROCEDURES

Ideally, the two previously described home-school program components would be combined with one which provides a systematic experience to parents in developing general behavior management skills. Such a program will require more than mere information giving. Parents need guided practice in behaving differently toward their child. They require practice defining problem behaviors, analyzing possible factors involved in their development and maintenance, and in devising behavior management strategies. Second, parents may profit from discussion of general preventative strategies. Instead of dealing with problems after they arise, parents need to know what they can do to provide those positive experiences which will render less likely the appearance of problems of learning and management. Finally, parents frequently will find it necessary to modify their own behavior. They must develop new control over the stimulus events which cue their own behaviors in relation to their child. And as they begin to behave differently they must find sources of reinforcement to strengthen and maintain their new child-rearing practices. Parents are frequently under the strong control of their child's inappropriate behaviors. Reinforcement to the parents for engaging in new child-interaction behavior must come from external sources such as school personnel. As the parents succeed in behaving differently toward their child and as they recognize concomitant positive changes in the child's behavior, this social feedback will provide sufficient reinforcement to maintain their new behavior.

In developing the specific content of a systematic program in behavior management, the teacher may devise a program which delineates the principles presented in previous chapters, or the teacher may use books that have been written specifically for parents. The books by Becker (1971), Patterson and Gullion (1968), Patterson (1971), and Smith and Smith (1966) are available for this purpose.

PART VI

Supplementary Readings
and Audiovisual Materials

Supplementary Readings
and Audiovisual Materials

SUPPLEMENTARY READINGS

The following references are suggested for the reader who wishes to gain additional information about the topics of behavior management. The references include materials of a technical level comparable to that of the present book as well as more advanced materials.

Ackerman, J. M. *Operant conditioning techniques for the classroom teacher.* Glenview, Ill.: Scott, Foresman and Co., 1972.

Becker, W. C., Engelmann, S., & Thomas, D. R. *Teaching: A course in applied psychology.* Chicago: Science Research Associates, 1971.

Becker, W. C., Thomas, D. R., & Carnine, D. *Reducing behavior problems: An operant conditioning guide for teachers.* Urbana, Ill.: Educational Research Information Center Clearinghouse on Early Childhood Education, 1969.

Bijou, S. W., & Baer, D. M. *Child development. Systematic and empirical theory.* Vol. I. New York: Appleton-Century-Crofts, Inc., 1961.

Bijou, S. W., & Baer, D. M. *Child development. Universal stages of infancy.* Vol. II. New York: Appleton-Century-Crofts, Inc., 1965.

Blackham, G. J., & Silberman, A. *Modification of child behavior.* Belmont, Calif.: Wadsworth Publishing Co., 1971.

Clarizio, H. F. *Toward positive classroom discipline.* New York: John Wiley and Sons, 1971.

Deibert, A. N., & Harmon, A. J. *New tools for changing behavior.* Champaign, Ill.: Research Press, 1970.

Gardner, W. I. *Behavior modification in mental retardation.* Chicago: Aldine, 1971.

Haring, N. G., & Phillips, E. L. *Analysis and modification of classroom behavior.* Englewood Cliffs, New Jersey: Prentice-Hall, Inc., 1972.

Krumboltz, J. D., & Krumboltz, H. B. *Changing children's behavior.* Englewood Cliffs, N. J.: Prentice-Hall, 1972.

Kunzelmann, H. P. (Ed.) *Precision teaching.* Seattle: Special Child Publications, Inc., 1970.

Meacham, M. L., & Wiesen, A. E. *Changing classroom behavior: A manual for precision teaching.* Scranton, Pa.: International Textbook Co., 1969.

O'Leary, K. D., & O'Leary, S. G. *Classroom management: The sucsuccessful use of behavior modification.* New York: Pergamon Press, Inc., 1972.

Staats, A. W. *Child learning, intelligence and personality.* New York: Harper and Row, 1971.

Sulzer, B., & Mayer, G. R. *Behavior modification procedures for school personnel.* Hinsdale, Ill.: Dryden Press, 1972.

Tharp, R. G., & Wetzel, R. J. *Behavior modification in the natural environment.* New York: Academic Press, 1969.

Vernon, W. M. *Motivating children: Behavior modification in the classroom.* New York: Holt, Rinehart and Winston, 1972.

Watson, L. S. *How to use behavior modification with mentally retarded and autistic children.* Columbus, Ohio: Behavior Modification Technology, 1972.

AUDIOVISUAL MATERIALS

The audiovisual materials listed provide illustration of the application of various behavior management principles to young children with learning and behavior problems.   The film *Who Did What to Whom* is especially useful in training observers to identify specific behaviors and to identify the specific behavior management procedures being used to influence these behaviors.

Films and Videotapes

1. *A step behind.* A three film series:
   GENESIS.   (16mm/color/25 min.) Demonstrates a behavior management approach to teaching basic self-help skills of eating, dressing, and toileting.
   ASK JUST FOR LITTLE THINGS. (16 mm/color/20 min.)

Three life skills—ambulation, personal hygiene and attending—are taught. Parent is taught to train child in the home.
I'LL PROMISE YOU A TOMORROW. (16 mm/color/20 min.) Designed to teach the basic skills in preparation for placement in community special education setting. Demonstrates teaching of the basic use of words and simple sentences, of following directions, and of group participation.
(These three films are available from Hallmark Films, Inc., 1511 E. North Avenue, Baltimore, Maryland.)

2. *How to use tokens in teaching.* (16 mm/color/8 min.) Teacher demonstrates the proper way to use tokens in preschool education. (Audio Visual Center, 746 Massachusetts, University of Kansas, Lawrence, Kansas 66044)

3. *Rewards and reinforcement in learning.* (16 mm/B&W/25 min.) Shows teaching child to lace shoe, to walk independently of support, and remediation of an articulation problem. (Behavior Modification Productions, P.O. Box 3207, Scottsdale, Arizona 85257)

4. *Spearhead at Juniper Gardens.* (16mm/B&W/40 min.) Demonstrates preschool and remedial education research project. Reinforcement principles are used to enhance language skills of preschool children and to motivate slow-learning grade school children. (Audio Visual Center, 746 Massachusetts, University of Kansas, Lawrence, Kansas 66044)

5. *Behavior modification in the classroom.* (16 mm/color or B&W/24 min.) Use of operant conditioning and modeling to strengthen task-oriented behavior in primary level children. Three classroom situations at different primary levels contrast behavior before and after use of behavior modification techniques. Methods of training teachers in use of behavior modification strategies are included. (Extension Media Center, University of California, Berkeley, California 74720)

6. *A demonstration of behavioral processes.* (16 mm/color/28 min.) Shows B. F. Skinner in classroom demonstrating use of learning principles. (Appleton-Century-Crofts Film Library, 267 West 25th Street, New York, New York)

√7. *Dare to do.* (16 mm/B&W/20 min.) Application of a behavior modification system is demonstrated in a third grade classroom in a New York ghetto area. (Synchro Films, 43 Bay Drive West, Hintington, New York 11743)

8. *Who did what to whom.* (16 mm/color/17 min.) Film designed to provide opportunity to practice behavior analysis of everyday interactions. Each of 40 short scenes is followed by five seconds of black leader so that projector may be stopped and the scene discussed. The behavior principles of positive and negative reinforcement, punishment, and extinction are shown in scenes in home, school, and office. (Research Press Co., 2612 N. Mattis Avenue, Champaign, Illinois 61820)

9. *Behavior modification: Teaching language to psychotic children.* (16 mm/color/42 min.) Reinforcement and stimulus fading illustrated as methods of teaching speech to psychotic children. (Appleton-Century-Crofts Film Library, 267 West 25th Street, New York, New York)

10. *Behavioral analysis classroom.* (16 mm/color/20 min.) Demonstrates classrooms which use behavior analysis techniques and token reinforcement systems. Shows how parents are used to supplement the regular teaching staff. (Audio Visual Center, 746 Massachusetts, University of Kansas, Lawrence, Kansas 66044)

11. *Self-help skill videotape.* Demonstrates in detail a behavior modification program for teaching self-help skills. Principles considered are reinforcement, successive approximation, chaining, prompting and fading, and stimulus control. This tape can be used as an introduction to behavior modification.
Language videotape. Summarizes a program for teaching receptive language and speech. All steps used to develop language skills are described. Demonstrates use of reinforcement, successive approximation, chaining, prompting and fading principles.
Social-recreational videotape. Describes a program for teaching psychotic and retarded children to play games, and to develop frustration tolerance, eliminate psychotic behaviors and develop social interaction between children. Illustrates application of behavior modification principles to game situations. (These three videotapes may be obtained from Behavior Modification Technology, P.O. Box 23161, Columbus, Ohio)

Bibliography

Abbott, M. S. Modification of the classroom behavior of a "disadvantaged" kindergarten boy by social reinforcement and isolation. *Journal of Education*, 1969, 151, 31–45.

Ackerman, J. M. *Operant conditioning techniques for the classroom teacher*. Glenview, Ill.: Scott, Foresman and Co., 1972.

Addison, R. M., & Homme, L. E. The reinforcing event (RE) menu. *National Society for Programmed Instruction Journal*, 1966, 5, 8–9.

Allen, K. E. Behavior modification: What teachers of young exceptional children can do. *Teaching Exceptional Children*, 1972, 4, 119–127.

Allen, K. E., & Harris, F. R. Elimination of a child's excessive scratching by training the mother in reinforcement procedures. *Behavior Research and Therapy*, 1966, 4, 79–84.

Allen, K. E., Hart, B. M., Buell, J. S., Harris, F. R., & Wolf, M. M. Effects of social reinforcement on isolate behavior of a nursery school child. *Child Development*, 1964, 35, 511–518.

Allen, K. E., Henke, L. B., Harris, F. R., Baer, D. M., & Reynolds, N. J. Control of hyperactivity by social reinforcement of attending behavior. *Journal of Educational Psychology*, 1967, 58, 231–237.

Allen, K. E., Turner, K. D., & Everett, P. M. A behavior modification classroom for Head Start children with problem behaviors. *Exceptional Children*, 1970, 37, 119–127.

Baer, D. M., Peterson, R. F., & Sherman, J. A. The development of imitation by reinforcing behavioral similarity to a model. *Journal of Experimental Analysis of Behavior*, 1967, 10, 405–416.

Baker, J. G., Stanish, B., & Fraser, B. Comparative effects of a token economy in nursery school. *Mental Retardation*, 1972, 10, 16–19.

Bandura, A. *Principles of behavior modification.* New York: Holt, Rinehart and Winston, 1969.

Bandura, A., Grusec, J. E., & Menlove, F. L. Vicarious extinction of avoidance behavior. *Journal of Personality and Social Psychology*, 1967, 5, 16–23.

Bandura, A., & Menlove, F. L. Factors determining vicarious extinction of avoidance behavior through symbolic modeling. *Journal of Personality and Social Psychology*, 1968, 8, 99–108.

Barrett, B. Behavior modification in the home: Parents adapt laboratory-developed tactics to bowel-train a 5½-year-old. *Psychotherapy: Theory, Research, and Practice*, 1969, 6, 172–176.

Becker, W. C. *Parents are teachers: A child management program.* Champaign, Ill.: Research Press, 1971.

Becker, W. C., Engelmann, S., & Thomas, D. R. *Teaching: A course in applied psychology.* Chicago: Science Research Associates, 1971.

Becker, W. C., Madsen, C. H., Arnold, C. R., & Thomas, D. R. The contingent use of teacher attention and praise in reducing classroom behavior problems. *Journal of Special Education*, 1967, 1, 287–307.

Bereiter, C., & Engelmann, S. *Teaching disadvantaged children in the preschool.* Engelwood Cliffs, N.J.: Prentice-Hall, 1966.

Bettelheim, B. *Love is not enough.* New York: Free Press, 1950.

Bijou, S. W. The technology of teaching young handicapped children. In S. W. Bijou and E. Ribes-Inesta (Eds.) *Behavior modification: Issues and extensions.* New York: Academic Press, 1972. Pp. 27–42.

Bijou, S. W., & Sturges, P. T. Positive reinforcers for experimental studies with children-consumables and manipulatables. *Child Development*, 1959, 30, 151–170.

Birnbrauer, J. S., & Lawler, J. Token reinforcement for learning. *Mental Retardation*, 1964, 2, 275–279.

Birnbrauer, J. S., Wolf, M. M., Kidder, J. D., & Tague, C. E. Classroom behavior of retarded pupils with token reinforcement. *Journal of Experimental Child Psychology*, 1965, 2, 219–235.

Bricker, W. A., & Bricker, D. D. A program of language training for the severely language handicapped child. *Exceptional Children*, 1970, 37, 101–111.

Briskin, A. S., & Gardner, W. I. Social reinforcement in reducing inappropriate behavior. *Young Children*, 1968, 24, 84–89.

Brown, P., & Elliott, R. Control of aggression in a nursery school class. *Journal of Experimental Child Psychology*, 1965, 2, 103–107.

Buell, J., Stoddard, P., Harris, F. R., & Baer, D. M. Collateral social development accompanying reinforcement of outdoor play in a preschool child. *Journal of Applied Behavior Analysis,* 1968, 1, 167–173.

Bushell, D., Wrobel, P. A., & Michaelis, M. L. Applying "group" contingencies to the classroom study behavior of preschool children. *Journal of Applied Behavior Analysis,* 1968, 1, 55–61.

Camp, W. L., & Lathen, L. A successful classroom program for emotionally disturbed children. *Training School Bulletin,* 1967, 64, 31–38.

Carlson, C. S., Arnold, C. R., Becker, W. C., & Madsen, C. H. The elimination of tantrum behavior of a child in an elementary classroom. *Behavior Research and Therapy,* 1968, 6, 117–119.

Clarizio, H. F. *Toward positive classroom discipline.* New York: John Wiley and Sons, 1971.

Daley, M. F. The "reinforcement menu:" finding effective reinforcers. In J. D. Krumboltz & C. E. Thoresen (Eds.) *Behavioral Counseling.* New York: Holt, Rinehart and Winston, 1969. Pp. 42–45.

Deci, E. L. Work—who does not like it and why. *Psychology Today,* 1972, 6, 57–58.

Eisenberg, L. The autistic child in adolescence. *American Journal of Psychiatry,* 1956, 112, 607–612.

Ferster, C. B. Positive reinforcement and behavioral deficits of autistic children. *Child Development,* 1961, 32, 437–456.

Garcia, E., Baer, D. M., & Firestone, I. The development of generalized imitation within topographically determined boundaries. *Journal of Applied Behavior Analysis,* 1971, 4, 101–112.

Hall, R. V., Axelrod, S., Tyler, L., Grief, E., Jones, F. C., & Robertson, R. Modification of behavior problems in the home with a parent as observer and experimenter. *Journal of Applied Behavior Analysis,* 1972, 5, 53–64.

Hamblin, R. L., Buckholdt, D., Ferritor, D., Kozloff, M., & Blackwell, L. *The humanization processes: A social, behavioral analysis of children's problems.* New York: John Wiley and Sons, 1971.

Harris, F. R., Johnston, M., Kelley, C. S., & Wolf, M. M. Effects of positive social reinforcement on regressed crawling of a nursery school child. *Journal of Educational Psychology,* 1964, 55, 35–41.

Hart, B. M., Allen, K. E., Buell, J. S., Harris, F. R., & Wolf, M. M. Effects of social reinforcement on operant crying. *Journal of Experimental Child Psychology,* 1964, 1, 145–153.

Hart, B. M., & Risley, T. R. Establishing use of descriptive adjectives in the spontaneous speech of disadvantaged preschool children. *Journal Applied Behavior Analysis,* 1968, 1, 109–120.

Hart, B. M., Reynolds, N. J., Baer, D. M., Brawley, E. R., & Harris, F. R. Effect of contingent and non-contingent social reinforcement on the cooperative play of a preschool child. *Journal of Applied Behavior Analysis*, 1968, 1, 73–76.

Hartung, J. R. A review of procedures to increase verbal imitation skills and functional speech in autistic children. *Journal of Speech and Hearing Disorders*, 1970, 35, 203–217.

Hawkins, R. P., Peterson, R. F., Schweid, E., & Bijou, S. W. Behavior therapy in the home: Amelioration of problem parent-child relations with the parent in a therapeutic role. *Journal of Experimental Child Psychology*, 1966, 4, 99–107.

Heitzman, A. J. Effects of a token reinforcement system on the reading and arithmetic skills learning of migrant primary school pupils. *Journal of Educational Research*, 1970, 63, 455–458.

Herman, S. H., & Tramontana, J. Instructions and group versus individual reinforcement in modifying disruptive group behavior *Journal of Applied Behavior Analysis*, 1971, 4, 113–119.

Homme, L. E., deBaca, P. C., Devine, J. V., Steinhorst, R., & Rickert, E. J. Use of the Premack principle in controlling the behavior of nursery school children. *Journal of Experimental Analysis of Behavior*, 1963, 6, 544.

Hopkins, B. L., Schutte, R. C., & Garton, K. L. The effects of access to a playroom on the rate and quality of printing and writing of first and second-grade students. *Journal of Applied Behavior Analysis*, 1971, 4, 77–87.

Horner, R. D. Establishing use of crutches by a mentally retarded spina bifida child. *Journal of Applied Behavior Analysis*, 1971, 4, 183–189.

Johnston, M. K., Kelley, C. S., Harris, F. R., & Wolf, M. M. An application of reinforcement principles to development of motor skills of a young child. *Child Development*, 1966, 37, 379–387.

Kirby, F. D., & Toler, H. C. Modification of preschool isolate behavior: A case study. *Journal of Applied Behavior Analysis*, 1970, 3, 309–314.

Kozloff, M. A. *Reaching the autistic child: A parent training program.* Champaign, Ill.: Research Press, 1973.

Krumboltz, J. D., & Krumboltz, H. B. *Changing children's behavior.* Englewood Cliffs, N.J.: Prentice-Hall, 1972.

Lahey, B. B. Modification of the frequency of descriptive adjectives in the speech of Head Start children through modeling without reinforcement. *Journal of Applied Behavior Analysis*, 1971, 4, 19–22.

Larsen, L. A., & Bricker, W. A. A manual for parents and teachers of severely and moderately retarded children. *IMRID papers and reports*, Vol. V, No. 22. Nashville: George Peabody College, 1968.

Levin, G. R., & Simmons, J. J. Response to food and praise by emotionally disturbed boys. *Psychological Reports*, 1962, 11, 539–546.

Lindsley, O. R. Technical note: A reliable wrist counter for recording behavior rates. *Journal of Applied Behavior Analysis*, 1968, 1, 77–78.

Lovaas, O. I. Interaction between verbal and nonverbal behavior. *Child Development*, 1961, 32, 329–336.

Lovaas, O. I. Control of food intake in children by reinforcement of relevant verbal behavior. *Journal of Abnormal and Social Psychology*, 1964, 68, 672–678.

Lovaas, O. I. A behavior therapy approach to the treatment of childhood schizophrenia. In J. P. Hill (Ed.) *Minnesota symposia on child development.* Vol. I. Minneapolis: University of Minnesota Press, 1967. Pp. 108–159.

Lovaas, O. I. A program for the establishment of speech in psychotic children. In H. Sloane and B. MacAulay (Eds.) *Operant procedures in remedial speech and language training.* Boston: Houghton Mifflin, 1968. Pp. 125–154.

Lovaas, O. I., Berberich, J., Perloff, B., & Schaeffer, B. Acquisition of imitative speech by schizophrenic children. *Science*, 1966, 151, 705–707.

Lovaas, O. I., Freitas, L., Nelson, K., & Whalen, C. The establishment of imitation and its use for the development of complex behavior in schizophrenic children. *Behavior Research and Therapy*, 1967, 5, 171–181.

Madsen, C. H., Becker, W. C., Thomas, D. R., Koser, L., & Plager, E. An analysis of the reinforcing function of "sit down" commands. In R. K. Parker (Ed.) *Readings in educational psychology.* Boston: Allyn and Bacon, 1968.

Mager, R. F. *Preparing instructional objectives.* Palo Alto, Calif.: Fearon Publishers, 1962.

Mahoney, K., Van Wagenen, R. K., & Meyerson, L. Toilet training of normal and retarded children. *Journal of Applied Behavior Analysis*, 1971, 4, 173–181.

Martin, G. L., England, G., Kaprowy, E., Kilgour, K., & Pilek, V. Operant conditioning of kindergarten class behavior in autistic children. *Behavior Research and Therapy*, 1968, 6, 281–294.

Martin, J. A. The control of imitative and nonimitative behaviors in severely retarded children through "generalized instruction-following." *Journal of Experimental Child Psychology*, 1971, 11, 390–400.

Mattos, R. L. A manual counter for recording multiple behavior. *Journal of Applied Behavior Analysis*, 1968, 1, 130.

McClain, W. A. The modification of aggressive classroom behavior through reinforcement, inhibition and relationship therapy. *Training School Bulletin*, 1969, 65, 122–125.

Metz, J. R.   Conditioning generalized imitation in autistic children. *Journal of Experimental Child Psychology,* 1965, 2, 389–399.

Mischel, W.   *Introduction to personality.*   New York: Holt, Rinehart, and Winston, 1971.

Montenegro, H.   Severe separation anxiety in two preschool children: Successfully treated by reciprocal inhibition. *Journal of Child Psychology and Psychiatry,* 1968, 9, 93–103.

Nordquist, V. M.   The modification of a child's enuresis: Some response-response relationships. *Journal of Applied Behavior Analysis,* 1971, 4, 241–247.

O'Connor, R. D.   Modification of social withdrawal through symbolic modeling. *Journal of Applied Behavior Analysis,* 1969, 2, 15–22.

O'Leary, K. D., & Becker, W. C.   The effects of the intensity of a teacher's reprimands on children's behavior. *Journal of School Psychology,* 1968, 7, 8–11.

O'Leary, K. D., Kaufman, K. F., Kass, R. E., & Drabman, R. S.   The effects of loud and soft reprimands on the behavior of disruptive students. *Exceptional Children,* 1970, 37, 145–155.

Packard, R. G.   The control of "classroom attention:" A group contingency for complex behavior. *Journal of Applied Behavior Analysis,* 1970, 3, 13–28.

Paloutzian, R. F., Hasazi, J., Streifel, J., & Edgar, C. L.   Promotion of positive social interaction in severely retarded young children. *American Journal of Mental Deficiency,* 1971, 75, 519–524.

Patterson, G. R.   An application of conditioning techniques to the control of a hyperactive child.   In L. P. Ullman and L. Krasner (Eds.) *Case studies in behavior modification.*   New York: Holt, Rinehart and Winston, 1965.   Pp. 370–375.

Patterson, G. R.   *Families.*   Champaign, Ill.: Research Press, 1971.

Patterson, G. R., & Brodsky, G.   A behavior modification programme for a child with multiple problem behaviors. *Journal of Child Psychology and Psychiatry,* 1966, 7, 277–295.

Patterson, G. R., Cobb, J. A., & Ray, R. S.   A social engineering technology for retraining aggressive boys.   In H. Adams and L. Unikel (Eds.) *Georgia symposium in experimental clinical psychology.*   Vol. II.   Oxford: Pergamon, 1970.

Patterson, G. R., & Gullion, M. E.   *Living with children: New methods for parents and teachers.*   Champaign, Ill.: Research Press, 1968.

Patterson, G. R., Jones, R., Whittier, J., & Wright, M. A.   A behavior modification technique for the hyperactive child. *Behavior Research and Therapy,* 1965, 2, 217–226.

Pendergrass, V. E.   Timeout from positive reinforcement following persistent, high-rate behavior in retardates. *Journal of Applied Behavior Analysis,* 1972, 5, 85–91.

Perline, I. H., & Levinsky, D.   Controlling maladaptive classroom behavior in the severely retarded. *American Journal of Mental Deficiency*, 1968, 73, 74–78.

Premack, D.   Toward empirical behavior laws: I.   Positive reinforcement. *Psychological Review*, 1959, 66, 219–233.

Quay, H. C., Werry, J. S., McQueen, M., & Sprague, R. L.   Remediation of the conduct problem child in the special class setting. *Exceptional Children*, 1966, 32, 509–515.

Reynolds, N. J., & Risley, T. R.   The role of social and material reinforcers in increasing talking of a disadvantaged preschool child. *Journal of Applied Behavior Analysis*, 1968, 1, 253–262.

Rimland, B.   *Infantile autism.*   New York: Appleton-Century-Crofts, 1964.

Risley, T. R.   The effects and side effects of punishing the autistic behavior of a deviant child. *Journal of Applied Behavior Analysis*, 1968, 1, 21–34.

Risley, T. R., & Hart, B.   Developing correspondence between the non-verbal and verbal behaviors of preschool children. *Journal of Applied Behavior Analysis*, 1968, 1, 267–281.

Risley, T. R., & Wolf, M. M.   Establishing functional speech in echolalic children.   In H. Sloane and B. MacAulay (Eds.) *Operant procedures in remedial speech and language training.* Boston: Houghton Mifflin, 1968. Pp. 157–184.

Risley, T. R. M., & Wolf, M.   Establishing functional speech in echolalic children. *Behavior Research and Therapy*, 1967, 5, 73–88.

Rosenberg, H.   Contingency management for the educable retarded. *Journal for Special Educators of the Mentally Retarded*, 1971, 8, 46–50.

Ross, D. M., Ross, S. A., & Evans, T. A.   The modification of extreme social withdrawal by modeling with guided participation. *Journal of Behavior Therapy and Experimental Psychiatry*, 1971, 2, 273–279.

Salzberg, B. H., Wheeler, A. J., Devar, L. T., & Hopkins, B. L.   The effect of intermittent feedback and intermittent contingent access to play on printing of kindergarten children. *Journal of Applied Behavior Analysis*, 1971, 4, 163–171.

Sibley, S. A., Abbott, M. S., & Cooper, B. P.   Modification of the classroom behavior of a disadvantaged kindergarten boy by social reinforcement and isolation. *Journal of Experimental Child Psychology*, 1969, 7, 203–219.

Sloane, H. N., & MacAulay, B. D. (Eds.) *Operant procedures in remedial speech and language training.*   Boston: Houghton Mifflin, 1968.

Smith, J. M., & Smith, E. P.   *Child management: A program for parents.*   Ann Arbor, Mich.: Ann Arbor Pub., 1966.

Spradlin, J. E., & Girardeau, F. L.   The behavior of moderately and severely retarded persons. In N. R. Ellis (Ed.) *International review of research in mental retardation.* Vol. I. New York: Academic Press, 1966. Pp. 257–298.

Staats, A. W. *Child learning, intelligence and personality: Principles of a behavioral interaction approach.* New York: Harper and Row, 1971.

Stuecher, U. *Tommy: A treatment study of an autistic child.* Arlington, Va.: The Council for Exceptional Children, 1972.

Sulzbacher, S. I., & Houser, J. E. A tactic to eliminate disruptive behaviors in the classroom: Group contingent consequences. *American Journal of Mental Deficiency,* 1968, **73**, 88–90.

Sulzer, B., & Mayer, G. R. *Behavior modification procedures for school personnel.* Hinsdale, Ill.: Dryden Press, 1972.

Tharp, R. G., & Wetzel, R. J. *Behavior modification in the natural environment.* New York: Academic Press, 1969.

Thomas, D. R., Becker, W. C., & Armstrong, M. Production and elimination of disruptive classroom behavior by systematically varying teacher's behavior. *Journal of Applied Behavior Analysis,* 1968, **1**, 35–45.

Twardosz, S., & Sajwaj, T. Multiple effects of a procedure to increase sitting in a hyperactive retarded boy. *Journal of Applied Behavior Analysis,* 1972, **5**, 73–78.

Ullman, L. P., & Krasner, L. (Eds.) *Case studies in behavior modification.* New York: Holt, Rinehart and Winston, 1965.

Vernon, W. M. *Motivating children: Behavior modification in the classroom.* New York: Holt, Rinehart and Winston, 1972.

Wahler, R. G. Setting generality: Some specific and general effects of child behavior therapy. *Journal of Applied Behavior Analysis,* 1969, **2**, 239–246. (a)

Wahler, R. G. Oppositional children: A quest for parental reinforcement control. *Journal of Applied Behavior Analysis,* 1969, **2**, 159–170. (b)

Wahler, R. G. Some ecological problems in child behavior modification. In S. W. Bijou and E. Ribes-Inesta (Eds.) *Behavior modification: Issues and extensions.* New York: Academic Press, 1972. Pp. 7–18.

Wahler, R. G., Sperling, K. A., Thomas, M. R., Teeter, N. C., & Luper, H. T. The modification of childhood stuttering: Some response-response relationships. *Journal of Experimental Child Psychology,* 1970, **9**, 411–428.

Wahler, R. G., Winkel, G. H., Peterson, R. F., & Morrison, D. C. Mothers as behavior therapists for their own children. *Behavior Research and Therapy,* 1965, **3**, 113–124.

Walters, R. H., Parke, R. D., & Cane, V. A. Timing of punishment and the observation of consequences to others as determinants of response inhibition. *Journal of Experimental Child Psychology,* 1965, **2**, 10–30.

Ward, M. H., & Baker, B. L.   Reinforcement therapy in the classroom. *Journal of Applied Behavior Analysis,* 1968, 1, 323–328.

Wasik, B. H., Senn, K., Welch, R. H., & Cooper, B. R.   Behavior modification with culturally deprived school children: Two case studies. *Journal of Applied Behavior Analysis,* 1969, 2, 181–194.

Watson, L. S.   *How to use behavior modification with mentally retarded and autistic children.*   Columbus, Ohio: Behavior Modification Technology, 1972.

White, G. D., Nielsen, G., & Johnson, S. M.   Time-out duration and the suppression of deviant behavior in children.   *Journal of Applied Behavior Analysis,* 1972, 5, 111–120.

Whitman, T. L., Zakaras, M., & Chardos, S.   Effects of reinforcement and guidance procedures on instruction-following behavior of severely retarded children.   *Journal of Applied Behavior Analysis,* 1971, 4, 283–290.

Wiesen, A. E., & Watson, E.   Elimination of attention seeking behavior in a retarded child.   *American Journal of Mental Deficiency,* 1967, 72, 50–52.

Williams, C. D.   The elimination of tantrum behavior by extinction procedures. *Journal of Abnormal and Social Psychology,* 1959, 59, 269.

Wolf, M., Risley, T., Johnston, M., Harris, F., & Allen, E.   Application of operant conditioning procedures to the behavior problems of an autistic child: A follow-up and extension.   *Behavior Research and Therapy,* 1967, 5, 103–111.

Wolf, M., Risley, T., & Mees, H.   Application of operant conditioning procedures to the behavior problems of an autistic child.   *Behavior Research and Therapy,* 1964, 1, 305–312.

Zeilberger, J., Sampen, S. E., & Sloane, H. N.   Modification of a child's problem behaviors in the home with the mother as therapist. *Journal of Applied Behavior Analysis,* 1968, 1, 47–53.

Author Index

Subject Index

Abnormal behavior, 16, 20
Abnormal learning experiences, 20, 21
Aggressive behavior:
  and aversive stimuli, 152
  behavior management program for, 297–300
  description of, 295
  extinction-induced, 142
  learning of, 296–297
  modified through:
    extinction, 135, 138, 139–140, 298
    modeling, 299
    reinforcement of competing behavior, 135, 137–138, 298, 299
    time-out, 298
  positive reinforcement of, 139, 296, 297, 299
  related to punishment, 152
  role of modeling in, 149, 297
  verbal, 138
Alternative responses (*see* Competing behaviors)
Analysis of behavior, 251–255
Apathy, pattern of, 35–36
Attention:
  deficits of, 28–30
  in observational learning, 129

  skills, 27
  span, 10
    short, 28, 29, 109, 308
Atypical, 8
Autistic behavior patterns:
  behavior management programs for, 17, 155, 308–311
  characteristics of, 307–308
  early infantile, 307
  kindergarten program for, 311
  parent training program for manangement of, 311
  speech difficulties in, 309–311
  and types of reinforcing events, 64, 308–309
Aversive events:
  conditioned (secondary), 111
  and control, 151
  defined, 41
  disadvantages in use of, 149–154
  and negative reinforcement, 42, 112
  primary, 111
  procedure of developing new, 111, 112
  and time-out procedure, 154–158
  use of, in reducing behavior, 148–167

19